The German Nation and Martin Luther

A. G. Dickens was born in Yorkshire in 1910. He took a First in History at Magdalen College, Oxford, and became a Fellow of Keble College. During the Second World War he served in the Royal Artillery. From 1949 to 1962 he was Professor of History in the University of Hull, and from 1962 to 1967 Professor of History at King's College, London. Since the latter date he has been Director of the Institute of Historical Research in the University of London. He is a Fellow and the Foreign Secretary of the British Academy; a Fellow of the Society of Antiquaries and of the Royal Historical Society.

Among his other books are: *Thomas Cromwell and the English Reformation* (1959), *Reformation and Society in Sixteenth Century Europe* (1966), *Martin Luther and the Reformation* (1967), *The Counter Reformation* (1968), and *The Age of Humanism and Reformation* (1972). *The English Reformation* (1964) is also available in Fontana.

The German Nation and Martin Luther

A. G. Dickens

FONTANA/COLLINS

First published by
Edward Arnold (Publishers) Ltd 1974
First issued in Fontana 1976
Copyright © A.G. Dickens 1974

Made and printed in Great Britain by
William Collins Sons & Co. Ltd , Glasgow

Preface

Short histories of the Reformation are plentiful enough and this present book does not seek to add to their number. Instead it explores what I take to be the central problem of Reformation history: to identify the intellectual and social forces which got Luther's revolt off the ground. Having dealt rather summarily with the long preparatory phase, it examines in more detail the crucial years c. 1517–30. I have depicted these years as uniquely important, because they saw Lutheranism become an ineradicable feature of German society. I reject the traditional course of the narrative, which concentrates on Luther's theology and then moves through the Knights' and Peasants' Wars to the princely Reformation. I see the creative and irrevocable events largely in terms of the urban Reformation, a movement effectually springing from the new dynamic added by the preachers, pamphleteers, and printers to the old turmoil of city politics. Passing from ideas into society itself, my later chapters thus seek 'explanations' at the local level. But 'grass-roots' history is harder to write than the history of states and princes, and in my terms there would appear no early prospect of composing even a mildly 'definitive' history of the German Reformation. Having spent some thirty years acquiring a tolerable grasp of the main sources and secondary authorities in print, the author of such a work would then need the prolonged services of a large team of researchers amid the manuscripts of a host of German cities and provinces. To part-time sexagenarian scholars like the present writer, the utter impossibility of the assignment becomes almost comforting! Nevertheless, it does not exonerate us from thinking on a big scale, from reading the voluminous researches of our contemporaries, from staking out some of the ground, from propounding some hypotheses for our successors to prove or disprove.

This necessarily modest essay began its career at Trinity College, Cambridge, as the Birkbeck Lectures for 1969–70 and I am grateful to the Master and Fellows—especially to Walter Ullmann—for this early encouragement. I am also indebted to the Folger Shakespeare Library, which enabled me to dispose of the main burden of writing in the relative peace of Washington, D.C. Almost every paragraph owes a debt to personal friends. Merely to list them would seem an elaborate exercise in name-dropping, since through many undeserved strokes of fortune I have come to know most of the American leaders in this field, together with some few of their equivalents in Germany. My special thanks are due to that master of the period Gerald Strauss, who generously read the typescript and put right some of its faults. Again, I owe not a little to my younger associate Bob Scribner, whose recent researches at Erfurt and elsewhere have enabled me to sample vicariously the excitement of new discovery among German manuscript-sources. And in regard to the paragraphs on Erfurt, it could be said of us: *Si Scribnerus non scripsisset, Dicens non dixisset.* After that, my readers who recall the famous saying about Lyra and Luther should be prepared for anything!

A. G. DICKENS
Institute of Historical Research
January 1973

FOOTNOTES

The footnotes are less concerned to document the text than to give a broad notion of the books I have used, and still more to help readers who want to consult the main secondary sources. Among the latter, however, I have tried to select those which provide good reference to the primary sources. Most notes refer to items given in the Bibliographies, and so need cite only authors' names, or at most short titles. Some notes do, however, provide more specialized references omitted from the Bibliographies, and in these cases full titles, dates and places are included. Throughout, where no place of publication is given, the book was published in London. In general, abbreviations are avoided, except for some of the standard works of reference, which appear in a brief separate Bibliography.

PREFACE TO THE FONTANA EDITION

Since this book originally went to press in 1973, a certain amount of significant research in these fields has appeared. R. W. Scribner has summarized important aspects of his earlier research in 'Civic Unity and the Reformation in Erfurt', *Past & Present*, no. 56, February 1975. Equally relevant is his article 'Why was there no Reformation in Cologne?' in *Bulletin of the Institute of Historical Research*, xlix, no. 120, November 1976. Steven E. Ozment has worked along complementary lines in *The Reformation in the Cities. The Appeal of Protestantism in Sixteenth Century Germany and Switzerland* (New Haven and London, 1975). Gerald Strauss has meanwhile supplied a disconcerting postscript: 'Success or Failure in the German Reformation', *Past & Present*, no. 56, May 1975. It should also now be observed that a major co-operative project based at the University of Tübingen will in course of time greatly enlarge our knowledge of Reformation-origins in numerous German cities.

I submit one correction. The reference (pp. 201–2) to the lack of a Lutheran Foxe or Crespin is in a sense true, yet it ignores the contribution of the Ulm pastor Ludwig Rabus (*Historien der . . . Bekennern und Martyrern*, Strassburg, 1554–8). Though so large a part of his collection concerns ancient and late medieval times, and though his place in Reformation history cannot compare with those of the major martyrologists, it should nevertheless have been taken into account.

Contents

Central Europe in

Stralsund
ck
POMERANIA
Danzig
EAST PRUSSIA
Ermeland
ANDENBURG
Berlin
tenberg
zig
Mühlberg
NY
Dresden
ickau
POLAND
SILESIA
Prague
Cracow
BOHEMIA
Moravia
HABSBURG-HUNGARY
Passau
IA
Vienna
AUSTRIA
Salzburg
A
TURKISH HUNGARY

rmation Period

1

Nationalism and Anticlericalism: Prophecy and Piety

The Protestant Reformation has not infrequently been 'explained' by reference to movements of thought, politics and public opinion apparent only on the very eve of Luther's revolt. Such short-term analysis betrays not merely a weak grasp of historical causation but also a singular lack of feeling for the power of tradition over the German mind. Doubtless these explanations have been welcomed by ardent admirers of the medieval Church, who want to view the Reformation as a sudden conspiracy, a vast confidence trick played upon a pious and orthodox nation. Conversely, the same analysis also appeals to the Protestant hagiographer who wants to enjoy a one-man circus a whole revolution created by the heroic spirit and energy of Martin Luther. Admittedly, it would be possible to react overnuch against short-term explanations. Even the present account will place great stress upon the impact of humanists and pamphleteers at work during the years after 1500. These men perfected and consummated the efforts of their predecessors to stir up a German nationalism which was predominantly anti-Italian and anti-papal. Yet we must begin with an account of those predecessors, some of them humanists, yet others with their roots far deeper in the struggles, the grievances, the culture of the Middle Ages. Luther rather than the Habsburgs became the beneficiary of the Hohenstaufen emperors! The humanists provided new weapons for a very old campaign. They appealed to emotions grounded upon centuries of struggle, since German patriotic sentiments had from time immemorial been directed most often against the popes, and they had been clearly expressed by intellectuals, ecclesiastics and politicians long before humanism began to touch Germany.

One effective forerunner of the German Reformation should thus be recognized in the anti-papal prejudices created by those interminable conflicts between empire and papacy, conflicts mainly originating in the Investiture Contest of the eleventh and twelfth centuries. By the time of Emperor Lewis IV (r. 1314–47), the first issues had become subsidiary, yet he had still to fight defensively against papal pressures, and these pressures were now arising from a succession of French popes established at Avignon. During the same period more purely ideological crises also became sharper within the Church itself, even though they were to reach their first peaks elsewhere, and in later decades, following the careers of Wycliffe and Huss. Meanwhile amongst the champions of the Emperor Lewis the two best-known and least orthodox, Marsiglio of Padua and William of Occam, were not even Germans by origin. The weight and character of the German movement can be assessed not by reference to rootless radicals at the imperial court but in the writings of solid, conservative German churchmen, such as Lupold of Bebenburg (d. 1362) and Conrad of Megenberg (d. 1374). We may best begin the story with its least sensational characters, important by the very fact of their four-square qualities.

Men such as these did not desire military campaigns against papal territories: still less did they condone any threat of heretical schism. After a distinguished academic and ecclesiastical career, Lupold occupied the important bishopric of Bamberg during the last decade of his life.[1] His *Tractate on the Laws of the Kingdom and the Empire* appealed to historical origins as well as to natural law, Roman law and canon law, in order to demonstrate the independence of empire from papacy. Like Dante and others long before, Lupold maintained that over and above his German kingdom the emperor had every right to exercise a world jurisdiction. In the imperial oath made to the pope he saw only an assurance of support, not an admission of papal overlordship.

---

[1] F. Hertz, pp. 183–5, summarizes some leading ideas. For standard works see A. Senger; H. Meyer; R. Most.

Coronation by the pope merely acknowledged the emperor's privilege as the highest international power. And a century before Lorenzo Valla's textual criticism displayed the Donation of Constantine as a forgery, Lupold had already denounced it as apocryphal and unauthentic. His *Tractate* cannot be dismissed as an academic thesis intended merely for discussion in the law-schools, since as early as 1341 it was translated into German. Of more direct interest from our Reformation viewpoint is the fact that it was printed in 1508 at the instance of the patriotic humanist Wimpfeling, even as the tide of anti-papal thought began to attain new heights. It became a favourite text of those Alsatian humanists who formed the spearhead of German nationalism. Though Lupold himself had been little concerned either with clerical abuses or with the events of the imperial-papal struggle in his own day, he had all the same professed an ardent patriotism for the German fatherland and deplored the malice of the many enemies who had plucked feathers from the imperial eagle.

Even those who upheld some papalist causes might also strive to arouse German patriotism. Lupold's slightly younger contemporary, Conrad of Megenberg, had a more versatile literary approach.[2] Theologian and philosopher, he became in 1337 head of the cathedral school of St. Stephen in Vienna, later acquiring a canonry at Regensburg. He composed the first German-language handbook upon physics and astronomy. He also anticipated the enthusiasm of the German humanists for regional history in his writings on the bishopric of Regensburg. But so far from being a political imperialist, Conrad believed that the Avignon popes had right on their side in the struggle against the Emperor Lewis. In his opposition to the extreme claims of Marsiglio and Occam, he called the former a heretic and attacked the whole philosophical scheme of the latter. Just as conservatively he wrote against the heretical Beghards and blamed the intrigues of the friars for many of the problems of Christendom. His work of 1355 *On the Translation of the Empire* accords to the

[2] H. Ibach; F. Hertz, pp. 185–6. Further details on his treatises appear in the two articles, respectively by P. Schneider and H. Grauert, in *Historisches Jahrbuch*, xxii (1901). On his *Lacrimae ecclesiae*, attacking heretics and friars, see R. E. Lerner, *The Heresy of the Free Spirit in the later Middle Ages* (Berkeley, 1972), pp. 55–7.

popes a degree of supremacy over the emperor which Lupold would scarcely have admitted. On the other hand, so long before the Conciliar Movement, Conrad qualifies papal authority by asserting the right of a General Council to depose a pope. He also elevates the emperor as a world monarch above all other kings, while he defends with warmth the right of the German nation to possess the Holy Roman Empire. More pointedly than Lupold, he stresses the valour and other noble qualities of the Germans, as opposed for example to the chivalrous but luxury-loving character of the French. To the German nation and its emperor there had been divinely ordained the transfer of a world authority. This *translatio* had long been associated with the coronation of Charlemagne in the year 800, and had become a commonplace among German writers several generations before its dramatic exploitation by the humanists. To their minds the Holy Roman Empire and the German nation had been conjoined by an event of history transcending all the failures of actual emperors and imperial institutions.

To this situation the earlier fifteenth century added not only further patriotic attitudes but also harsher criticisms of ecclesiastical misrule, criticisms reflecting upon the papal curia and in some cases foreshadowing the anticlericalism of the period of Hutten and Luther. The eventual claims of Celtis and other patriotic humanists concerning the scientific prowess of the Germans were long anticipated by Conrad Kyeser of Eichstätt (1366 to after 1405), whose richly illustrated manuscript *Bellifortis* (1405) deals with military engineering and other technical aspects of warfare. In comparing the achievements of the nations, Kyeser claimed for his own not merely outstanding courage in war but a superior prowess in mechanical inventiveness and in the arts and crafts as a whole. He even made his own minor contribution to the cause by prophesying the invention of the hot air balloon.[3] A few decades later his claims would have been easier to substantiate, when Germans were teaching the other nations to print from movable type. Still more would he have had cause to rejoice in Dürer's Nuremberg, where metal

[3] On Kyeser: *ADB*, lii, p. 769; B. Gille, *The Renaissance Engineers* (1966), pp. 58–66. A facsimile of the original ms. at Göttingen was edited by C. Quarg (Düsseldorf, 2 vols., 1967).

workers laid the basis for the precision instruments necessary to the rise of modern science. But already before these developments German technology also received praise from Enea Silvio, soon to become Pope Pius II (r. 1458–64), who singled out German excellence in both mathematics and building.[4] Unlike most Italian humanists of his day, Enea was far from ungenerous toward the transalpine barbarians amongst whom he lived so long. His earnest condescension once caused him to shed tears of emotion when he heard even an English layman making a speech in good humanist Latin!

It seems one of history's stranger ironies that this conciliarist-turned-papalist should have done so much to educate the Germans into cultural self-confidence. His praise for the nation arose in the course of his so-called *Germania*, the treatise countering a letter from Martin Mair, chancellor to the arch-bishop of Mainz. In congratulating Enea on his elevation to the cardinalate, Mair had taken the opportunity to press the grievances of the German Church, already a familiar subject at the Council of Basle, that notable focus of German resentment against the papal curia. But by this time (1457) Enea already had his eye upon the papacy, to which he would in fact succeed a few months later. This being so, his response to Mair was couched in subtle terms. Not only did he seek to refute charges of papal misgovernment and rapacity: he also flattered the Germans by dwelling on their wealth and their cultural achievements. So how could anyone seriously argue that this splendid nation had been pauperized by Roman exactions? Having described over twenty magnificent German cities known to him, he stressed the faithfulness of the rulers and prelates to the see of Rome, attributing all the restiveness reported by Mair to the volatile and ungrateful rabble. This cunning answer produced results Enea could not have foreseen but which he entirely deserved. German scholars and patrons were encouraged to take their cultural pretensions ever more seriously: they cited with pride the high opinions of this eminent Italian humanist. On the other hand officialdom and scholars alike resented more bitterly than ever the manifest opposition of the papacy toward reform

---

[4] References to the texts and a synopsis of the debate with Enea Silvio are in G. Strauss, *Manifestations*, pp. 35ff.

and fiscal moderation. As will become apparent, the controversy between Mair and Enea was never forgotten: the great humanist Wimpfeling specifically revived it in 1515 on the very eve of Martin Luther's revolt.

Even a brief anthology of medieval anticlericalism could hardly fail to include some formidable extracts from the earlier writings of that greatest German of his day, Cardinal Nicholas of Cusa (1400–64), whose birthplace Cues amid the vineyards of the Moselle still contains the hospital which he founded. Nicholas came late enough to observe Italian humanism, but he declined to become a sycophantic admirer of its verbal elegances. As for that leading patron of humanism, the Roman papacy, the conversion of Nicholas to its support came only in 1437, after his many years of support for conciliar reform at Basle. He had also advocated a peaceful reconciliation with the Hussites and a vigorous campaign to discipline the Catholic clergy as a whole. Though he ultimately accepted the cardinalate, Nicholas could nevertheless be cited to the effect that Church government depends on consent, and that occupants of parochial benefices should be elected by their parishioners, bishops by their clergy and people, archbishops by their bishops, all indeed upon the same lines as the election of popes by cardinals. In his *Concordantia Catholica* (1431–3) he exalts the emperor as a supernatural world ruler and divinely appointed guardian of the Faith: he rejects the claim that the imperial office had been a donation from the papacy. Observing that Charlemagne had been crowned by the pope, he deliberately selects Otto I as the first German to be invested with the empire. In his conciliar days Nicholas also believed that a General Council could depose a pope. He protested against the undue involvement of the Church in politics, against the encroachments of the popes upon the investiture of bishops, and against the extortion of money from the German people by means of papal taxation. He was a proud German patriot as well as a champion of the empire.[5]

[5] On the political thought of Nicholas, see E. Bohnenstädt; G. Kallen, 'Die politische Theorie im philosophischen System des Nikolaus von Cues' in *Historische Zeitschrift*, clxv (1942); G. Strauss, *Pre-Reformation Germany*, p. 220, n. 20; F. Hertz, pp. 206–10; F. L. Borchardt, pp. 42–5. On his aspirations as a churchman see E. Iserloh. A general account by E. F. Jacob is in F. J. C. Hearnshaw, *The Social and Political Ideas of Some*

A more consistent critic of the papacy was the jurist and diplomat Gregor Heimburg (d. 1472), a many-sided intellectual who had enjoyed the respect and friendship of Enea Silvio. Even so at the Diet of Frankfurt in 1456 he and his former pupil and fellow-jurist Martin Mair inspired the Electors to formulate the *gravamina* of the German nation against the papacy and to demand a Pragmatic giving the German Church a measure of independence similar to that enjoyed by the French Church under the Pragmatic Sanction of Bourges (1438). Three years later, at the Mantua congress of 1459, Gregor acted as spokesman of the German princes against that same pope's crusading plans, and was put under the ban of the Church by his former admirer. Of course, little respect was accorded to this papal censure by the German rulers, and Gregor continued to receive important political commissions. He even helped in Prague to direct the markedly anti-Roman policy of the tolerant Hussite king of Bohemia, George of Podêbrady. Heimburg and Mair enunciated conciliar theory but probably with little genuine desire to see a General Council reassembled. They certainly counselled King George to use the threat of a Council in order to extort from the pope the command of the army being raised to fight the Turks. The charges Gregor levelled against the papacy have been compared with those brought by Luther: corruption and financial exploitation; the forgery of documents purporting to accord worldly powers to Rome; policies calculated to incite frequent civil wars within the empire. Again, like the Hussite and Protestant Reformers, Gregor did not hesitate to draw pointed contrasts between the conduct of the papacy and the examples set by Christ and his disciples in the Gospels.[6]

During these middle decades of the fifteenth century, a tradition developed whereby the successive Diets of the empire enumerated the grievances of the nation (*gravamina nationis germanicae*) against the papacy.[7] Deriving initially from complaints prepared during the Council of Constance, they attained clarity and prominence in the Frankfurt Diet of 1456 and were

Great Thinkers of the Renaissance and Reformation (1925), pp. 32–59. On the writings of the Basle-Florence background, see H. O. Burger, ch. 3.

[6] P. Joachimsohn; F. Hertz, pp. 211–12; further references in *NDB*.

[7] A general history of the *gravamina* is provided by B. Gebhardt. A translation from those of 1521 is in G. Strauss, *Manifestations*, pp. 52–63.

thereafter constantly reiterated by the princes and prelates. These sponsors were chiefly concerned to diminish papal exactions and papal appointments to benefices; they openly aspired to win concessions as favourable as those accorded to the French Church. In later years the Emperor Maximilian was to utilize the traditional *gravamina* during his attempts to obtain a settlement with the papacy; and in 1510 he employed the humanist Wimpfeling to abbreviate and re-draft the list. Nevertheless it soon expanded once more. Too seldom observed by historians is the fact that the very Diet of Worms which in 1521 condemned Luther's doctrines also drew up a fresh list specifying no less than 102 papal abuses. Even at this point the long story of orthodox protest does not end; it became a heritage of the Catholic Habsburgs. The impact of the *gravamina* upon the middle and lower orders of German society is hard to ascertain, yet it should probably rank high among those long-term influences which we are now seeking to disentangle.

The struggle between the emperors and their opponents was not only conducted on the practical plane shared by jurists, diplomats, scholars and ecclesiastical administrators. Since the thirteenth century or earlier, it had also been fought in terms of rival prophecies. To us irrational, even ludicrous, this was a *milieu* wholly natural to the medieval mind, which based belief and action upon 'received' patterns of the future, just as readily as upon patterns of the past gained from history. And one might well concede in passing that such an answer to human fears and aspirations is little more irrational than some of the forms taken by the modern myth of progress or that of socialist revolutionary optimism. At all events, prophecy continued to flourish, powerfully reinforced by the ever-growing cult of astrology, in High Renaissance Europe. Some of its favourite exponents were obscure members of the clerical proletariat, though they sometimes seem to display another class-affinity, appealing as they obviously did to unprivileged townsmen, a class which had aspirations to share in the government of their cities, having hitherto drawn very meagre dividends from rising urban prosperity.

Late medieval and sixteenth-century prophecy could boast few fresh or original ideas. To a striking extent it continued to

adapt the elements supplied by that imaginative systematizer
Joachim of Fiore (d. 1202), the Calabrian abbot whose works
had set forth a trinitarian scheme of history with three ages:
those of Father, Son and Spirit.[8] The first two, corresponding
respectively with the reigns of the Old and the New Testaments,
were now drawing to a close. About 1260, predicted Joachim, a
series of religious orders would re-convert the world and usher
in the third age: that of the Spirit. Scarcely had the prophecies
gained circulation than the Mendicant Orders were founded and
attained great influence. Embraced in later years by the Spiritual
Franciscans, Joachism promoted religious trends disquieting to
the governors of Church and state. The prophet's cloudy phrases
regarding a Universal Emperor and an Angelic Pope were
amplified by countless pseudo-Joachite writings: they soon
descended into the political arena, particularly into the conten-
tions between empire and papacy, Germany and France. The
movement divided into what might be called anti-German and
pro-German factions. Though patronized by the Hohen-
staufens, Joachim had predicted a German emperor who would
prove to be the scourge of the Church, while his papalist followers
awaited the Angelic Pope, who would establish a new theocracy
throughout the world. But on the pro-German side, there arose
more persistent and popular expectations of a messianic reforming emperor. According to some beliefs he would be the new
Charlemagne, a title which in due course encouraged French
publicists to snatch at the Empire for their own nation, claiming
the role successively for their kings Charles VI (r. 1380–1422)
and Charles VIII (r. 1483–98). The invasion of Italy by the
latter provided a vigorous but short-lived stimulus to this
French vaticination. And finally in 1519, on the election of
Charles V as emperor, there was no lack of triumphant Germans
and Burgundians who insisted upon seeing the long-awaited
imperial Messiah in the stolid young Habsburg, who had just
inherited not merely the name but also a huge empire comparable with that of Charlemagne.

Yet more influential in Germany became the figure of
imperialist prophecy known as 'the third Frederick'. This

[8] M. Reeves, pts. 3 and 4, gives details regarding these works. On the
Third Frederick, see also N. Cohn, ch. 5.

fantasy had remained popular since the fall of the Hohenstaufen dynasty with the death in 1250 of Frederick II, whose Sicilian court and habits had strangely failed to destroy his credibility as German emperor. To papalists, the threatened third Frederick naturally seemed an Antichrist, yet to numerous German believers in prophecy he appeared not merely a national and secular hero, but one with a strong inclination toward social as well as ecclesiastical reform. Some day, perhaps very soon, the new Frederick would arise and inaugurate a veritable kingdom of God on earth, expropriating the rich, overthrowing the Church of Rome and reducing both the Jews and the foreign nations to submission. While certain impostors were executed before they could carry this mission far, the fable easily attached itself to some actual emperors, even to the improbable Sigismund. Its most obvious beneficiary was the Habsburg Frederick III (r. 1440–93), but his singularly feeble conduct of affairs brought rapid disillusion to all save the most credulous. This Frederick proved the least Messianic figure one could conceive. Nevertheless, bolstered by their amazing pattern of dynastic marriages, the Habsburgs somehow managed to ride the surf of imperial prophecy. Immense expectations clung to Frederick's son Maximilian I, to his grandson Philip of Burgundy (d. 1506) and, we have just observed, to his great grandson Charles V. Such dreams were no perquisite of courtiers, authors or astrologers. They also attracted the populace, because they included not merely the apotheosis of emperor and nation but the promise of a new deal within German society.

Obviously enough, as a purifier of the Church the Messianic prince may also be viewed in the context of the Reformation. He found various fifteenth-century champions such as the author of the Latin tract *Gamaleon*, dated variously 1409 and 1439, which prophesied the coming of a future emperor who would crush the French, the Hungarians, the Slavs and the Jews. In a Germany exalted above the other nations, this ruler would destroy the Romanist clergy and install in Mainz a native patriarch of the German Church under his close control.[9] In 1439 there appeared that far more influential treatise, the *Reformation of Sigismund*, which has set modern scholars critical problems of

[9] M. Reeves, pp. 332–3.

great complexity. Within the general orbit of South Germany and Switzerland, both locality and authorship continue to be disputed, but with little hope of agreed solutions. And if in fact, as was once supposed, the treatise was influenced by some of Emperor Sigismund's officialdom, it certainly cannot represent even a tentative imperial programme. In its early forms it may possibly have been a scheme submitted to the Council of Basle by a priest called Frederick of Lantnaw; then reshaped by a lay admirer who added the prophecy placed in the mouth of Sigismund. This concluding passage claims that Frederick of Lantnaw is none other than the long-awaited Messiah-King, and that he will soon embark upon his apocalyptic task, beginning with the destruction of the avaricious prelates and merchants. Such wild prophecy apart, the *Reformatio Sigismundi* advocates a more or less reasonable socialism intended to benefit the common people.[10] Guilds and trading monopolies should be cancelled; wages, prices and taxes codified, game-laws and enclosures of commons abrogated, serfdom abolished and the towns opened to liberated serfs. In every town a salaried municipal physician should be appointed, treat patients without charge and dispense free medicines to the poor. Despite his attacks on the guilds, the author places his main hopes in the towns, which had generally backed the emperors in their struggles with the popes. But he also calls upon those other traditional imperialists, the knights, whom he urges to take a more active part in this reorganization of society. From the princes and the greater nobles he has no such expectations, though he reserves his chief hatred for the Church, especially for the monastic orders as distinct from the parish clergy.

With much justice, Count zu Dohna has urged that the *Reformatio* should be regarded as a conservative programme of reform rather than as a truly revolutionary document. It did not call for immediate subversive action; rather did it urge its readers to stand on the side of the priest-king when he should come to establish a new rule of law in the world. Again, in the passages

[10] N. Cohn, pp. 113–14; and p. 400, n. 113 refers to the commentaries by Bezold and Peuckert. The work was edited by K. Beer (Stuttgart, 1933) and from a better ms. by H. Koller (Stuttgart, 1964). For recent criticism and the authorship problem, see L. Dohna; K. Mommsen.

where appeals are made to 'the little people', these words do not mean the proletariat but the 'poor in spirit', blessed not only in the Beatitudes but by the *devotio moderna* of the late Middle Ages. It would hence appear that when von Bezold called it 'the trumpet of the Peasants' War', he was casting the book for a role never intended by its author. Not without reason the latter has been characterized as an earnest thinker more closely related to the *Imitation of Christ* (which appeared five years earlier) than to the peasant rebels and the apocalyptic radicals of the 1520s. Yet the intentions of a writer do not exhaust the social and political significance of his work. The actual influence of the *Reformatio Sigismundi* upon later generations appears to have been far from negligible, and it deserves a more detailed analysis than it has hitherto received. Luther himself quoted the tract, and the points of agreement suggest that, when in *Christian Nobility* he came to excogitate his own social programme, he may have been affected by some of its proposals. A great deal of its phraseology proved susceptible—like some of Luther's own—to radical interpretations. Again, its wide and lasting dissemination cannot be doubted. After early circulation in many manuscripts, it was printed in 1476, and it proceeded to attain a dozen further editions by 1720.

The appearance and the popularity of the *Reformatio* marks the split between the literature of nationalism proper—henceforth best represented by the humanists—and the literature of protest. The latter, it is true, often continued to invest the German nation with a special, even a dominant role in history. Yet it expended much of its wrath upon self-criticism, and prophesied the nation's renewal only in the furnace of internal revolution. Humanist nationalism will be dealt with in the next chapter; yet it would be simplistic to imagine either that cool scholarship dominated the years around 1500, or that the learned men devoted themselves solely to philological and historical studies, leaving the world of reformist prophecy to semi-educated and obscure fanatics. Though by no means limited to central Europe, the mood of restlessness, of expectancy, of indefinable anxiety invaded all classes of the German people. The mental world of Joachim of Fiore had never been livelier than on the eve of Martin Luther's revolt. The basis of that extremist sectarianism we associate most readily with the second quarter of the sixteenth century was laid long before 1500, a fact which suggests that we should view the total career of Luther as a braking-force as well as an acceleration of history. The spirit of unrest took innumerable forms. Amongst the less-educated classes there was a growth not only of an inward religiosity but of a craze for pilgrimages and miracles. As the future would show, the persistence of the *Bundschuh*, the economic striving of the peasantry had by no means absorbed the whole of their infinite restlessness. On the other side, erudite men like Abbot Trithemius (d. 1516), his pupil Paracelsus (d. 1541) and Agrippa of Nettesheim (d. 1535) embraced alchemy and astrology as keenly as anyone had ever embraced sober classical studies.[11] Like their mental inferiors they too yearned to discover the keys to the hidden forces, the formulae by which men might break through into a fresh knowledge and wisdom, might transcend the limitations of the unsatisfactory workaday world. At the opposite extreme represented by the art of conjuring, the *Faustbuch* of 1587 tells the legend of the charlatan from a godly Lutheran viewpoint, as a terrible example of the unprincipled quest for knowledge and power. Meanwhile German art, both popular and sophisticated, assumed an ever stronger Expressionist character, culminating at last in the terrific imagery of Dürer, of Hieronymus Bosch, of the Isenheim altarpiece. Even the later critics of the established order found it hard to extricate themselves from this apocalyptic world. That important tract *The Burden of the Church* (*Onus Ecclesiae*, written 1519, published 1524 and 1531) has long been attributed, though upon disputed evidence, to the distinguished jurist and theologian Berthold, bishop of Chiemsee.[12] Whoever he was, this writer has much to say about the hard facts and the moral abuses, especially those concerning the covetous and warlike aristocrat-prelates of Germany. Yet he also revives the old prophecies of Joachim in order to build up a terrible picture of the coming last days of the world. At the same time the professional astrologers made their calculations and emerged with portents of

---

[11] J. Lortz, i, p. 115; on Paracelsus see G. H. Williams, pp. 196–8.
[12] H. Werner, *Die Flugschrift Onus Ecclesiae 1519* (Giessen, 1901); L. Pastor, *History of the Popes* (1891–1953), vii, pp. 294–6.

revolutionary change, sometimes with enough direct hits and near-misses as to suggest that foresight as well as luck had managed to influence the serene witness of the stars.

Amongst these German prophecies a steady authority was attained by the *Prognosticatio* of Johann Lichtenberger, the first edition of which is dated 1488.[13] Outside the book, little is known concerning the author, save that he came from Alsace and served as court astrologer to the Emperor Frederick III. Though he sometimes used the pseudonym 'Peregrinus Roth', he was no fictitious personage, since others of his respected profession acknowledged him as their teacher. To its innumerable German editions can be added thirteen in Latin and Italian, published between 1490 and 1532 at Modena, Venice and Milan. Lichtenberger's work attained a perennial popularity rivalling that of *Old Moore's Almanac* in eighteenth- and nineteenth-century England. Within a few years great sales were enjoyed even by its imitators, amongst which was the *Prognosticon* (1496) by Joseph Grünpeck, historiographer and secretary to the Emperor Maximilian. Before long the satirists directed their shafts against such easy targets and produced farragos of monstrous and nonsensical prophecies. And early in the seventeenth century Johannes Kepler was still warning his readers that, absurd as unskilled astrology had become, they should not throw out the scientific baby with the superstitious bathwater—an early version of a since overworked metaphor. Meanwhile, reinforced by some forty or fifty lurid woodcuts, Lichtenberger's prophecies foretold, sometimes in mildly figurative terms, what so many educated men expected without the aid of the celestial science: a general overturning of the present social and ecclesiastical order.

It has been rightly remarked that the prophetic portions of his book bear but slight relation to the astrological portions, the latter being based upon the work of his contemporary Paul of Middelburg, who in 1492 produced an invective denouncing Lichtenberger's superstitions. The prophecies themselves mingle themes drawn from both the anti-German and the pro-German descendants of Joachim, but the latter tradition strongly predominates. Amid the forthcoming tribulation of Christianity,

[13] On Lichtenberger and associated writers: M. Reeves, pt. 3, ch. 5, especially pp. 347–51; H. Gravier, ch. 1.

Lichtenberger foresees a saviour-emperor at once chastizing and renewing the Church. Moreover, he clearly attaches this role to the Habsburgs. The marriage of Maximilian with Mary of Burgundy will make him the new Charlemagne, a ruler with his nucleus of power in those Burgundian lands once central to the Carolingian empire. In detail, Lichtenberger's prognostications turned out to be by no means the least accurate of their kind. He was roughly right in promising a series of violent disasters for the nation during the years 1523–5; right (though unoriginal) in predicting special calamities for the Church and the clergy; yet wrong in suggesting that the liberties won by the Swiss would soon be diffused across the heartland of Germany. Amongst those of the next generation who sponsored the republication of Lichtenberger was Martin Luther himself, yet in his preface of 1527 Luther cast doubts upon astrological prediction and denied that it could owe anything to divine revelation. One of his real aims was to show the papalists that Lichtenberger's sentence of doom upon their Church had not, as they had badly wanted to believe, been fulfilled merely by the Peasants' Revolt.

Meanwhile there had sprung forward other champions of social revolution, prepared to intensify the programme of the *Reformatio Sigismundi*. They are most strikingly represented by the *Book of a Hundred Chapters*, written not long after 1500 by an anonymous enthusiast now called 'the Revolutionary of the Upper Rhine'.[14] Weighting the scales rather unfairly in his own favour, this prophet announces that God will give the wicked world a respite in order to observe what will come of the divine commands about to be transmitted in his present tractate. These commands centre upon a brotherhood soon to be recruited from monogamous men of legitimate birth. Wearing uniforms marked by a yellow cross, the members will arise from the Black Forest to reign for a thousand years. They will slaughter all sinners, including the reigning emperor and 'the great men, both in the Church and among the laity'. The well-fed clergy, from

---

[14] H. Haupt; N. Cohn, pp. 114–23; F. L. Borchardt, pp. 116–19; translations from the *Book of a Hundred Chapters* are in G. Strauss, *Manifestations*, pp. 233–47. The first full edition, by G. Zschäbitz and A. Franke, was published in Berlin as recently as 1967.

the pope and the simoniacal prelates down to the unchaste monks, nuns and friars, will be killed at the rate of 2,300 a day over a period of four-and-a-half years. The moneylenders, price-fixers and profiteers will share their fate. Nor does the Revolutionary omit a historical appeal. He asserts that the primitive Germans had held all property in common until their social structure had been wrecked by the Romans, whose evil influences had been continued by the Church of Rome. The Germans had been the genuine chosen people not merely since Charlemagne but since the Creation. Until tongues became diversified at the Tower of Babel, the human race had spoken German, and the patriarch Japhet had migrated to Europe, bringing that language to Trier. From this capital a European empire had spread, Alexander (long a great figure in medieval German literature) being among its national heroes. By contrast there had also emerged the Latin peoples, who despite their shallow and corrupt character, had successfully conspired to overthrow the teutonic way of life. Yet now the day of cleansing and retribution was at hand. Having occupied western Europe and driven out the Turks, the new emperor would conquer the Holy Land and offer the Muslims a choice between death and baptism. The spiritual authority of Mainz would replace that of Rome, but at Mainz the German patriarch would administer the Church entirely under the rule of this emperor, the true spiritual and temporal leader of the human race. The latter was assigned to head a new brand of Christianity, and this would replace that of the historical Jesus, whose message had been only for the Jews.

One need hardly warn modern readers against exaggerating the importance of this outburst from a half-crazed, half-calculating extremist. Although many obscure confederacies and brotherhoods, both secular and religious, already existed by 1500, it remains hard to believe that such prophecies can have been fully credited by any considerable readership. Moreover, unlike the *Reformatio Sigismundi*, the *Book of a Hundred Chapters* did not go into print: it survives in only one manuscript and might well be regarded as a symptom rather than a cause of unrest and anti-clericalism. Nevertheless some of its ideas do seem to have influenced peasant prophets and rebels not long after its composition, while its bloodthirsty proposals find obvious later analogies in the programmes of that violent wing of Anabaptism foreshadowed by the more intellectual fanatic Thomas Müntzer and represented by the activist groups among the German sectarians of Luther's day.[15] Here came the desperate climax of the long and hopeless dream. As Norman Cohn has remarked, fantasies doubtless reflected the disappointment of the common people, who had cast successive emperors—Sigismund, Frederick III and Maximilian—for eschatological roles they had all signally failed to play. The vision of a German empire renovated and reborn finds here its feverish apotheosis, even as the ambitious policies of Maximilan crumbled, even as Berthold of Henneberg and the reformist Electors strove soberly but in vain to reassemble the nation around a more strictly constitutional monarchy.

One may scarcely attempt a sketch of Luther's more remote background without reference to the religion of the common people, who despite their besetting economic and social grievances responded but sluggishly to the manifestos and ideologies of jurists, prophets and classical scholars. Indeed, we can read few paragraphs by modern German historians concerning the century before Luther's advent without encountering the shibboleth *Frömmigkeit*, that special Catholic piety which, according to Janssen and his successors, enwrapped the German nation of that day. Supposedly more simple, more intense, more widespread than that of other nations, this virtue is often made the prelude to a particular view of the Lutheran Reformation we have already mentioned: the view which regards it as a sudden, unpredictable bolt from the blue, a swift aberration imposed by a small minority of religious innovators and politicians upon this traditionalist Catholic nation.[16]

The present writer must confess openly to a certain scepticism concerning any unique national piety, and to a belief that the

[15] Guidance through G. H. Williams, index, s.v. 'Violence'.

[16] The best introduction to German popular religion in this period is in W. Andreas, ch. 3; further bibliography in S. Skalweit, pp. 425–6. In addition to the detail in Janssen, see also J. Lortz; W.-E. Peuckert; P. Wunderlich; and the article by B. Moeller, 'Frömmigkeit in Deutschland'. On Luther's own attitudes to saints and superstitions see O. C. Clemen, *Luther und die Volksfrömmigkeit seiner Zeit* (Dresden and Leipzig, 1938). On heretical groups, see C.-P. Clasen, 'Medieval Heresies in the Reformation.'

sudden acceptance of Protestantism by some communities concealed a longstanding instability. By a selective use of the sources one could depict a similar spectacle of primitive devotion in the Netherlands, in England, in Spain, and even in many areas of Renaissance Italy itself. All these countries could boast a popular religion of devout observance: all of them produced religious literature and art ranging from peasant integrity to febrile religiosity. And if lay gifts to the Church be a yardstick, these other nations must have poured at least as much per head into ecclesiastical buildings and charities as did the German laity. The present writer may be a victim of cultural chauvinism, but he cannot help feeling more deeply impressed by late medieval English cathedrals and parish churches than by their German equivalents. In both countries all such activities need to be further revalued by reference to class differentials. And so far as concerns the Germans, what an immense volume of evidence attests forces very different from those of the steady (but dull!) quality evoked by the words *pietas* and *Frömmigkeit*. The prevalent reality is better expressed by that other favourite term: *Volksreligiosität*. But was there ever an age—even in the social history of German *Angst*—more apprehensive, more questioning, more profoundly disturbed than the age of Dürer? Did any western society give clearer evidences of a tension between the boredom of its daily round and its aspiration toward new spiritual and intellectual powers? Did any declare with such frequency and conviction that the times were out of joint? When one has sampled the literature of question and protest[17] one need only turn to Dürer, who seems to stand on the pinnacle of genius not in order to isolate himself but to observe and to express the deep, unquiet spirit of his nation. If there did exist some unique element in the German soul, it stands revealed in the *Melancolia*, *The Four Horsemen*, *The Knight, Death and the Devil*. But that something is emphatically not *Frömmigkeit*. Could a less suitable term be invented to describe it?

If, however, we obstinately reject all these complications and counter-signs; even if we end by taking this German folk piety at the value current among the more insular German historians, it nevertheless fails to make Luther's Reformation a surprising and unpredictable outcome. As elsewhere in northern Europe,

[17] G. Strauss, *Manifestations*, pp. 208–22.

the 'popular' devotion ran along two courses. On the one hand came the religion of observances, of saint-placating, of Indulgence buying. This ran counter to the creative intellectual and spiritual trends of late medieval Christianity. The Council of Trent was to prune its luxuriance and, but for the natural reactions aroused among the Catholic establishment by Luther's violence, might well have pruned if far more drastically. On the other hand there flowed the new piety, the *devotio moderna*, its mainstream coming from the Netherlands and lower Rhineland, its ultimate sources lying in both the German and the Netherlandish mystics of the fourteenth century.[18] In its rank-and-file this was a bourgeois rather than a folk movement. In addition, its social effectiveness derived from clerical writers and from that semi-clerical order of social workers and school-founders, the Brethren of the Common Life. Its contemplative origins ensured that it could embrace only the minority of lay men and women having some natural flair for spiritual endeavour. By powerful implication at least, it rejected or ignored the rival religion of petty observances and prelatical fund-drives. Directly or by close proxy, its adherents received inspiration from a special literature: they found themselves committed to mental disciplines too rigorous for the minds of common men. Nevertheless a number of spiritual writers—presumably backed by a far greater number of confessors and counsellors—had been insisting that contemplative values could be attained even by lay men and women involved in the struggle to earn their daily bread and raise their families. Fragments of biography and the large sales of the *Imitation of Christ* indicate that the response to this challenge had become considerable throughout western and central Europe: even in England it merged with the powerful native parallel represented by Rolle and Hilton. Nevertheless the *devotio moderna* and its analogies had distinct limits, not merely because they were impervious to common minds, but because they proved so vulnerable to the blows of Luther and the Anabaptists.

The *Imitation of Christ* and the lesser devotional works of the movement were in no small measure destined to be forerunners and victims of the Reformation as well as pillars of the Counter

[18] On the advance of the *devotio* deep into Germany, see the three articles by W. A. Landeen. Skalweit cites B. Windeck, *Die Anfänge der Brüder vom Gemeinsamen Leben in Deutschland* (Bonn Dissertation, 1951).

Reformation. Everybody knew that the books of the *devotio moderna* were modern books: they could not expect to survive competition with a fine translation of the Bible, since the quest of this generation became ever more a quest for authority. Yet even had this competition never occurred, why should the vaunted German *Frömmigkeit* have disposed the nation to adhere loyally to the papacy of Alexander VI, of Julius II, of Leo X? Before the Counter Reformation what kinship had these pieties—superstitious or sophisticated—with such an adherence? Still less can they have fostered a loyalty toward those blue-blooded secularists the prince-bishops, who imposed such awful burdens upon the credibility of the German Church. The *devotio* offered a Quakerish programme of withdrawal and rejection, not a programme of ecclesiastical revolution. Yet it had obvious links with Protestantism, which also sought to replace observance-religion by heartfelt and exacting religion. On the other hand, in the Netherlands, where it had been more widely successful than in Germany, it seems to have retained the strength to compete with Luther's propaganda. Moreover in Bavaria, where Catholicism in its days of weakness enjoyed some un-usually effective political support, a surviving Catholic devotion doubtless helped the great Jesuit revivalist Peter Canisius around the middle of the sixteenth century. Despite these particular situations, it remains difficult to avoid the opinion that some German historians have not only made too much of German piety on the eve of the Reformation, but under the influence of nineteenth-century notions of orthodoxy have connected it too directly with the claims of Rome. Piety as expounded by the Indulgence-pedlar Tetzel was not even a frail wall around the papal position: it was a breach in that wall, beckoning to any determined attacker. Even the very different *devotio moderna* remained in Germany a somewhat tenuous and ambivalent factor. How many German lives is it likely to have directed? In the face of this unanswerable question we are at least entitled to question the more inflated claims. This much we may venture to say: that throughout much of Germany the new piety proved an Icarus with waxen wings, soaring for a time yet all too readily brought down by the stern heat of evangelical and sectarian Christianity.

2

Humanism and the National Myth

Though we have reserved the German humanists for separate treatment, we must insist that they never inhabited the vacuum within which modern surveys seem apt to place them.[1] They never constituted a race apart: with uneven abilities they sought to grasp the message of the ancient world and no one among them attained the character of a purely classical scholar. Like the other publicists we have already discussed, they were deeply involved both with German folk-legend and with the old imperial patriotism. They played an important and increasing role in their country's vernacular literature, and ultimately they acted as midwives to the Lutheran Reformation. Until this last phase arrived, most of them stood nearer to the conventional pieties or to the *devotio moderna* than to the secularist tendencies

---

[1] An introduction to German humanism is in W. Andreas, ch. 8. L. W. Spitz, *Religious Renaissance*, provides an admirable series of the main figures: another portrait gallery is provided by R. Newald. Among the more comprehensive general accounts are those by H. O. Burger; H. von Srbik. Seminal articles are those by B. Moeller; G. Ritter; and P. Joachimsen, the last being especially brilliant. Showing a good grasp of ideas and social background, U. Paul surveys the broad problem of the rise of the national consciousness in Germany. He stresses (chs. 1, 3) the importance of the Councils of Constance and Basle as foci. F. L. Borchardt provides a good analysis of the mythology of German origins; on pp. 327–32 he assesses the work of his predecessors. Amongst these T. Bieder, H. Dannenbauer, F. Gotthelf (slight), U. Paul, H. Riess, and P. H. Stemmermann appear in the Bibliography below. The last-named forms a good concise survey, moving forward to the seventeenth century, and providing material (chs. 5, 6) on early collections of Roman inscriptions. Later humanist historiography is considered in my ch. 10 below.

which had been for some time invading the ranks of the Italian humanists. It is true that German university circles played a great part in the rise of humanism, and that some princely patrons of the newer universities favoured studies clearly concerned with the education and the service of princes. Again, it has been argued that in Germany the rival scholastic studies were less deeply entrenched than in France and England. On the other hand, within the universities the humanists could not rapidly create self-sufficient empires since, despite the plethora of new foundations, the teaching patterns underwent a minimum of change. Endowments continued to flow mainly into the traditional studies, not into the pockets of those who wandered from one university to another, desiring only to impart and practise the *studia humanitatis*. Many of the classical enthusiasts had to find a precarious teaching function within the *trivium*, which still comprised the arts programme undertaken by freshmen. Outside their common love of the ancient world, the German humanists displayed a wide variety of intellectual, social and religious convictions. It is not easy to make a 'movement' out of men so different in temperament, activity and achievement as Agricola, Brant, Wimpfeling, Reuchlin, Mutian, Celtis, Hutten and Pirckheimer. And though Erasmus was often counted—sometimes even by himself—among the 'German' scholars, he remained both by origin and choice an uprooted cosmopolitan without any warmth of attachment to German national sentiment, let alone toward the empire.

Unlike some of the literary trends just described, humanism followed a historical, not a prophetic principle, building upon the past rather than upon the future. The main relevance of the past for the present enquiry lies in the deductions drawn by Germans of the fifteenth and sixteenth centuries from the early history—either true or mythological—of their own nation. In this field the humanists inherited and did not create an ideological context. The recent acute examination of this 'Renaissance myth' by Professor Borchardt shows clearly that throughout most of the fifteenth century popular writers rather than humanists dominated the scene. And while humanists duly took command around 1500, this popular element lingered on for another century or more.

From around the time of the Council of Constance (1414–18) numerous German chroniclers and literary men had been reading and speculating about the obscure origins of the Germanic peoples. As yet they lacked help from the one solid authority, the *Germania* of Tacitus. Instead, they employed wild etymological guesses to produce stories which, however absurd in the eyes of modern readers, can be assigned a creative role in the evolution of the German mind. For example, soon after 1418 Gobelinus Persona compiled a world history, the *Cosmodromium*, which amid a wealth of entertaining ancedote set forth fabulous origins for the Lombards, Goths, Huns, Saxons, Franks and English. The Franks undoubtedly came from Troy, though there remained doubt about the details. Some people alleged that a group of their fugitives elected one Francio as their leader and then adopted his name. But according to a rival story they had been at first enslaved by the Romans, then liberated by the Emperor Valentinian, so receiving the name 'Franks' or free men. Meanwhile the Saxons had descended from faithful survivors of the army of Alexander the Great and, having migrated to the Caucasus, had taken their name from the *Saxum Marpesiae*. Again, when the early Goths attacked Scythia, some monstrous witches (called in the Gothic tongue *Alirunae*) fled to the woods and coupled with fauns and satyrs. Thus they gave birth to the ferocious Huns, whom they tormented as babies in order to make them cruel. In such writings the transition from fable to history is a gradual one, and it usually becomes noticeable to us with the emergence of a few true facts concerning the Merovingian period.

Naturally, the Bible could also be made to yield attractive dividends to these makers or adaptors of myths. In particular the family of Noah provided an unimpeachable antiquity for the German race. Some writers relate how Japhet came to Europe after the flood, along with his sons Gog and Magog. Rather more convincingly, Noah was discovered to have begotten post-diluvial offspring, including Tuisco, who gave his name to the Germans, the *Teutsch*. Better still, the moon (*Mond*) and the sun (*Sonne*), venerated by the ancient Germans, were derived from Tuisco's son and daughter-in-law, Mannus and Sunno! It should not, however, be supposed that either humanists or pre-humanists attained anything like a consensus of opinion on these stories.

Drawing from the Old Testament, ancient history and geography, medieval legend and German nomenclature, the game offered infinite permutations. Decade after decade it appealed to men of learning, while the advent of humanism, instead of imposing more sceptical attitudes, enriched the subject-matter and fertilized the imagination.

As befitted a superior mind, Nicholas of Cusa approached these speculations with restraint. On the other hand, with perverse ingenuity and labour, Abbot Trithemius and others composed bogus sources in order to attain verisimilitude. Toward these latter, literary scholars have been most indulgent, pointing out with truth that Trithemius did not live in the age of Ranke. Yet one may doubt whether notions of historical veracity were regarded with general contempt in Germany around 1500. If so, a marvellous change occurred within the following half century, after which Sleidan, as we shall see, enunciated Ranke's ideals almost in Ranke's words. Whatever the case, this game of myths was played by some Germans with no little skill. More successfully than their French and English rivals, they managed to provide an atmosphere of erudition. They became particularly adept at demolishing a fantastic story with a barrage of objections, merely to replace it by another story at least equally fantastic, but now invested with an air of critical acumen. Yet from our present viewpoint, the chief significance of this mythologizing literature lies in its contribution to the legend of a nation resplendent in antiquity, valour and simple piety. Even before God took the empire from the less deserving Romans, here in the northern forests had flourished the obvious recipients of empire, the noblest Romans of them all. Here at least the German authors stood united: that egregious scholar who established etymological and historical links between Vestal Virgins and Westphalian nuns only provided an extreme case. And when we have finished laughing at the myths, we should surely accept them as a serious ingredient in the patriotism not only of semi-literate townsmen but of the humanists, who doubtless felt themselves different from their benighted predecessors, yet remained for several decades emotionally conditioned to reinforce rather than to destroy the imagined origins of their uniquely virtuous nation.

To exemplify the complex situation of the German spirit on the eve of the Reformation, we might possibly explore the mind and art of Albrecht Dürer. Instead we shall cite the less subjective spectacle of Sebastian Brant (*c.* 1458–1521), the famous author of *The Ship of Fools*.[2] Brant's position within the humanist ranks cannot be challenged. Reared in the leading schools of that rising tradition at Schlettstadt and Basle, well known for his *Varia Carmina* of 1498, he enjoyed the friendship of Reuchlin and received a veritable panegyric from Erasmus. He stood prominent among those who addressed their careful hexameters and distichs to the oft-lauded Maximilian. On the other hand, he wrote much in German, including his immensely popular *Ship of Fools* (1494), and he found a vast readership among townsmen innocent of humanist learning. In this dualism of courtly and popular appeal, he seems a forerunner of the Reformation publicists. He deliberately translated his own and others' Latin verses into German, and he succeeded not only in turning from Latin to vernacular writing but in gradually strengthening his German style throughout his career. Again, his work shows profound debts to medieval German sources, while he became distinctly committed to the Joachite prophecies, relating them publicly to Maximilian. Certain of his minor poems call upon the latter to assume a commanding role in world history, while in 1498 he published a new edition of Aytinger's *Revelations of Methodius* (1496), both his own preface and the text of the book foretelling Maximilian's destiny as victor over the infidel and as renovator of the Church. As late as 1518 Brant was addressing verses of exhortation to Maximilian. On the other hand, this activity cannot be regarded as a screen to cover either heretical or socialist aspirations. A fervent Christian piety often breathes through his verse in both languages. His devotion to the Virgin caused him and other Strassburgers (including Jakob Locher, who translated *The Ship of Fools* into Latin) to be attacked by the Dominicans, who in common with the majority of scholastic

[2] On Sebastian Brant see C. Schmidt, vol. i, bk. 2; U. Paul, ch. 10; H. O. Burger, pp. 258–63. *Das Narrenschiff*, ed. M. Lemner (Tübingen, 1962) has the 1494 text, with the additions of 1495 and 1499. An able translation is that by E. H. Zeydel, *The Ship of Fools* (New York, 1944, 1962). Note also W. Gilbert, 'Sebastian Brant; Conservative Humanist' in *Archiv für Reformationsgeschichte*, xlvi (1955).

opinions had long opposed the controversial doctrine of the Immaculate Conception. And so far as concerns secular affairs, it cannot be claimed that Brant foreshadows the literature of social protest. *The Ship of Fools* anticipates Erasmus' *Praise of Folly* in ridiculing impartially the weaknesses of every class. The author detests greed and ostentation wherever he finds it, not least in ambitious men striving to rise from the class into which they have been placed by providence. He does not spare the sins of the peasants, even though his attitude toward the working masses remains far from ungenerous. He cannot be accused of anti-papal tendencies, even though he regards the emperor as the most likely source of church reform. One of his few positive enthusiasms is manifested in the passage calling upon the nation to back Maximilian and so restore the glories of the empire. Zeydel thus translates these lines:

> The Germans once were highly praised
> And so illustrious was their fame,
> The Reich was theirs and took their name;
> But soon we found a German nation
> That brought its own realm ruination...
> But all you lords, you states and kings,
> Do not permit such shameful things!
> If you'll support the ship of state
> It will not sink but bear its freight.
> Your king is all benignity,
> He'll don for you knight's panoply,
> Rebellious lands he will subdue,
> But you must help, he needs you too.
> The noble Maximilian
> He merits well the Roman crown.
> They'll surely come into his hand,
> The Holy Earth, the Promised Land,
> He'll undertake it any day
> If he can trust in you and may.[3]

The German humanists who grew to maturity before 1500 inherited such patriotic and imperial traditions; yet, while they often criticized abuses, they displayed no systematic pattern of

[3] *The Ship of Fools*, trans. E. H Zeydel (New York, 1962), pp. 320-21.

anticlerical, conciliarist or anti-papal attitudes. The 'father of German humanism', Rudolf Agricola (1444–85), showed himself an exceptionally conventional son of the Church.[4] A genial Petrarchan, he made only mild references to the need for ecclesiastical reform. Invited by the local bishop in 1484 to address a clerical synod at Worms, he concentrated upon the dignity of the priesthood and its privileged role in the mystery of transubstantiation. His final work, the congratulatory oration to the newly elected Innocent VIII, passed beyond the bounds of civil eulogy and hailed Rome as the world-centre from which there would henceforth radiate the salvation of man. A tradition that Agricola joined with his master Wessel Gansfort to attack clerical celibacy and exalt Justification by Faith was cited long afterwards by Melanchthon, yet it has rightly been dismissed as in all likelihood a mixture of faulty recollection and wishful thinking. Scarcely less clerical by upbringing and temperament was that more accomplished humanist Jacob Wimpfeling (1450–1528), yet he became an arch-patriot, one whose patriotism was directed not merely against complacent Italians like Enea Silvio, but against the French menace. As a fellow-countryman of Brant in Alsace—in fact the son of a saddler at Schlettstadt—he came from the province which had most reason to assert its national character.[5]

In 1501 Wimpfeling published his *Germany; in Honour of the City of Strassburg*, a short treatise intent to prove that the Germans had not inherited the imperial office through the Gauls but directly from Rome. Though the names of the ancient Roman emperors show that they derived from several provinces, in no cases were they French, while since Charlemagne all the emperors had clearly sprung from noble German families. To show Pepin's nationality, Wimpfeling uses a curious if popular argument. German mothers commonly warn their children that one cannot do something 'even were one as wise as King Pepin'. Obviously the authors of such a national proverb would never have cited the example of a French king! It seems fair to add that

[4] L. W. Spitz, *Religious Renaissance*, ch. 2.
[5] *Ibid.*, ch. 3 and pp. 301–6 provide guidance on the large Wimpfeling literature. A long account of his life and works is in C. Schmidt, vol. i, bk. 1, while vol. ii, bk. 1 has chapters on his collaborators and disciples. Note also F. L. Borchardt, pp. 98–103.

Wimpfeling also produces more solid evidence for his thesis, based on spoken language and personal names at the court of Charlemagne. He also enters the geopolitical sphere by arguing that the Franco-German frontier is formed by the Vosges, not by the Rhine; and his work was to be reprinted and quoted by German patriots when Louis XIV began his threat against Alsace. A weightier book was Wimpfeling's *Epitome of Germanic Affairs* (1505), a well-organized history of the Germanic peoples since the days of Tacitus. In its concluding section it praises not only their faithfulness, valour and generosity but also the outstanding cultural achievements of the nation. Those special regional elements which so often underlay the national patriotism of the period do not fail to appear. Printing, we are told, developed in Strassburg before being carried by Strassburgers into Italy. As for the sculptures of Strassburg Cathedral, they had aroused the wonder of Enea Silvio, and would indeed have been recognized as perfect even by Phidias and the sculptors of antiquity. These enthusiastic passages in no way conflicted with an occasional attack not only upon Rome but upon papal influences within the German Church. Like many others of the establishment Wimpfeling sometimes criticized simony, concubinage and the misuse of the canon law: he demanded better schools for the people and intervened in the old conflict between the secular and the regular clergy. Yet he had no fresh solutions to offer the Church. In September 1510 Maximilian, having cursed Julius II in a private letter to his daughter Margaret, consulted Wimpfeling on ecclesiastical reform and elicited from him a document which began in the best tradition of the *gravamina* with a list of abuses emanating from Rome: the revocation by popes of agreements made by their predecessors, their interferences with the election of German prelates, their trafficking in Indulgences for money, their summoning of cases to Rome. Wimpfeling adds that the overburdened people of Germany may well follow the Bohemians into schism from Rome. But when it comes to a remedy the author seems to capitulate. The emperor should plead with the Holy Father to accord better treatment to his German sons. After all, more energetic actions might alienate the three ecclesiastical Electors or even bring down an interdict from Rome. The friars would raise the people against the emperor: it was even conceivable that the pope would imitate his medieval predecessors and deprive Maximilian of the imperial crown.

Five years later Wimpfeling dedicated a more strongly worded manifesto[6] to a most appropriate German recipient: Albrecht of Mainz, the young sybarite whose grasping for luxury and power were about to provoke the Indulgence scandal and Luther's revolt. It began with a tribute to Martin Mair, sometime chancellor of that archdiocese, and then took the form of a belated response to Mair's adversary Enea Silvio, Pope Pius II. The points are ably made, the issues by no means outdated. Enea had argued that Germany should feel profoundly indebted to Rome for her initial conversion to Christianity. Wimpfeling now replied that Rome herself had been converted by St. Peter, a Jew from the Holy Land. And for that matter, Rome should also feel indebted to Germany. 'Have not two of our compatriots invented the noble art of printing, which makes it possible to propagate the correct doctrines of faith and morals throughout the world and in all languages?' He then lists the time-honoured grievances: the citation of suits to Rome for trivial reasons, the bestowal of benefices on unworthy men, non-residence and pluralism, lack of hospitality and the ruin of church buildings, simony, back-biting and immorality among the priesthood. The Council of Basle had been inspired when it decreed that a third of all benefices should go to men well-versed in the Bible. The weight of papal taxation on poor burghers, clerics and peasants had become insupportable, and a violent insurrection against the Church might well be imminent. 'It would not take much for the Bohemian poison to penetrate our German lands.' And with similar prescience Wimpfeling finally alluded to the moral and financial blight occasioned by the preaching and sale of Indulgences. In fact he made very many of the criticisms so soon to be made by Luther; yet again, in the last resort, he saw no course beyond verbal remonstrance. Predictably enough, Wimpfeling rejected the stronger remedies advocated by Hutten and the theological revolution urged by Luther. So he lived on into a lonely old age in a world ever more foreign and violent. His roots lay very deep in the Catholic past.

[6] Passages are translated in G. Strauss, *Manifestations*, pp. 40–48.

Joachimsen has reminded us that all the three famous Alsatians, Geiler, Brant and Wimpfeling, criticized ignorant monks, yet wanted to become hermits in the Black Forest; and that all three were enthusiastic disciples of Gerson and his mystical theology.

This loyalty and caution, so characteristic of the age-group, recurred even in the case of Johannes Reuchlin (1453–1522), a scholar far more deeply and bitterly involved in the struggle against ecclesiastical reaction.[7] Reuchlin's relations with scholasticism and Biblical humanism—and consequently with the Reformation—have been commonly oversimplified. His misfortunes dated from 1509, when the converted Jew Johannes Pfefferkorn obtained a commission from the emperor to perambulate Germany and confiscate Jewish books. When in the next year conflicting pressures induced Maximilian to suspend this campaign, the thwarted Pfefferkon slandered Reuchlin in print, asserting that he had accepted bribes from the Jews and that a Jewish scholar had written works claimed by Reuchlin as his own. The distinguished Hebraist, who had already advised the emperor against the destruction of Jewish literature, descended into the arena and rent his adversary asunder in the pamphlet *Augenspiegel*. When the latter suffered a counter-attack from the ultra-conservative theologians of Cologne, Reuchlin also turned upon them in a *Defence against his Cologne Calumniators*. Nevertheless both his tracts were suppressed by the imperial government and condemned also by the theological faculties of Louvain, Mainz and Erfurt. Thenceforward he had to encounter a personal foe immensely more formidable than the vulgar Pfefferkorn: this was Jakob van Hochstraten, a Cologne Dominican and inquisitor of heretical pravity within Germany. Late in 1513 Hochstraten tried to summon Reuchlin before his court of Inquisition, but fell foul of the privileges claimed by the archbishop of Mainz. An

[7] L. W. Spitz, *Religious Renaissance*, ch. 4 and his article in *Archiv*. J. H. Overfield minimizes the 'humanist *versus* obscurantist' element in the Reuchlin affair, and stresses antisemitism. For more traditional views, see e.g. H. Holborn, *Ulrich von Hutten*, pp. 53ff., and F. G. Stokes. On Erasmus and Reuchlin, see the article by C. S. Meyer in *Moreana*. A basic bibliography on Reuchlin is in E. G. Léonard, pp. 30–32. On the position and attitudes of the Jews themselves see H. H. Ben-Sasson and L. I. Newman.

appeal having been made to Leo X, that pope remitted the case to the bishop of Speyer, who thereupon denied that the *Augenspiegel* was heretical, and even ordered Hochstraten to leave Reuchlin in peace. Yet with a dogged pertinacity worthy of a better cause, Hochstraten went off to Rome and spent the next six years in further efforts to get Reuchlin's views condemned. Having regrettably divided not only the rulers but the scholars of Europe, he at last succeeded; and on the papal verdict against the *Augenspiegel*, the tired Reuchlin accepted the decision and was allowed to die in peace.

By the time the inquisitor had won this hollow victory, the nature of the struggle had changed, and it was harming the Church more than the original anti-Jewish campaign could possibly have done. Yet at no stage did the Reuchlin affair attain that heroic simplicity accorded to it by so many historians of humanism. During its earlier stages, it was a conflict between antisemitic zealots and the leading Christian Hebraist, who needed to collaborate with learned Jews and to preserve Cabbalist literature. In addition, Reuchlin was a trained lawyer, who believed that Jews were no heretics and that their legal rights should be rigorously maintained. But if the Cologne theologians were attacking humanism in general, at least they betrayed no sign of the notion, while the humanists for their part, at least until 1514, displayed no evidence of alarm, or indeed much overt interest in Reuchlin's problems. Even in the later stages, not a few failed to develop a warm partisanship. In particular Erasmus never gave Reuchlin more than perfunctory support, and having little personal interest in Hebrew studies characteristically despised the whole affair as a sordid interference with his own noble project to unite and inspire Christendom. Mutian's backing also remained guarded, and in his correspondence he questioned Reuchlin's conduct. All the same, between 1514 and 1516 the battle-front did widen perceptibly. A number of the younger humanists publicly rallied to the cause of Reuchlin, and they began to impugn the scholarship of his opponents. In some eyes at least, the fight had now become a fight between scholastic theologians and humanists. For the first time Reuchlin himself began asking whether he was being attacked for daring to conduct a linguistic enquiry into the sacred texts.

Despite these widening queries, the matter might have continued in the main to revolve around the status of Jewish books, but for Crotus Rubeanus and Ulrich von Hutten, authors of the *Epistolae Obscurorum Virorum* (1515, 1517). These new contestants purported to discover a vast conspiracy by the theologians to suppress not merely Hebrew studies but humanist criticism as a whole, especially as applied to the Scriptures. Needless to add, wherever humanists flourished this larger tension had never lain far below the surface. That many theologians held a superstitious regard for the text of the Vulgate and a corresponding suspicion of Greek and Hebrew studies can likewise be demonstrated. Yet the unattractive character and aims of Reuchlin's adversaries should not encourage the simplified legend of a straight conflict between humanist enlightenment and scholastic obscurantism. Symbolizing the complexities of the situation, the prime target of the *Epistolae*, Ortwin Gratius, was no austere Thomist. However antisemitic, Ortwin remained a humanist, and had been praised as such by none other than Wimpfeling. And as for Reuchlin himself, he stood in somewhat remote detachment from his self-appointed champions of the *Epistolae*, especially from Hutten, while it remains a notorious fact that he survived to repudiate Luther. Platonist and Cabbalist, Reuchlin had as a public figure some disabilities not wholly unlike those of the scholastics whom he despised. A cool theologian rather than a Pauline existentialist, abtruse and esoteric in his approaches to Christianity, he belonged to an élite and felt no desire to lead young anticlericals or practical reformists. Nevertheless his career acquired the utmost significance in its relation to that of Luther. At the very moment of the latter's revolt, when the *Letters of Obscure Men* had just brutally simplified the issues, Reuchlin was still locked in combat with his persecutors; and some of his humanist allies mistakenly supposed that he and Luther were fighting a common battle against the entrenched forces of darkness and reaction. At the later stage when the humanists perceived the distinctions through the haze of enthusiasm, most of the older generation among them—and indeed some of the younger—withdrew support from Luther.

Within the conservative generation must be placed Mutian (Conrad Muth or Mudt, 1471–1526), the leader of the most

renowned humanist group outside Alsace.[8] Once a pupil of the
Brethren of the Common Life at Deventer, he never abandoned
the inward-looking pietism of the *devotio moderna*. Though more
of a formal philosopher—and a neoplatonist—than the other
leading German humanists, he never lost the distrust of the
devotio for intellectualism and he wrote toward the end of his
life, 'The peasant knows many things which the philosopher
does not know. Christ our life died for us: this I believe as most
certain.' Was this not a conscious recollection of the *Imitation
of Christ*?

> For though you knew the whole Bible by heart and the sayings
> of all the philosophers, what does it profit you without the
> love of God and without his grace?...Surely a humble peasant
> who serves God is better than a proud philosopher, who,
> neglecting himself, labours to understand the system of the
> heavens.

But Mutian did not, like Karlstadt in later days, denounce
learning and seek to follow the dictates of peasant wisdom.
A famous teacher at Erfurt and a canon at nearby Gotha, he built
up the humanist circle which included Georg Spalatin, Luther's
friend and later champion at the Saxon court. For a modern
reader who conventionally regarded Mutian as a mere conservative, his actual writings would contain some surprises. He
makes frequent attacks on ceremonial religion, on salvation by
observances, on clerical ethics, on Rome as a veritable inferno of
criminal practices. And even as late as 1521 he could express a
certain admiration for Luther. Nevertheless, like most scholars
of his age and devotional background, Mutian ended by rejecting
the Reformer's mature thought. By contrast with Luther's
anthropology, he retained an Erasmian confidence in human
freedom and moral capability.

Amongst the major humanists a thoroughgoing nationalism
found its successive champions in Conrad Celtis (1459–1508)

[8] L. W. Spitz, *Religious Renaissance*, ch. 7, and his article 'The Conflict
of Ideals'; also H. O. Burger, ch. 9. On Mutian's background at Erfurt:
P. Kalkoff; F. W. Kampschulte; R. W. Scribner. A main source is *Der
Briefwechsel des Mutianus Rufus*, ed. C. Krause (*Zeitschrift des Vereins für
hessische Geschichte und Landeskunde, Neue Folge, Supplement* 9, Kassel,
1885).

and in the much younger Ulrich von Hutten (1488–1523). Compared with Celtis—whose tirades sometimes suggest the literary poseur—Hutten was a deep-dyed anticlerical nationalist. Celtis may nevertheless be ranked among the founders of the new secularist German humanism. Whereas his contemporaries remained half theologians and philosophers, whereas they hesitated to stage an outright attack on the time-honoured disciplines and the scholastic world, Celtis showed himself temperamentally secular and militant.[9] Both he and Hutten were *poetae*, wandering scholars without deep roots in government and society. They bore at least a family resemblance to Burckhardt's archetypal man of the Renaissance, free from ecclesiastical pieties, enjoying self-reliant combat with the forces of reaction, savouring women and wine to the full and glorying in the unlimited potential of man. Both at an early age fell victims to syphilis. It is an ironical but undeniable fact that such men helped to prepare the nation for Luther's revolt.

Already in 1487 the young Celtis was crowned at Nuremberg by Frederick III as the first native poet laureate of the empire. He also became the first humanist to lecture on Tacitus in a German university. In 1500 he published the *Germania* in a student-edition, and with it a poem *Germania Generalis* heralding the composition of a *Germania Illustrata*, a treatise on topography and history intended to be his masterpiece. Though Celtis never completed this work, his fine description of the origins, institutions and customs of Nuremberg (written in Latin but translated by 1495) survives as a sample of the grand design. Patriotism had come of age: the Germans could feel more confident that they had inherited the empire as a result of their intellectual merits. Before Erasmus flayed Italian cultural arrogance in his *Praise of Folly*, Celtis performed a similar operation in his *Five Books of Epigrams*. Wherever in later days

[9] See L. W. Spitz, *Conrad Celtis*, and ch. 5 of his *Religious Renaissance*; U. Paul, ch. 7; H. O. Burger, chs. 7, 8; F. L. Borchardt, pp. 106–9; L. W. Forster; L. Sponagel; H. Rupprich, *Der Briefwechsel des Konrad Celtis* (Munich, 1934). His work in German history and topography is discussed in G. Strauss, *Sixteenth Century Germany*, while his *Norimberga* was attractively edited by A. Werminghoff, *Conrad Celtis und sein Buch über Nürnberg* (Freiburg, 1921). On the epic *Ligurinus*, see the edition by J. Sturm, *Der Ligurinus* (*Studien und Darstellungen*, viii, ed. H. Grauert, Freiburg, 1911).

we notice Italians like Guicciardini still applying the word
barbari to foreigners, especially to teutons, we should be
reminded not merely of the revolt of Martin Luther but of many
earlier decades of German anger. In 1492 the address of Celtis
at the inaugural ceremonies of the university of Ingolstadt rang,
in the words of Lewis Spitz, 'with a fervour not unlike that of
Fichte's *Speeches to the German Nation*'.

> Resume, O men of Germany, that spirit of older time where-
> with you so often confounded and terrified the Romans. Behold
> the frontiers of Germany: gather together her torn and
> shattered lands! Let us feel shame, yes, shame I say, to have
> let our nation assume the yoke of slavery and pay tribute to
> foreign barbarian kings.[10]

And he continues to bid his countrymen wrest their ports from
the Poles, win their entrance to the ocean from the Danes, link
up with their minority groups still separated from the main body
of the nation. And he does not forget to curse the foreign traders
from the south—doubtless he had mainly the Venetians in
mind—who at once drain Germany of her vast natural wealth
and stimulate her people's demand for luxuries. The occasion
at Ingolstadt should not be regarded as unique. For example, a
parallel speech came from the humanist Heinrich Bebel, who,
when crowned laureate in 1501 by Maximilian, responded with a
classic outburst of wounded national pride, looking back at a
glorious past and lauding the heroic exercise of Christian
virtues by the Germans.[11]

Though he discovered the renowned Roman itinerary map
called the Peutinger Table, the interest of Conrad Celtis in the
search for German source-materials was not limited to those
of antiquity. More especially he rediscovered (and printed in
1501) the tenth-century plays in the manner of Terence by
Roswitha, abbess of Gandersheim. He also found the epic
Ligurinus which commemorated the exploits of Frederick
Barbarossa; and he stood among those who celebrated the
technical discoveries of the Germans, from gunpowder to the

[10] L. W. Forster, pp. 45–7.
[11] G. Strauss, *Manifestations*, pp. 64–72, translates a large part; cf. also
F. L. Borchardt, pp. 109–14.

art of printing, the blessings of which latter he proclaimed in verse. By the same token, he lost few opportunities to record his patriotic distaste for Italians, Bohemians and Jews. In short, Celtis must be regarded as the writer in whose hands romantic literary nationalism took final shape and organization. He founded humanist sodalities to publicize the new studies and he left numerous active disciples: such men as Johannes Cuspinian, Rhagius Aesticampianus, Vadianus and Aventinus.

Celtis was by no means the first patriot to exploit the *Germania* of Tacitus, to glorify by that unique shaft of light the primitive valour and simplicity of the nation. The sole extant copy of this text had been discovered in a German monastery by the Italian scholar Enoch of Ascoli, and had been printed at Nuremberg in 1473. Alongside this source could be laid the story of the destruction of the Roman legions by Arminius, narrated by Tacitus in the *Annals*, a work printed in Venice as early as 1470, though not until 1515 with the addition of its 'lost' books. Tacitus did not remain the permanent preserve of scholars, since in 1526 Eberlin von Günzburg—an important Lutheran and social pamphleteer in his own right—published a vernacular translation of the *Germania*. Altogether the discovery and popularization of Tacitus contributed strongly to the self-confident, not to say aggressive attitudes of German intellectuals and of their half-educated followers.[12] There arose and spread that appealing image of teutonic integrity which ended by capturing the impressionable Machiavelli and, alongside his more factual admiration for the orderly government and civic spirit of German cities, served to reinforce his charges of decadence against the Italians. Could any discoveries have come more opportunely for scholars north of the Alps? From being barbarians in the outer twilight, the Germans had become exemplars in the school of social and even political thought. Or, to put the matter in less complimentary terms, long before the explorers discovered the noble savage, his prototypes can be traced in at least two sources: the cult of Tacitus and the praise accorded by the *devotio moderna* to the pious wisdom of simple men.

[12] P. Joachimsen, 'Tacitus im deutschen Humanismus'; F. L. Borchardt, ch. 4.

Even when supplemented for later historical periods by the *Nibelungenlied*, by Einhard's *Life of Charlemagne*, by the discoveries of Celtis, Tacitus did not fully satisfy the voracious appetites of the patriots, who clutched eagerly at forgeries purporting to enlarge the authentic sources. Indeed, an Italian led the way. The Dominican Annius of Viterbo, suitably enough an eminent Vatican official under Alexander VI, had published a collection of spurious pieces under the title *De Commentariis Antiquitatum*, among them a 'vanished' work attributed to Berosus, an actual historian of the third century. This forgery established the tale that Noah made his son Tuisco his favourite heir and sent him to take possession of the lands between the Rhine and the Don, a territory to be called Deutschland after its first king, or *Germania* by another derivation so tortuous as not to be worth retailing. The fraud, later countenanced in good faith by reputable historians like Aventinus, was half believed by many readers even after its demolition by the finer critical intelligence of Beatus Rhenanus, in his *Three Books of Germany* (1531).

It cannot be claimed that the forgers were all smart Italians, and in any case their inventiveness must be seen in the context of the period. For example, in England the Arthurian legend was still being taken as literal truth: it survived not merely in historiography but in the political propaganda of the early Tudor kings. In Germany the respected friend of Celtis, Johannes Trithemius (1462–1516), abbot of Sponheim, published in 1514 a *Compendium of the Origins of the Frankish Race, from the Twelve Last Books of Hunibald*. Here a fictitious author had been created in order to supply some badly-needed information concerning the early Franks. More pardonably, Trithemius had also produced in his *Ecclesiastical Writers* (1494) and his *Illustrious Men of Germany* (1495) extensive biographical collections showing how the Germans had shone with godly learning and culture ever since their conversion to Christianity. Nourished thus by truth and fable alike, ultra-patriotic literature continued to gush forth during the years immediately preceding the revolt of Martin Luther. Even fellow humanists criticized the superlatives used by Pirckheimer's friend Irenicus (Franz Friedlieb, 1495–1559) in his *Exegesis Germaniae*

(1518), a gigantic monument of patriotism containing 488 chapters.[13]

Of such effusions, one of the more interesting is that of Johannes Nauclerus (Vergenhans, c. 1425–1510): *Chronicles of Memorable Things of Every Age and All Peoples*, an attempt at a universal history apparently seeking to supplant the one published at Nuremberg in 1492 by yet another friend of Celtis, the physician Hartmann Schedel.[14] Nauclerus, an old man at his death in 1510, illustrates the fact that extreme nationalism could grip not merely the younger generation but some of the senior German humanists. A tutor and diplomat in the service of the house of Württemberg (which rewarded him with various benefices), he compiled his *Chronicles* with the help of other scholars during the last two decades of his life, and he brought the story to the year 1500. Published posthumously at Tübingen in 1516, this history was hailed as a major literary achievement and it attained many editions, one as late as 1675. It still preserves a mild interest since it incorporates a vast number of sources, among them both the pseudo-Berosus and parts of genuine chronicles since lost. Not all its attitudes could have seemed modish after 1500. Though Nauclerus criticized simony and other abuses, he again belonged to the generation which retained a modicum of respect for the papacy, having visited Rome in 1482 with his pupil and patron Count Eberhard of Württemberg. Yet this respect did not prevent him from becoming in certain passages a vigorous exponent not only of patriotic imperialism but of something akin to pan-German racialism. Of Charlemagne's coronation he writes: 'On that day the Roman Empire was transferred from the Greeks [i.e. Byzantines] to the Germans in the person of Charles the Great'; and he asks which other nation under heaven has ever since shown such sincerity, so many great-hearted nobles, so many

[13] A survey and bibliography on Trithemius by P. P. Volk is in *Rheinische Vierteljahrsblätter*, xxvii (1962). See also U. Paul, ch. 8; H. O. Burger, p. 352; F. L. Borchardt, pp. 127–35. On the work of Irenicus see F. L. Borchardt, pp. 144–8. G. Strauss, *Manifestations*, pp. 72–4 translates a passage.

[14] On the biography of Nauclerus, I can add little to *ADB*. Interesting points are made by F. L. Borchardt, pp. 120–24. The British Museum has a copy of *Memorabilium omnis aetatis et omnium gentium chronici commentarii* (Tübingen, 1516).

mighty soldiers. He urges the German princes of his own day to maintain these splendid traditions, since 'God chose you before others, and gave you the monarchy of the world so that you should rule all nations'. Looking backward beyond Charlemagne, he develops the legend of Noah and Tuisco to mean that the German nation was the aboriginal, the dominant stock of Europe; in Wallace Ferguson's words, 'the *Urvolk* of Europe and later...the conquerors whose blood and vigor were injected into the British, French and Italian nations during the victorious era of the *Völkerwanderungen'*.[15]

Within the nationalism of the humanists there often existed regional elements, tending to a more detailed treatment and more fulsome praise of the author's regional *Stamm* and his background in historical topography. Commonly the patronage of some prince or city can be shown to have influenced such emphases. Nauclerus clearly leaned toward the Hohenstaufen house of his native Swabia. Under court patronage his much younger and more sophisticated successor Aventinus (Johann Turmair, 1477–1534) wrote his *Annals of the Dukes of Bavaria* in 1519–21 and translated them into German in 1526–33. Though unpublished for a further half-century, this attractively-written work became for two hundred years a standard interpretation of both Bavarian and German history within the context of universal history.[16] Though still misled by sources like the pseudo-Berosus, the ambitions of Aventinus to recover the regional past may be regarded as one of the more original contributions of the German humanists to historiography. This approach to history had parallels elsewhere in Europe, as in the county historians of Tudor England. But these English units were commonly too small to stimulate creative thinking, and on the whole the Germans had a better chance to avoid the parochial antiquarianism which has always tended to emasculate regional history in England. On the other hand, one may well detect in this approach the Achilles' heel of German intellectual nationalism. From the first their patriotic attitudes were so often

---

[15] W. K. Ferguson, *The Renaissance in Historical Thought* (Cambridge, Mass., 1948), p. 35.

[16] Aventinus is the subject of G. Strauss, *Historian in an Age of Crisis.* The same author's *Sixteenth Century Germany* admirably surveys the broad theme of topographical and regional historiography.

qualified by both universalist and regionalist thinking as to lessen the inspiration they could have provided for a comprehensive German national state similar to those evolving in France, England and Spain. Writers like the court historian of Bavaria could boast a sincere German patriotism, yet in the event their work tended to serve the needs of the princes, whose territorial states, strengthened in the long run by Reformation and Counter Reformation, were to provide the substitutes for a German national state. In this as in other senses, the *Stamm* became an ancestor of regional dynasticism. Despite this resemblance to his predecessors, Aventinus did not merely re-echo the themes of Nauclerus and the old generation. He displayed strong leanings toward Lutheranism and showed little regard for the papacy. His treatment of the national myth combines old and new attitudes. While carefully glossing over those passages of Tacitus which report the pagan practices of the ancient Germans, he not only accepts the shadowy Tuisco but credits him with the establishment of a monotheistic faith without a priesthood. He naturally follows Tacitus in praising the dress, diet and morals of the ancient teutons, uncorrupted by trade and the modern craving for luxury. Yet he can also see the story in Tacitus from the standpoint of the Romans, who inevitably, even naturally, would regard the Germanic barbarians as we regard the Turks. And like others of his day, Aventinus contrasts ancient simplicity and austerity with the guzzling and gourmandizing of his own day, the excesses which (as Luther too was saying) drew the scorn of other nations upon the Germans.

As we enter the years of Luther's revolt, we may possibly dispel certain misconceptions by drawing attention to three characteristics of developing German nationalism: its imperialist tendencies, its anti-French aspects, and its capacity to interest all the German-speaking populations. As it absorbed Tacitus, together with mythological accretions and racialist fancies, humanist nationalism did not shed its regard for the Holy Roman Empire, or for the individual Habsburg emperors of the day. Ulrich von Hutten and his contemporaries went on believing—or felt it necessary to affect belief—in the reformist role of the emperor, and they too received Charles V in a most hopeful spirit when in 1519 he succeeded the still popular

Maximilian. Again, national sentiment was directed against Italy and the papacy, but these were by no means the sole targets. German writers had not forgotten the tradition of resentment springing from the old quarrels at Prague and from the disastrous failures of the crusades led by Germans in 1421–30 against the Hussites. Occasionally they still sought to dismiss the Czechs as ignorant barbarians. Again, we have already observed that sentiment could be directed against France, the more so since some major centres of humanism like Strassburg and Schlettstadt lay in Alsace, upon which the French crown already had aggressive designs and where a pro-French party existed. It was Wimpfeling who directed feeling against the French, and he was followed by several other Alsatians like Sebastian Brant, Thomas Wolf and Hieronymus Gebwiler. These attitudes were naturally welcome to Maximilian, who had received bitter affronts from the French monarchy and needed friends in frontier provinces remote from the main centres of Habsburg influence. Alsatian Germanism had good reason to become intensified upon his death, when Francis I actively sought to be elected emperor. Later on the Catholic humanist Thomas Murner ridiculed the more extreme manifestations of this patriotism, even though he too had no doubt that his province and his people were German.

Confronting these phenomena as a whole, we should in present terminology speak of Germanic rather than of German nationalism, since they were far from being bounded by Bismarckian frontiers or even by those of the functioning Holy Roman Empire of that day. Many of these humanists failed to share the European cosmopolitanism of Erasmus, yet they displayed what might be somewhat paradoxically called a pan-German cosmopolitanism, which put them at ease throughout German-speaking lands with extremely varied political and social backgrounds. The phenomenal expansiveness of Lutheranism within these bounds was thus preceded by the expansiveness of a teutonic humanism, turning ever more from the Latin to the German language. This tendency could flourish even within the cities of the Swiss Confederation, which had long ago extracted themselves from the framework of the Empire. Language and literature provided very solid ties between the politically divergent sections of the German-speaking world. Among the more accomplished and productive classical scholars of the early sixteenth century was Vadianus (Joachim von Watt, 1484–1551), who was born and died at St. Gallen, where he also served as burgomaster.[17] Becoming in due course a loyal adherent of Zwinglianism, he studied Swiss antiquities and left a scholarly history of the famous Abbey of St. Gallen. On the other hand Vadianus was no narrow Swiss patriot armed with the traditional distrust for the Habsburgs, those former oppressors of Swiss nationhood. He had also studied, taught and attained the office of rector in the University of Vienna. Moreover his early fame there reached such a height that, in 1514, he too received the laureate crown from Maximilian. Like Aventinus, he could combine universal with regional history, but his writing indicates a pronounced anti-papalism and a Germanic patriotism based upon veneration for the Frankish monarchy and the Holy Roman Empire.

It need scarcely be added that the survival of imperialism and its re-clothing in humanist costumes occurred also in the congenial atmosphere of Maximilian's shifting court and under his patronage in Vienna, where the emperor fostered a group of intellectuals devoted not only to scholarship but to glorifying his personality and his struggles against the popes and the French. The atmosphere was well established by his quasi-autobiographical writings—the verse epic *Teuerdank* and the prose *White King*—conceived by Maximilian though composed with the aid of Markus Treitz and other ghost-writers.[18] Essentially non-comprehending where the deeper aspirations of humanism

[17] On Vadian, see p. 119, n. 7 below.
[18] On Maximilian's humanists, and the emperor as publicist, see R. Zinnhobler; P. Diederichs; H. von Srbik, vol. i, ch. 2; H. O. Burger, pp. 396–401. On his historiographer Cuspinian, see U. Paul, ch. 9. For several other important references see S. Skalweit, pp. 423–4, 428. Among the older biographies, E. Heyck, *Kaiser Maximilian I* (Bielefeld and Leipzig, 1898) is concise and well illustrated; others are by Heinrich Ulmann (2 vols., Stuttgart, 1884–91, repr. Vienna, 1967); R. W. S. Watson (1902); G. E. Waas (New York, 1941); R. Buchner (Göttingen, 1959); H. Wiesflecker (vol. i, Munich, 1971). A bibliography on imperial reform is in S. Skalweit, pp. 423–4. For comment see K. S. Bader in G. Strauss, *Pre-Reformation Germany*, pp. 136–61; H. Baron, 'Imperial Reform and the Hapsburgs, 1486–1504. A New Interpretation' in *American Historical Review*, xliv (1938–9).

were concerned, Maximilian grafted an Italianate yearning for eternal fame upon old chivalric ideals. He used scholars and printing presses just as he used Peter Vischer, Albrecht Dürer and Hans Burgkmair to further his repute and his dynasticism. A romantic, gallant and affable egotist, Maximilian never allowed the interests of the German nation to obstruct his Habsburg family ambitions. On the other hand it seems all too likely that the writings of Brant, Wimpfeling and Celtis encouraged that view of his office which depicted him as a direct and functioning successor to the ancient Roman emperors, and in particular prompted his fruitless interventions in Italy. In one of his memorandum-books (1501–5) is the entry: 'In this office his Majesty gave eight secretaries enough to write, in order that his Majesty might outdo Julius Caesar'. In the *White King* he claimed to be more than a knight-errant without fear or reproach. Sincerely enough, he believed himself a great master of statecraft and war, comparable with Caesar. He even imagined that his servants were incapable of injustice or corruption, and that everywhere in his dominions men might travel and trade without fear: two claims quite notoriously untrue. All these visions were fostered by his own humanists, but the hard-headed princes and cities repeatedly took very different attitudes when urged to provide money for his campaigns. Few emperors can have made greater unwitting contributions toward that distrustful particularism which kept Germany divided. And at least one humanist, the nobleman Hans von Hermansgrün, friend of Reuchlin and pupil of the famous Roman classicist Pomponius Laetus, circulated at the time of the Worms Diet in 1495 a Latin manuscript *Somnium* deploring Maximilian's failure to become a great German emperor.[19] It described the writer's dream of a great assembly at Magdeburg, where three visitors of superhuman stature—Charlemagne, Otto I and Frederick Barbarossa—suddenly appeared. The last-named thereupon delivered a long oration deploring the decay of the old national spirit and discipline, the triumphs of France over German lands and interests, the slothfulness of Maximilian

[19] U. Paul, ch. 11; and *ADB* s.v. Hermansgrün. I have so far failed to obtain H. Flecker, 'Der Traum des Hans von Hermansgrün' in *Festschrift Karl Eder* (Innsbrück, 1959).

which allowed these disasters. And needless to add, as the gathering stood amazed and ashamed, Hans von Hermansgrün awoke from his Germanic dream! But at the same Diet of 1495 Hermansgrün actually proposed that radical measures, even the creation of a German patriarchate in place of the papacy, should be taken if Alexander VI should attempt to transfer the imperial office to the King of France. Among those less sophisticated and critical, Maximilian's glittering pantomime did not seem unimpressive.

The vision of a lion of justice, a mighty ruler, a Germanic Caesar, lived on when Maximilian died among his faithful 'poets' and warriors at Wels, and when men turned to the grandson whom they expected to redeem his many failures and realize his impossible designs. And in retrospect it can at least be added that Maximilian stood prominently amongst those rulers who played a part in the expansion of German humanism from an academic cult into an optimistic creed of reform, aspiring to influence opinion throughout all classes of society. Of course, in the event some of the humanists would move opinion in directions very different from those anticipated by the emperor and by other munificent princely patrons. One of these patrons was to be none other than that transalpine equivalent of Leo X: Albrecht of Mainz. The very factor we have somewhat absurdly labelled 'pan-German cosmopolitanism', partly humanist yet partly based on medieval literature and popular legend, was destined greatly to broaden the scope of the Lutheran Reformation. It might still further have united the Germanic world but for the stubborn theological and apolitical conservatism of Martin Luther, when in 1529 he quarrelled with Zwingli at Marburg. But the Swiss were by no means the only neighbours capable of receiving such influences. German medieval colonization and trading enterprise had long since created far-flung outposts in the Scandinavian and east Baltic ports, in the Netherlands and England, again in Bohemia and in the Transylvanian cities remote from the Reich. These Germans of the *diaspora* were to embrace Luther's cause almost to a man. Not a little of their instant enthusiasm must have sprung from the new factor represented by Luther's tracts and vernacular Bible, yet the channels had been constantly kept open by other forces, notably that sense of Germanic identity fostered by scholars and literary men throughout several generations, and especially by the humanists and their publishers.

In the transition from humanism to Lutheranism, no figure was more influentially—or more debatably and ambivalently—concerned than Ulrich von Hutten.[20] Born in 1488 of a knightly Franconian family, he never ceased to stress his privileges and duties, his warrior code as a nobleman of the Holy Roman Empire. Yet to this feudal inheritance Hutten added an unusually sound school training in the abbey of Fulda. This he augmented by some years of wandering from university to university. In the dignified manner of the day he sponged upon anyone who would relieve his poverty, yet all the time he was acquiring from other itinerants like Crotus Rubeanus and Rhagius Aesticampianus—and indeed from the Erfurt circle—both elegance and eloquence in Latin verse and prose. Championing Wimpfeling against monkish opponents, he developed a ferocious anticlericalism foreign to Wimpfeling, an anger which later made him contribute so formidably to the deadlier combats around Erasmus and Reuchlin.

Having briefly soldiered with Maximilian in Italy, Hutten accepted office in the household of Albrecht of Mainz, though his views and temperament could hardly have squared less with the role of an ecclesiastical courtier. After enraging the Dominicans by his polemical attacks, Hutten departed to study in Italy (1515–17), where he received a warm welcome from several admirers. At Bologna his Greek studies equipped him to become an accomplished disciple of Lucian, whose dialogues he imitated with marked success in his later controversial writings. On his return to Germany, Conrad Peutinger presented him to the declining emperor, who included him amongst the poets laureate.

From this point Ulrich von Hutten became ever more deeply involved in politico-ecclesiastical pamphleteering. Having expressed ardent admiration for Luther's stand against Indulgences,

[20] The life by H. Holborn, originally published in German, was revised for the translation by R. H. Bainton, and remains the best biography of Hutten. See also L. W. Spitz, *Religious Renaissance*, ch. 6; F. G. Stokes; T. W. Best, *The Humanist Ulrich von Hutten: a Reappraisal of his Humor* (Chapel Hill, N.C., 1969); German bibliography in S. Skalweit, p. 429.

he also attained intimacy with the leader of the knightly faction, Franz von Sickingen, whom he persuaded to back both Luther and Reuchlin. Having helped Crotus Rubeanus to savage Reuchlin's Dominican foes in the *Letters of Obscure Men* (1515), he soon afterwards composed and published on his own account a second volume of the *Letters*, more political and more bitter than the first. In 1518 he edited Valla's *Donation of Constantine* with a sarcastic dedication to the pope. Less-known but equally striking examples of his devotion to the historic imperialist cause can be found in his discovery and publication of anti-papal tracts written in former times. Some of these had arisen from the period of the Avignonese Captivity, but one, which had been recently discovered at Fulda, emanated from the far more distant struggle between Henry IV and Gregory VII. This tract Hutten dedicated to Archduke Ferdinand, with a clear call to the young Habsburg to overthrow the temporal power of Rome.

A further vital stage in Hutten's career came in 1519, when he translated one of his own treatises into German. Thenceforth he commonly wrote in the vernacular, appealing like Luther directly to the masses. By this time even the carefree curia of Leo X had become alarmed and sought to procure his arrest. He thus fled to join Sickingen, and but for an illness which kept him out of the Knights' Revolt, he would doubtless have gone down fighting with his friend. Though at first the fugitive was received favourably in some of the Alsatian towns, Erasmus and other cautious people refused to see him. More disastrously, he had now reached an advanced stage of his illness. Sheltered at last by Zwingli, already in his heyday as leader of the early Swiss Reformation, Hutten died a lonely death in August 1523 on the island of Ufenau in Lake Zürich. Into his thirty-five years of life he had crowded a great deal of experience and passion.

By any standards Hutten can be claimed as a remarkable writer, a master of Latin prose and verse who during his last years achieved a German style scarcely less effective than that of Luther. Of his vehement dedication to causes there can be no question. Oblivious to the cost, he threw himself into literary protest, and he drew more deeply than any humanist upon that heritage of romantic patriotism we have sought to describe. His early death, his unfinished mission, his ideals incapable of realization, do not deprive his career of historical meaning: it forms a bridge between the earlier manifestos of German humanism and the great outburst of popular pamphleteering which must soon engage our attention. And that his protest paved the way for Luther's protest cannot reasonably be denied. On the other hand any cool analysis (which Hutten himself would have been the first to scorn) must reveal internal disharmonies both intellectual and emotional, conflicting forces which greatly lessened his impact as a public figure. He failed to understand the dichotomy between his chivalrous pride on the one hand and empire, people and cities on the other. Like so many knights, he championed an imperial tradition against the rising power of the princes. Yet he thought no more clearly on these matters than did the stupid rank-and-file of his social class. He did not grasp the conflict between the idea of German monarchy and that of world empire. While he enjoyed the intellectual life rendered possible by the walled cities, he stood all too close to the robber-knights who kidnapped merchants and held them to ransom. He could express hatred for townsmen, traders and bankers without realizing his own profound debts to the urban culture these enemies had created. His attitude toward Luther stands equally open to attack. An admirer of Luther's ecclesiastical revolt and social criticism, he took his place among the knights who threatened to use force if Luther were condemned at Worms. Indeed, just before that famous Diet, the papal legate Aleander saw on sale in Augsburg a print showing two figures conjoined: one was Luther with a book, the other Hutten in armour, fingering his sword. Above them the legend ran: *To the Champions of Christian Liberty*. But here was a popular image corresponding little with the facts of life. Hutten himself could not understand the theological and experiential forces which gave meaning and energy to Luther the man and the publicist. He did not share the other-worldly thinking which helped Luther to detach himself from those confusing elements of German society and politics which menaced the plan to rehabilitate Christianity. Hutten's literary and political being, made of softer materials than that of Luther, was eroded and split asunder by the violent streams of opinion which surrounded him. By the time these forces had thrust Hutten aside, certain new developments had begun to change the functions of humanism within German society. Its practitioners were no longer merely university teachers or 'poets' hovering on the fringes of academic and courtly society. In considerable number humanists—or rather jurists with good humanist backgrounds—were entering politics and administration as executive officials in the service of princes and cities. Something not unlike the old 'civic humanism' of Florence was reborn in a multitude of transalpine settings. Certain of these practical men were soon to play active parts in the spread of the Lutheran Reformation. Meanwhile the latter rose to its first crisis in the years 1520–21, when its programme attained a far greater political and theological definition, a clarity which challenged educated consciences to acceptance or rejection. Yet again, certain humanists united with bourgeois literary traditions to produce a flood of vernacular pamphlets, the vast majority of which not only supported Luther's cause but introduced a more positively religious emphasis into the protest of the German nation. Already by the year 1523, as Hutten lay dying on Ufenau, this torrent of popular writing attained its highest volume.

3

Luther's Debt to Humanism

The earlier career of Martin Luther overlapped with the climax of German humanism. When Celtis was crowned laureate in 1487, Luther was a child of four, living with his parents at Mansfeld. He matriculated at Erfurt in 1501, the year after Celtis published his student edition of Tacitus; and he entered the Augustinian convent in July 1505, almost contemporaneously with the appearance of Wimpfeling's *Epitome* and a few months before that of Reuchlin's *Rudiments of Hebrew*. In 1511, when Reuchlin attacked his enemies in the pamphlet *Augenspiegel*, Luther returned from his stay in Rome, then moved on from Erfurt to strengthen the teaching at the Saxon Elector's new university of Wittenberg. Here from 1512 until 1517 he was rapidly composing and delivering his lecture courses on *Genesis*, *Psalms*, *Romans* and *Galatians*, pieces unpublished until recent times, and yet of crucial importance in tracing his gradual attainment of an independent theology. The same year (1517) in which Hutten issued the second volume of the *Letters of Obscure Men*, Luther found Tetzel preaching Indulgences to raise money for Albrecht's purchase of the see of Mainz from the pope; and in October he broke through into history by publishing his *Ninety-five Theses* aimed not only against Indulgences but also against the sub-Christian outlook underlying the system. Five years younger than Luther, Hutten then excoriated the papacy in *Vadiscus* (1518), calling upon his friends to 'risk something for German liberty', at about the time when Luther, summoned to Augsburg, held his strident dispute with Cardinal

Cajetan. Finally in 1520, the year when Luther published his classic Reformation pamphlets, Hutten wrote his almost equally arresting *Apology* and some of his most effective dialogues.

In our present brief survey of Luther's own intellectual background and inheritance we propose to begin with the theme of humanism, and to pursue a somewhat more positive line than the one adopted by most modern theological historians,[1] who, even if they avoid equating humanism with that exiguous minority of Italian pagans, tend to equate it with the work of Erasmus. Whatever Luther's personal relations with Christian humanism, there has never been much doubt among informed scholars concerning its immense importance to the Lutheran movement. We have already shown how the humanists sharpened the resentment of the nation against Rome long before Luther made his appeal, a process unduly obscured in many accounts by an undue concentration upon the cosmopolitan and ambivalent figure of Erasmus. All are familiar with the support given by so many humanists during the movement's early critical phase, with their notable share in pamphleteering, with the ever-growing influence of Philip Melanchthon, whose teaching placed Wittenberg among the most renowned universities of Europe. Moreover one may scarcely overstress the historical importance in later years of a humanist-educated Evangelical clergy, and the injection of their moral and literary values into the school education of Lutheran Germany. Having recalled these varied historical connections, however, we have yet to delineate the role of humanism in the intellectual origins of the Evangelical religion, and more especially within Luther's own mind.

[1] At least since the pioneering survey by E. Zweynert (1895) most general accounts of Luther's work have included this theme. L. W. Spitz makes his *Religious Renaissance of the German Humanists* culminate in a valuable chapter on Luther; note his references (p. 345) to other publications. See also C. S. Meyer; J. C. Olin; H. von Schubert. Several prominent authorities (e.g. J. Lortz, i, pp. 336; H. Boehmer, pp. 28–30) make too little of that all-important theme: the application of humanist techniques to the Scriptures. Much relevant factual information appears in R. H. Fife, perhaps the best-referenced account in any language of Luther's earlier life. See also M. Greschat, 'Renaissance und Reformation' in *Evangelische Theologie*, xxix (1969), which gives general support to the argument of my present chapter.

The question, 'Was Luther a humanist?' would be at best a
semantic one. If a humanist must seem to step out from the more
lurid pages of Burckhardt, or must derive his inspiration solely
or largely from the restoration of ancient pagan values, Luther
must be excluded from the tribe. Yet by those naïve definitions,
humanism would have extremely little importance in sixteenth-
century Europe, since they fit so few figures of serious cultural
interest. The case is much the same with the question as to
whether Luther was a 'Christian humanist' or 'Biblical humanist'.
If to qualify for such titles a scholar must emerge from his
Biblical studies with the same answers as Erasmus, then Luther
would not qualify. Yet in that event neither would Reuchlin, nor
Lefèvre, nor Zwingli, nor Calvin. And if on the other hand one
argues that Luther was interested in substance, the humanists in
elegances of style, one is seriously, indeed quite ignorantly,
underestimating every major humanist of the age. The *studia
humanitatis* meant vastly more than the tricks of Ciceronian
Latin. In other words we are about to examine the somewhat
amorphous frontiers between a great but by no means always
consistent mind, and a complex, protean movement.

Martin Luther was ever a man of religious experience and
religious needs, a suffering mind stimulated, illumined, soothed
and confirmed by his theologian's approach to the Biblical
sources. Here is a truism immune from serious dispute, one may
hope even by those who would like to 'explain' Luther by
clinical psychology. Yet this cannot mean that humanism stood
detached from Luther's mental activities, and once we free our
minds from secular stereotypes of humanism (including Celtis
and Hutten!) we should find it easier to establish the relations of
both Luther and Lutheranism with the earlier movement. The
approach to the Scriptures, the habit of revising theology by a
new look at the Greek and Hebrew, the triumphant press-
campaign culminating in Luther's German Bible: all these
depended upon the application of established humanist techniques to the Biblical texts, techniques already so applied by
Colet, Erasmus, Reuchlin and others, and with which the young
Luther had been adequately furnished. While the Lutheran
movement seems unimaginable without the pre-existent
German nationalist humanism, the Reformer himself remains

equally unimaginable without the pre-existent Biblical humanism, and for that matter without humanist modes of appeal to the
layman. Every student of sixteenth-century history is accustomed
to the spectacle of Luther in 1525, as like a new Augustine he
savagely denounces Pelagius reborn in the *philosophia Christi* of
Erasmus; yet we should not minimize Luther's debts to the
school of which Erasmus had long been the admired leader. That
philological, historical and literary methods should be adduced
to reinterpret the Bible was a truly epoch-making event in
Christian history, the more so since the Bible had already
become the court of appeal against alleged papal, hierarchical and
popular deviations from Christianity.

Luther's debt to Erasmus went beyond the obvious debt of any
Biblical theologian to that most renowned champion of a
Scriptural Christianity. In his *Paraclesis* of 1516, the exhortatory
preface to his Greek and Latin edition of the New Testament,
Erasmus can sound like an ancestor of both Luther and the
Radicals.

> Indeed, I disagree very much with those who are unwilling
> that Holy Scripture, translated into the vulgar tongue, be read
> by the uneducated, as if Christ taught such intricate doctrines
> that they could scarcely be understood by very few theologians,
> or as if the strength of the Christian religion consisted in
> men's ignorance of it. The mysteries of kings, perhaps, are
> better concealed, but Christ wishes his mysteries published as
> openly as possible. I would that even the lowliest women read
> the Gospels and the Pauline Epistles. And I would that they
> were translated into all languages so that they could be read
> and understood not only by Scots and Irish but also by Turks
> and Saracens. Surely the first step is to understand in one way
> or another. It may be that many will ridicule, but some may
> be taken captive. Would that, as a result, the farmer sing some
> portion of them at the plough, the weaver hum some parts of
> them to the movement of his shuttle, the traveller lighten the
> weariness of the journey with stories of this kind! Let all the
> conversations of every Christian be drawn from this source.

The force of this relatively familiar passage is exceeded by that of
its successor, which Erasmus introduces by the reminder that

professional theologians are often too deeply concerned with mundane matters, just as monks who profess poverty and contempt of the world may be most worldly.

> To me he is truly a theologian who teaches not by skill with intricate syllogisms but by a disposition of mind, by the very expression and the eyes, by his very life, that riches should be disdained, that the Christian should not put his trust in the supports of this world but must rely entirely on heaven, that a wrong should not be avenged...that all good men should be loved and cherished equally as members of the same body, that the evil should be tolerated if they cannot be corrected...And if anyone under the inspiration of the spirit of Christ preaches this kind of doctrine, inculcates it, exhorts, incites and encourages men to it, he indeed is truly a theologian, even if he should be a common labourer or weaver. And if anyone exemplifies this doctrine in his life itself, he is in fact a great doctor.[2]

These were bold words even when Luther's revolt had not begun, when Erasmus was still the darling of the prelates, when no man could have foreseen the ultimate placing of his works upon the papal *Index of Prohibited Books*. By a strange irony they foreshadowed not only Luther's bringing of the Bible to the common people, but Luther's fate at the hands of the sectarian Radicals—for he in the long run suffered most from these same labourers and weavers, who thought Bible-reading fitted them to dispute the exegesis of that 'great doctor' Martin Luther. As events proved, revolutionary change lay less in mere Scriptural study itself than in the shift of Scriptural study from the university theologians to the semi-educated. This new social dimension, swiftly enlarged by cheap printing, made the cause of prelatical paternalism almost hopeless over large areas of Europe.

Again, the ultimate rejection of Luther by Erasmus should not be allowed to obscure the vital support given by the latter during the year 1520, when he addressed his *Axiomata* 'in behalf of the cause of Martin Luther, theologian' to the Elector Frederick of Saxony. 'There can be little doubt,' writes Professor Olin, 'that Erasmus' counsel, so favourable to Luther, confirmed and

[2] J. C. Olin, pp. 96–8.

encouraged Frederick in his policy of protecting Luther at this critical juncture.' Some of the *Axiomata* have an irony and an economy resembling those of Luther's *Theses*.

> The origin of the case is evil: the hatred of letters and the desire for supremacy.
> Those who are conducting the case are open to suspicion, since all the best and closest to the Gospel teaching are said to be the least offended by Luther.
> The severity of the Bull [against Luther] offends all upright men as unworthy of the most gentle vicar of Christ.
> Only two universities [Cologne and Louvain] out of such a countless number have condemned Luther, and they have merely condemned him, not convicted him of error; nor are they in agreement.
> Luther is not soliciting anything; therefore he is less suspect; [but] the interest of others is being pressed.
> The world thirsts for the Gospel truth, and it seems to be carried in this direction by a longing ordained, as it were, by fate.[3]

From the outset the hatred of scholasticism shared by Erasmus and Luther had formed a major bond between them, the bond which initially attached the humanists to Luther's cause. Here Erasmus had long taken the lead, and never more effectively than in those letters to his friends which, circulated widely and often in print, set the tenor of humanist thought with merciless elegance. In the *Letter to Paul Volz*, first printed in 1518 as preface to a new edition of the *Enchiridion militis christiani*, he notes that war is now being prepared against the Turks.

> But what do you think would happen if we set before the vanquished—since I don't believe we shall kill them all—in order to win them to Christ, the works of Occam, or Durandus, or Scotus or Gabriel [Biel]...What will they think, what impression will they get—since they are surely men if nothing else—when they hear those thorny and intricate arguments about instances, formalities, quiddities and relationships? Especially when they see those great professors of

---

[3] Based on the translation in *ibid.*, pp. 147–9. Luther influenced Erasmus as well as *vice versa*: see R. G. Kleinhans, 'Luther and Erasmus, another Perspective' in *Church History*, xxxix (1970).

religion disagreeing about these matters among themselves
to the point that they frequently grow pale and insult and spit
at one another and sometimes even exchange blows, or when
they see the Dominicans fighting for their Thomas [Aquinas],
and the Franciscans guarding with joined shields their most
subtle and seraphic doctors; some speaking as nominalists,
others as realists. What indeed will they [the Turks] think
when they see the question is so difficult that it has never
adequately been settled what words should be used in speaking
of Christ? As though one is dealing with some wayward
spirit, who is evoked to your own destruction if prescribed
words are not carefully followed, and not instead with the
most merciful Saviour, who demands only that we live a pure
and simple life.[4]

At these moments, though we know well enough that a non-
Lutheran theology underlies the words of Erasmus, do we not
most clearly sense the superb vigour of that demolition by
which he cleared the ground for Luther?

Hard upon the heels of Reuchlin and Erasmus, Luther undertook a bolder re-examination of the original texts of the Scriptures. Vividly, as ever, he depicts a corner of the laboratory in his
letter of 30 May 1518 to his counsellor and superior Johann van
Staupitz. Here he recalls how the precepts of Staupitz 'like the
sharp arrows of the mighty', had prompted him to consult the
Greek text of St. Paul, and there to confirm that we are bidden
not, as in the mistaken Vulgate translation, to 'do penance', but
rather inwardly to repent or change our outlook.

After this it happened by the favour of the learned men who
taught me Hebrew and Greek that I learned that the Greek
word is μετάνοια, from μετά and νοῦν, in other words, from
'afterwards' and 'mind', so that penitence or μετάνοια is
'coming to one's right mind, afterwards'...All this agrees so
well with Paul's theology, that in my opinion, at least, nothing
is more characteristically Pauline. Then I progressed and saw
that μετάνοια meant not only 'afterwards' and 'mind' but also
'change' and 'mind', so that μετάνοια means change of mind
and affection, and this seemed to suggest not only the change
of affection, but also the mode of change, viz. the grace of

[4] Based on J. C. Olin, pp. 112–13.

God...Sticking fast to this conclusion, I dared to think that they were wrong who attributed so much to works of repentance that they have left us nothing of it but formal penances and elaborate confession. They were seduced by the Latin [of the Vulgate], for *poenitentiam agere* means rather a 'work' than a change of affection and in no wise agrees with the Greek...[5]

Here is a genuine glimpse of the Reformer in the making, a glimpse of photographic clarity compared with the cloudy speculations of modern psychologists. Luther's interpretation of Christianity depended on how one translated certain Greek words. To this matter he devoted long and anxious thought, and in later years in his open letter upon translating (1530) he explained his principles in reply to those who had objected to his translation of the text in *Romans*, iii. 28: *Arbitramur, hominem justificari ex fide absque operibus*. This Luther had rendered by the German equivalent of the sentence, 'We hold that man is justified without the works of the law, only by faith'. Admitting that the word *sola* does not appear in the Vulgate passage, he gives various examples to show that 'it is the way of German language to add the word "only", so that the word "not" or "no" may be more complete and clearer.' In short, a German translation must be in idiomatic German.

We must not, like these asses, ask the Latin letters how we are to speak German; but we must ask the mother in the home, the children in the street, the common man in the market place about this, and look them in the mouth to see how they speak, and afterwards do our translating.

Luther then cites other Pauline texts showing how repeatedly and explicitly the Apostle denies Justification by works. He nevertheless proclaims the demands of literal meaning, adding that in some passages he had preferred the lesser evil of doing some violence to the German language. 'Translating is not an art that everyone can practise, as the mad saints [i.e. Anabaptists and other Radicals] think; it requires a right

[5] Translated by P. Smith, *Life and Letters of Martin Luther* (1911), pp. 91ff.

pious, faithful, diligent, God-fearing, experienced, practised heart.[6]

In addition Luther knew well that exegesis involved far more than the accurate rendering of words and phrases: it involved comparative value judgments extending across the literature of the Bible. He was too good a humanist to become a fundamentalist by according equal authority to every part of the Bible, even though in certain cases he may have defended his obstinate convictions by what now seem fundamentalist arguments. But just as a secular humanist put Cicero's authority above that of late Latin writers, so Luther boldly listed in his Preface to the New Testament certain books of the Bible which in his view had greater authority than that of others, and indeed contained the core of the Christian message.

In a word, St. John's Gospel and his first Epistle, St. Paul's Epistles, especially *Romans*, *Galatians* and *Ephesians*, and St. Peter's First Epistle are the books that show you Christ and teach you all that it is necessary and good for you to know, even though you were never to see or hear any other book or doctrine. Therefore St. James' Epistle is really an epistle of straw, compared to them; for it has nothing of the nature of the Gospel about it...[7]

For this role in the field of Biblical humanism Luther had undergone a long preparation. Lewis Spitz has rightly said that 'Luther shared with the humanists a high regard for and even a fascination with languages', though he always regarded the latter as functional tools, and of course never so nobly used as when examining the Word of God. His Latin foundations had been laid in the old-fashioned grammar of Alexander of Villedieu, while upon entering the university of Erfurt be began an extensive course of reading both in the ancient authors and in their recent imitators like the Carmelite Baptista Mantuanus, who in his *Eclogues* (republished at Erfurt in 1501) had sought to write Latin verse purged of its heathen associations, and whom

[6] E. G. Rupp and B. Drewery, pp. 87–9, selected from H. E. Jacobs, *Works of Martin Luther* (Philadelphia, 1931–2, 1943), v, pp. 10ff.

[7] E. G. Rupp and B. Drewery, p. 94, from H. E. Jacobs, *Works of Martin Luther*, vi, pp. 439ff.

Wimpfeling had placed first among the modern classical poets in Italy. But the young Luther also read Ovid's *Heroides*, Vergil, Plautus, Cicero and Livy. In 1504 he is known to have attended an up-to-date lecture on Reuchlin's drama *Sergius* given by Hieronymus Emser of Ulm, who had made his way up to Erfurt and was later destined to become one of Luther's adversaries under the patronage of the Catholic Duke George of Saxony. Some of Luther's close friends like Spalatin and Crotus Rubeanus became members of the celebrated humanist circle assembled in Erfurt and nearby at Gotha by Mutianus, but he himself does not appear to have been in direct touch with the latter until 1516.[8] In later life he often quotes the classics from memory and in addition to the authors listed above displayed a creditable knowledge of Horace, Juvenal and Terence. His regard for Cicero brought him near to that famous passage of Zwingli, in which the Swiss Reformer expresses confidence in the salvation of the heroes of pagan antiquity. Luther is less sure but more humorous:

> Cicero is the best philosopher, for he felt that the soul is immortal...He wrote in earnest and did not fool like the Greeks Plato and Aristotle. I hope God will forgive such men as Cicero their sins. Even if he should not be redeemed, he will enjoy a situation in hell several degrees higher than that destined for our cardinal of Mainz.[9]

And knowing Luther, one feels certain enough that this last sentence was accompanied by a grin, and not intended as a formal bit of black Augustinian theology. Luther did not always lump together the Greeks in this cavalier fashion, and there are even occasions when he writes of the 'divine Plato'. Encouraged by these expressions, a philosopher has recently sought to detect in Luther's writings elements suggesting the influence of the Platonic Academy of Florence. Yet the evidence supplied seems too thin to carry conviction, the passages in question containing nothing more directly Platonic than Luther would automatically absorb from his prolonged study of St. Augustine. He likewise

    [8] R. H. Fife, pp. 51–6, 208–9, 415.
    [9] E. G. Rupp and B. Drewery, p. 144, from P. Smith, *Life and Letters of Martin Luther* (1911), p. 342.

encountered Neo-Platonist ideas in the Christian mystic Dionysius. And when he calls Plato 'divine', the epithet may be merely conventional, or intended to denigrate by contrast the father of all scholastic error: Aristotle.[10]

Whatever Luther's view of the Greek pagans, he had been working hard in Erfurt from 1509 both at his Greek and his Hebrew. He recalls purchasing about this time a copy of Reuchlin's *Rudiments of Hebrew*, published three years earlier, and throughout the decade which followed he hastened to secure all the best Biblical texts by Lefèvre, Reuchlin and Erasmus. Their glosses he often made his own. From the moment of his public revolt in 1517 Luther was corresponding with prominent humanists like Mutianus and Scheurl; and though at first the initiatives came from them, he later sought to win such valuable allies to the cause. That they valued Luther not merely as a publicist but as a scholar could be illustrated by many excerpts from their voluminous correspondence. Already in 1518 the historian Irenicus announces that all Germans honour Martin Luther on account of his 'outstanding erudition', while Bernhard Adelmann, the humanist canon of Augsburg, identifies the terms *doctus* and *Lutheranus*.[11]

The leading personalities involved in the early expansion of Luther's movement were all trained humanists, but nearly all considerably younger than their leader. Without their group enthusiasm the cause might never have surmounted its first obstacles, and it is a measure of genuine idealism that so many of these men changed their way of life, leaving the pursuit of letters to become pastors and preachers. 'Without humanism, no Reformation', writes Bernd Moeller, adding that revolutions are made by the young. Had it failed initially to capture this age-group amongst the 'progressive' people, Lutheranism would have taken a different and less formidable shape, both intellectually and socially. It might in that event have been taken over and reduced to ruin by the Radicals. On the other hand the humanist collaborators also tended to dispute Luther's

---

[10] See the review of T. Süss, *Luther* (Paris, 1969) by W. D. J. Cargill Thompson in *Journal of Ecclesiastical History*, xii (1971), p. 92.

[11] See e.g. H. Boehmer, pp. 267–70. On Adelmann's relations with Luther: R. H. Fife, pp. 418–20, 636–7.

interpretation of Pauline doctrine: not a few of these scholars, German as well as Swiss, soon wanted to modify his severe doctrine of Justification. Their natural inclinations tended to lead them in an Erasmian, even Pelagian direction: they wanted to accord some share in the process of salvation to the co-operative will of man. Most strikingly this became the case with Philip Melanchthon himself. Extravagantly praised by Luther, even his 'official' *Loci Communes* of 1521 and their revised version of 1535 survey the sources of Christianity with a cool humanist eye, and also with a convinced emphasis on the essential unity of philosophy and theology more reminiscent of Aquinas than of Luther and his Occamist predecessors. Unlike Luther he did not lose contact with Erasmus, either as a person or as a perennial source of inspiration. Again, it seems likely that few even among the intellectuals fully grasped Luther's curious doctrine of the Eucharist, on which issue many leaned from the first toward the far more rationalist solution of Zwingli. Without undue cynicism it has been suggested that Lutheranism rose from a series of misunderstandings. Yet is this not equally true of most revolutionary movements? Can any society in chronic tension follow integrated programmes? Whatever the case, humanist support ensured that Lutheranism contained that element called in our jargon 'Erasmianism'. Long held in check by the masterful personality of Luther, it erupted soon after his death in the bitter internal conflict between Philipists and Strict Lutherans, and it was terminated only in 1580 by the Formula of Concord.

Martin Luther's work as a translator of the Bible into German transcends all his achievements within the sphere of humanist scholarship. The hardest labours were by no means accomplished during his period of enforced sabbatical leave in the lonely 'kingdom of the birds' on the Wartburg. Illustrated by Cranach, his New Testament emerged in September 1522 soon after his reappearance in Wittenberg; but the Old Testament occupied a far larger share of his working life, since it was published in four parts, the last as late as 1534. In these stages he had at his elbow not only Melanchthon, but as significantly the Hebraist Johann Forster, one of Reuchlin's favourite students. Despite the radical differences of outlook between Luther and Reuchlin, the

former inherited not only the latter's own Hebraic scholarship
but also a common ancestry in Nicholas of Lyra (from Lire in
Normandy: d. 1340). This Franciscan master of Paris, a
primitive forerunner of humanist exegesis, had ranked high
among the influences which bore upon Reuchlin, while Luther
also possessed a close knowledge of his work.[12] Despite his early
date Nicholas had learned Hebrew and used the commentaries of
Jewish scholars. More important, though he had not wholly
abandoned the fourfold interpretation of the Scriptures, he had
set an important tradition of emphasis upon their literal meaning,
in his time too often overshadowed by allegorization. The direct
influence of Nicholas certainly remained wide even in the mid-
sixteenth century. The wills of clerics frequently prove that his
works were then still in use throughout Europe, while no fewer
than six printed editions of his *Postillae* were published between
1471 and 1508. Before Luther's time Lyra's principles had
already been taught by a succession of able masters at Erfurt.
The Reformer himself used and acknowledged the *Postillae*,
which helped him toward his rejection between 1516 and 1518 of
the old fourfold method. This he later ridiculed in good humanist
style, while not of course denying the allegorical content and
value of many passages. Again, he meant more than Lyra had
meant by the literal sense, for in that term he included the
prophetic sense of the Old Testament, which made it relevant
within a Christocentric religion. It is hence important to avoid
exaggerating Lyra's contribution to Luther's teaching, as
contemporaries of the latter so often did. Most of our present
chapter and the next form a denial of the smart simplification
'If Lyra had not lyred, Luther would not have danced'. This
epigram falls into the same class as the saying, also widely
repeated by contemporaries, that Erasmus laid the egg which
Luther hatched. If the facts had been half so clear as the epigrams, there would be little need for modern mental history.

Of Luther as of any other serious theologian, it goes without
saying that he rejected the secularist individualism flaunted by
some of the Italian humanists and in Germany by Celtis and
Hutten. He felt no attraction towards a humanism which fell

---

[12] References to Lyra, including his Rabbinical knowledge, are in *NCE*
s.v. Nicholas.

outside the Christian sphere. Yet some recent authorities have gone too far in writing that Luther had no understanding for the contemporary revaluation of man, and that 'his discovery was the discovery of a monk'. To the independent social and religious thought of the Italian humanists Luther devoted little attention, but one of them made a quite significant contribution to his development as a schismatic Reformer. This one, who also inspired both Erasmus and Hutten, was that disagreeable yet towering figure Lorenzo Valla (d. 1457), who had rediscovered important classical manuscripts and demolished the Donation of Constantine, upon which apologists had once confidently based papal authority. Valla had also established a canonical authority over the niceties of Latin style and had attacked the whole tradition of scholasticism. He even stood among those who had anticipated certain of Luther's own theological emphases. In his tract concerning free will and pre-destination, he had stressed the inscrutable mystery of the divine mind in relation to puny, powerless men. In *De Servo Arbitrio* Luther notes how Erasmus had attacked him on this issue by alleging that only Wycliffe and Valla stood on his side.[13] Valla certainly became for Luther a prime authority upon the evils of papal government in the Church. In 1520 it was Hutten who republished his treatise on the Donation, but a copy swiftly found its way to Luther, upon whom at this crucial moment it made a most powerful impression. Aroused by it, Luther immediately wrote to Spalatin one of his most violent letters on the Anti-christ of Rome.[14] In the same year he listed the great Italian critic along with Occam, Erasmus, Reuchlin and others as eminent scholars persecuted by reactionary theological faculties. Of Valla Luther bluntly wrote that he was 'also charged with the crime of ignorance by those who are in no way worthy to hand him a chamber-pot'. Many years later he continued to cite Valla when attacking the papacy. But to maintain a balanced picture, it might here be noted that in earlier days he had been similarly

[13] *Martin Luther on the Bondage of the Will*, ed. J. I. Packer and O. R. Johnson (1957), p. 109. On Valla see C. E. Trinkaus, 'Introduction to Valla' in E. Cassirer (ed.), *The Renaissance Philosophy of Man* (Chicago, 1948); E. Mühlenberg, 'Laurentius Valla als Renaissancetheolog' in *Zeitschrift für Theologie und Kirche*, lxvi (1969).

[14] *WA. Br.*, ii, p. 48 (no. 257, dated 24 February 1520).

moved to anger by reading Wimpfeling's *De Integritate*, with its strong attack on clerical abuses.

Fortunately Luther penned several passages defining his mature attitudes to humanism. While he stressed the transient character of all purely human culture, he firmly believed that the restoration of classical antiquity had been ordained by God as the pre-condition of a new understanding of Christianity. 'No one knew why God allowed the study of languages to come forth, until it was finally realized that it happened for the sake of the Gospel which he wished to reveal thereafter.'[15] Again, Mackinnon and other modern historians have drawn attention to that truly remarkable passage in the letter to Eobanus Hessus of 29 March 1523, where Luther urges him to incite the youth of Erfurt to the study of rhetoric and poetry.

> Do not give way to your apprehension, lest we Germans become more barbarous than ever we were by reason of the decline of letters through our theology. I am persuaded that, without a skilled training in literary studies, no true theology can establish and maintain itself, seeing that in times past it has invariably fallen miserably and lain prostrate with the decline and fall of learning. On the other hand, it is indubitable that there has never been a signal revelation of divine truth unless first the way has been prepared for it, as by a John the Baptist, by the revival and pursuit of the study of languages and literature... My ardent vow is that there should be as many poets and rhetoricians as possible, because I see clearly that by no other methods is it possible to train men for the apt understanding, the right and felicitous treatment of sacred things.[16]

In broader and still more important respects the attempt to dissociate Luther from humanist revaluations might persuade us grossly to truncate his total message to humanity.[17] The idea of a

[15] 'Niemant hat gewust, warumb Gott die sprachen erfür lies komen, bis das man nu allererst sihet, das es umb des Evangelio willen geschehen ist' (*An die Ratherren aller Städte* (1524) in *WA*, xv, p. 37).

[16] 'Ego persuasus sum, sine literarum peritia prorsus stare non posse sinceram theologiam...' (*WA Br.*, iii, 49–50). The above translation is from J. Mackinnon, *Luther and the Reformation*, iii, p. 216.

[17] For modern guidance on Luther's social and political views, consult especially F. E. Cranz: on their religious basis, note C. E. Trinkaus. Other relevant works are listed in E. G. Léonard, pp. 380–82 and in L. D. Stokes, pp. 32–5.

'monkish discovery' neglects his very serious and independent social thinking. However austere his anthropology, Luther developed a vital interest in the human relationships of this earthly life. His insistence upon the utter powerlessness and unworthiness of humanity applies to man's situation *coram Deo*, standing face to face with an infinitely pure and omnipotent Deity. It applies to the higher plane upon which the drama of Justification and salvation are enacted. But upon the earthly level (also pervaded by God) a man of faith can and should act joyously and courageously, trying to serve the community, seeking to be a 'little Christ' toward his followers. Upon this level Luther, as warmly interested in people as any man of religion before or since, delivered a most positive, a most activist message. He preached arduous training and lifelong exertion in the service of the commonwealth. As his enormous correspondence and his laborious personal counselling show, he respected and helped people as individuals. His own exchanges were natural and human; he could plead not guilty to that terrifying, diffused, statistical benevolence which characterizes so much twentieth-century highmindedness. Several of his writings envisage realistic programmes of social reform worthy to be placed alongside the most striking of those enunciated by humanists. In particular his *Christian Nobility*, while devoting only minimal attention to theological foundations or cultural ideals, says more about actual problems and possible solutions than his contemporaries said in far greater space. Hereabouts some illuminating comparisons might be made with More's *Utopia*, or for that matter with the grand but utterly unattainable *respublica christiana* which Erasmus hoped to make of European civilization by the propagation of humanist ideals. Nevertheless *Christian Nobility*, though so essentially non-speculative, could not possibly have been written before the humanists had created new attitudes to the life of man in his earthly setting.

Though Luther's economics were bedevilled by his archaic preferences for a simple agrarian economy, his social programme became advanced, creative, even relatively 'liberal'. It cannot fairly be dismissed as authoritarian, and it is not based upon any dim Biblical literalism. Luther played his part alongside Melanchthon in making Wittenberg one of the great trilingual universities of Europe. He also continued to say all the 'right' things about the need to multiply schools and to create public libraries, which latter scarcely existed in that day. He anticipated or stood alongside Vives and other Erasmians in demanding schools for girls as well as for boys. His gaze was never exclusively directed towards the arena of salvation; his earthiness never limited to the heaping of abuse upon the heads of his enemies. If he denigrated Reason as a false guide to the nature and purposes of God, he nevertheless believed that down on earth it was the God-given quality which controlled human relations and distinguished men from beasts. By the same token, he heartily believed that culture had its own justification within this transient world. He loved and played music; he admired Cranach and Dürer. He did not suppose that schools and universities existed simply to enable people to read and elucidate the Bible.

> It is reason enough for establishing the best possible schools for boys and girls, that the State (for its own well-being) make well-educated men and women for the better government of land and people, and for the proper nurture of children in the home.[18]

As for his proposed public libraries, they were to be organized along Christian humanist and pedagogic lines, with a deliberate bias against the old clerical-academic literature. He would naturally include Bibles in both the original tongues and in vernacular translation: he would exclude books on canon law, scholastic theology and philosophy. By contrast his attitude toward humanist literature is most amicable. The libraries must contain the works of classical authors, both pagan and Christian, together with the best authors on law, medicine, the arts and sciences. To these he would add histories and chronicles in the various languages, but especially those relating to German national history. At this point, however, caution seems required. Though he was, like his humanist predecessors, a patriotic German wishing to preserve the structure of the empire, Luther

---

[18] 'So were doch alleyn dise ursach gnugsam, die aller besten schulen beyde fur knaben und meydlin an allen orten auff zu richten' (*WA*, xv, p. 44).

advocated the study of secular history less as a means to inculcate patriotism than as an indication of God's will, insofar as this will had been expressed in the acts of men.[19] Melanchthon, as we shall observe in another context, followed the humanists more closely, making revelatory and moralistic history a pillar of his teaching programme. Yet in its extremer forms this pedagogic history cannot be fathered upon Luther in person, for he was never so simple as to regard the history enacted and written by man as any profound or complete vision of the divine will. Far below the comprehensible patterns of human history, God was directing a history of salvation, in detail quite incomprehensible to men. On this level, God works in a mysterious way by apparent contradictions and anomalies. What we call history does not in fact reveal the divine logic. Luther was too sophisticated to follow the more complacent humanist schoolmasters, Protestant or Catholic, with their 'history teaching by examples'. In other words he had seriously faced the awkward consequences of a belief in divine omnipotence.

Too often the element of secular utility in Luther's thought has been understressed by his pious biographers, yet they would surely be justified in regarding his secular structures as arising from religious and theological foundations. Closely allied to Luther's interest in living men and women is his basic teaching on the priesthood of all believers, his conviction that the clergy had not been commissioned by God as a separate and spiritually favoured order, but as men merely charged to perform special functions in Church and society. Conversely all callings, however simple, are also sacred when done in a spirit of love and service.

> A servant with this clause
> Makes drudgery divine,
> Who sweeps a room as for Thy laws
> Makes that and the action fine.

George Herbert's English hymn of the next century forms but a free translation of a famous passage in Luther. Here we may

[19] For Luther's views on history, see the stimulating work by J. M. Headley; E. Schäfer, who lists and classifies the books known to Luther; M. Schmidt. For some further humanist attitudes on history shared by Luther see L. W. Spitz, *Religious Renaissance of the German Humanists,* pp. 258–61.

observe one of Luther's most original, most imaginative and most vote-catching concepts. It might be argued that the priesthood of all believers and the sacred character of lay vocations had their modest origins in the *devotio moderna*, which did not merely deprecate the value of scholastic learning but asserted that a devout layman walked closer with God than did a bad monk. Moreover some authors in the mystical and pietist tradition had taught that a layman by assiduous effort might attain the same high spiritual experiences as those hitherto assumed to be within the preserve of the monastic life. Boehmer, who rightly claims a great advance for Luther's doctrine, nevertheless acknowledges that the notion of a lay calling had figured in numerous late medieval authors: Tauler, Gerson, Antoninus of Florence and the German Dominicans Johannes Nider and Markus von Weida.[20] Its connections with Christian humanism are perhaps less obvious, yet in this area it would seem mistaken to suppose that humanism merely staged a destructive attack upon the great clerical empire. The sociology of Christian humanism, from that of Erasmus downward, tended to envisage a divinely sanctioned commonwealth, within which men of all callings and classes played their parts under God. By the same token, the ideal picture of the psalm-singing ploughman was sketched by Erasmus long before the Reformers made him a reality.

Luther's thought on worldly society, on the calling of the layman, on the purposes of the state, hence owes debts to numerous predecessors, yet in the last resort it arises from his own doctrine of the Church, a largely original line of thought which can be traced back to his early writings. Luther could not find in the New Testament a clerically-orientated Church. For him the Church was God's people, the community of believers: he translated *ecclesia* as *Gemeinde* (community), *Gemeine* (congregation) or even *Versammlung* (assembly). In denouncing the Radicals, he repudiated the perfectionist and antiquarian notion that little flocks of true Christians should separate from the main body of church members and go off to recreate in precise detail the Church of the Apostles. On the other side, while he would not abandon the Catholic concept of 'the mystical body of Christ',

[20] H. Boehmer, pp. 134-5.

this body could not be built around the papacy and hierarchy, since it corresponded with the whole community of Christian believers knit together in Christ. The point is driven home with the usual brilliant metaphor:

> The result of being one with Christ is that we are also one among ourselves...As the grains of corn are ground, they blend with each other. None keeps its own flour but is mingled with that of others...So among Christians no one is for himself, but each one shows and spreads himself amongst his fellows in love.[21]

Unfortunately this challenge made all too little impact upon the actual conduct of the non-perfectionist majority. Had it been truly successful it must surely have modified the economic behaviour and the class divisions of secular society. Yet Luther's conservatism in regard to the latter and to the state has often been exaggerated by those who too simply took the Prussia of later days to typify Lutheran social and political practice. In fact Luther's restoration of the layman did not include the apotheosis of the secular state, an organism which in his view did not function upon the plane of salvation but upon that lower plane where man could exercise free will, and too often did so to tragic effect.[22] In his earlier works Luther tends to dismiss the state as a harsh bridle fastened by God upon unruly and criminal mankind, yet having marginal relevance to the life of the true Christian. Later on he regards it in somewhat more positive terms as ordained by God to govern Christians and non-Christians alike, yet still solely upon the worldly level. In other words the state does not contribute to the task of saving men; neither is it a 'Christian state', governing men's consciences and already integrated with the Church. Likewise a prince or a city councillor can be a Christian as an individual person, but he does not rule

[21] 'Und so wyr denn mit Christo eyn kuchen sind, so wirckt das selbige soviel, das wyr auch unter einander eyn ding werden...Seht, also sind wyr auch eyn brot, wenn wir glauben, das keyner is fur sich selbst, sondern ein yeglicher wyrfft und breyt sich unter den anderen durch die liebe' (*WA*, xii, p. 48). Cf. W. Pauck, p. 378; his ch. 3 deals broadly with Luther's concepts of Church and society.

[22] For a basic bibliography on the 'Two Kingdoms' see E. G. Léonard, pp. 380–82, and add the article by W. D. J. Cargill Thompson.

by virtue of his Christianity. Where rulers and magistrates partake in ecclesiastical administration, they do so as eminent members of the local Church or congregation. Luther stood adamant upon one distinction: that rulers must reform the Church yet exercise no authority over actual belief and worship. In effect he and his followers struck bargains with the secular powers. Lutheran churches were commonly reorganized and even administered by mixed commissions of state officials and divines, while secular governments allowed Luther and the divines to draw up catechisms and liturgies. Though the Church Orders went out over the seals of governments, to say that Lutheran princes and city councils 'prescribed the beliefs' of their subjects remains misleading; indeed their dealings with ecclesiastics and congregations did not differ fundamentally from those of medieval kings or of contemporary Catholic rulers. Even so, Luther's brave words on spiritual liberty uttered in 1520 came to mean less and less in terms of individual rights, until in 1555 the Peace of Augsburg finally sanctioned a wholesale forcing of consciences by the threat of exile, and promoted the transfer of dissidents between Lutheran and Catholic states. It seems likely that Luther, had he lived to see it, would have been desolated by the Peace of Augsburg. In the event the man who had so often in earlier days signed himself *Eleutherius*, the Liberator, did not live to see the blasting of his hope that the Word would sweep like a mighty tide throughout the whole empire, and that a German Evangelical Church would arise amid the general consent of rulers and people.

For the rest, Luther's political convictions remained somewhat typical of the middle and upper social orders. God may have stricken our princes with madness; they may be 'the greatest fools or the worst rogues on earth', yet Mr. Everyman (*Herr Omnes*) is manifestly unfitted to correct their faults. It was not during the Peasants' Revolt but four years earlier in *Christian Nobility* that Luther declared, 'I will side always with him, however unjust, who suffers rebellion, and against him who rebels, however justly'. On the other hand, he believed in the duty of passive resistance to ungodly commands: to suffer under the Cross was the one undoubted right of the Christian subject. Both principles he could base upon some solid New Testament texts. But it should not be imagined that his doctrine of non-resistance related merely to territorial princes, or even to the latter and the city-councils. Like that of most contemporary Germans, his sense of duty and patriotism revolved also around the concept of God-given empire. He watched with the utmost distress the growing rift between the emperor and a powerful block of Protestant princes and cities, and not until 1530 did he admit that in certain exceptional cases the princes of the empire had the right to resist the emperor by force. He nevertheless continued to use his waning, though never negligible, authority to oppose the slide toward civil war. With entire sincerity he continued to address Charles V in respectful, even affectionate terms, long years after the emperor's unswerving hostility toward the Evangelical religion had become manifest.

So far, therefore, as concerns Luther's heritage from humanism, the significant distinction seems to lie between his expansive social teachings and that reverse side of an ecclesiastical tapestry which has passed muster as his 'political thought'. In the social sphere he not only stood heir to Christian humanism but augmented this progressive heritage with his genial insight and enthusiasms. Yet in the political sphere, both theoretical and practical, a different situation obtained. Neither the humanists nor Luther were in our modern sense of the term 'political thinkers', and we do not make them such merely by placing their thought under this essentially more modern category. The German humanists inherited and also developed nationalism and imperialism. Luther broadly accepted their more temperate conclusions, duly modified by what he thought the Bible said about Church and state. Luther's younger contemporary and first full-scale biographer, Johannes Mathesius, laid especial stress on what Zeeden calls 'the German prophet *par excellence*, his mission covering Germany, his function that of a prophet to the Germans'.[23] This interpretation was to be duly revived by nineteenth-century historians, and so far as the more direct historical results of Luther's career are concerned, it remains far from inappropriate. On the negative side, he followed the nation's humanists in his inability to think much about non-German problems. As political crises developed he and the

[23] E. W. Zeeden, p. 22.

intellectuals of his party appealed increasingly to the Bible, even where it had the most dubious relevance to the tangled web of German politics. So far as practical influence on the course of politics was concerned, their situation degenerated year by year. Their capacity to resist the advances of princes and landlords has been exaggerated by many of their critics. Fundamental changes in the structure of empire and central European society had begun well before their time and could not be arrested by writers, preachers, theorists, whether Biblical or classical by inspiration.

Far-seeing, original, even influential as were Luther's attitudes toward the intellectual and spiritual fabric of earthly society, his gaze did not penetrate far upward into the dark clouds of high politics. But higher still, in a remote stratosphere and almost invisible to the naked eye, there hovered the still more impalpable concept of empire. During the last century historians have taught us to distinguish the components of empire more clearly than anyone could have distinguished them in Luther's day. As applied to the reign of Charles V, the term contained a gross dichotomy between the ever more Spanish-centred dynasticism of the Habsburgs and the medieval dream—itself a strange dichotomy—of an *imperium* which should be at once German and universal, functional and mystical. As politicians, neither Luther nor his humanist associates were sufficiently wide awake to deliver the German nation from this muddled dream.

4

Theological Influences on Luther

That Luther's closest followers came to regard his mission as unique, original and divinely ordained cannot be denied. Justus Jonas writes that other preachers crawl and stutter in comparison with this man, who commands 'an ocean of words and deeds... He can make all things plain whereas we altogether can do nothing.' Melanchthon dubs Bugenhagen a grammarian, himself a logician and Jonas a rhetorician, 'but Luther is everything, a miracle among men; what he speaks and writes grips the heart and leaves behind a wonderfully deep impression.' And it was not just by way of a literary flourish that Bugenhagen in his valedictory oration identified him with the Angel of the Apocalypse, seen by St. John flying in mid-heaven, bearing an eternal gospel to all men and nations. 'The angel that cried out "Fear God and give the praise" was Doctor Martin Luther.'

These men were not simple, impressionable burghers but eminent humanists brought up in the critical world of Erasmus, Reuchlin and Lefèvre. Whatever values may now be placed upon Luther's attempt to reinterpret Christianity, one must at least credit him with a charisma and a communicative power almost unique in the history of modern western religion. This aspect of his personality and public career cannot be regarded as dependent upon forerunners; it depends no more upon them than the power of a radio transmitter upon singers, actors or programme-planners. We must later discuss these prophetic and projective gifts alongside the relatively new science of printing, which obviously amplified, yet just as obviously did not create, such unusual gifts. Likewise, while this chapter aims to identify and discuss the many religious thinkers of all periods who foreshadowed and stimulated Luther, it should not be interpreted as an attempt to 'explain' the man or the movement solely or even chiefly in terms of 'influences' which came to bear upon his mind or upon those of his hearers.[1] Luther's mind and programme, Luther's impact on history ranged far beyond any mere group of historical influences which modern scholars can detect and analyse. The fact remains that the man—and still more the movement—could not have arisen without a singularly powerful and complicated heritage, which must somehow be disentangled. Yet in this task we too closely resemble archaeologists trying to recreate a living culture from a mass of pitiful coins and potsherds—the difference is that we have enough evidence in some areas to convince us of our poverty in others.

So far the present writer has sought to distinguish some features of Luther's undeniably creative relationship with humanism. Which should we regard as his other major intellectual debts? What remained truly original in his thinking? Conversely, how far was he revivifying old concepts by means of new imagery and verbal definition, by the magic of personality? Again, which of his ideas became cataclysmic within European society and hence make special demands upon historians? Amongst the essentials we have already encountered one, though it cannot be pronounced original to Luther: the primacy of Scriptural evidence over ecclesiastical tradition. Upon this rock every structure of the Protestant Reformation was founded. We have encountered, or shall shortly encounter, certain other basic elements in Luther's thought: the non-freedom of the human will in matters concerning salvation; the 'theology of the Cross'; above all the sinner's Justification by Faith, through the imputation (the reckoning to his credit) of the merits of Christ.

[1] The present writer's notions on Luther's theology are mainly based on such well-known secondary authorities as Atkinson, Boehmer, Bornkamm, Ebeling, Gerrish, Headley, Lau, McDonough, Pauck, Pelikan, Rupp, Saarnivaara and Watson, all listed in the Bibliography. We still lack an exhaustive and systematic review of Luther's relations with his predecessors, but H. A. Oberman's *Forerunners of the Reformation* is informative on certain aspects. The literature on individual 'sources' is voluminous: for a selection, see E. G. Léonard, pp. 370–71.

Yet before proceeding further with these great issues even a historian little versed in eucharistic theology cannot avoid some reference to this other vexed topic, if only because its negative influence proved so powerful. More than any other issue it prevented the German Reformation from becoming a Germanic Reformation. Here Luther's theology grew out of a veritable passion to produce a literal meaning for the words 'This is my Body', while nevertheless rejecting the notion of a priestly sacrifice or miracle, together with the 'Aristotelian' doctrine of transubstantiation. His early studies of d'Ailly and Biel encouraged him to accept the ubiquitous presence of the glorified Body of Christ, extended in space and—without any priestly miracle—inevitably present in the elements of bread and wine. By contrast, he had been repelled by passages in the earlier writers like Wessel Gansfort, who seemed to undervalue the literal interpretation. This confrontation came to a head as early as 1521, when the elderly Dutch lawyer Cornelius Hoen (d. 1524) sent his younger friend Hinne Rode to Wittenberg in order to convince Luther of the truth of a symbolic and commemorative doctrine of the eucharist. With him Rode took not only a copy of Hoen's own able essay *A Most Christian Letter* (to be published by Zwingli in 1524) but also some recently rediscovered manuscripts by Gansfort.[2] Again, long before his critical encounter with Zwingli in 1529, Luther had clashed heavily with his own former friend and colleague Karlstadt on this matter of a Body 'corporeally extended in space'. Zwingli he regarded as an extremist closely identified with adversaries like Hoen and Hoen's disciple Karlstadt. He thus came to Marburg in 1529 with a closed mind, wholly unprepared to consider seriously the Zwinglian commemorative and symbolic interpretations of the Lord's Supper. In the great hall of Landgrave Philip's castle he began the decisive debate by chalking the words *Hoc est corpus meum* on the table between his party and the Zwinglians, and announcing, 'I take these words literally; if anyone does not, I shall not argue but contradict.' Luther thus suffered the two Reformations, which could agree on fourteen articles of faith, to split asunder and drift into

[2] H. A. Oberman, *Forerunners of the Reformation*, pp. 252, 268ff; G. H. Williams, pp. 35–7.

enmity over this fifteenth article of the eucharist. For historical purposes, his Marburg decision proved final and in the decades which followed, Luther's own solution to the problem of the eucharist failed to commend itself to any other reformed Church. At home it had all the advantages of a dogma unintelligible to the common man. There can be few such instances where the monumental conviction of a theologian has produced political and social effects of a comparable magnitude: yet these effects worked almost entirely to the advantage of Luther's Catholic opponents. Even in the seventeenth century eucharistic doctrine still divided Lutheran from Calvinist, thus becoming one of the many unearned bonanzas of the Habsburgs.

Less personal in origin, yet of far greater spiritual and social force, was Luther's 'theology of the Cross', which can be traced as early as the *Lectures on the Psalms* (1513).[3] Thenceforth it became a marked feature of the *Ninety-five Theses* and their *Explanations* (1517)—and again of Luther's theses in the Heidelberg Disputation of April 1518. This important teaching does not merely call for response to Christ's redeeming sacrifice: it asserts that if a man is one of those chosen by God, his life will also be lived amid some degree of spiritual suffering. That the latter could be intermittently acute Luther had experienced in his own case. 'Thus we know', he wrote in his copy of Tauler's sermons, 'that God does not act in us, unless he first destroys us by the Cross and suffering.' That these agonies could be a sign of God's favour, and not the reverse, Luther took to his great comfort and expressed in his own writing. In due course he contrasted the theology of the Cross with the theology of glory, the illusion of the scholastics that a knowledge of God can be gained from reason, philosophy and the world of nature. This concept did not, however, spring from him or from any single mind. He did not even wrest it purely from his own studies of *Corinthians* or of St. Augustine. For him one of its main sources lay in the familiar writings of the German mystics, especially in the sermons of the Strassburg Dominican Johann Tauler (d. 1361), published in 1508, studied by Luther on the advice

[3] The theme appears in most of the theological books; cf. especially P. S. Watson, ch. 4; E. G. Rupp in C. S. Meyer, *Luther for an Ecumenical Age*.

of his superior Staupitz, then recommended by him to Spalatin and to others of his correspondents. Tauler became one of his permanent inspirations. He found a similar consolation in the *Theologia Germanica*, which he or a friend probably discovered in some Thuringian monastery. In 1516 he edited and published it with an appreciative introduction, this being the earliest of his published works. Though the treatise is now thought to have been written in the late fourteenth century by a priest of the Teutonic Order at Sachsenhausen, Luther in fact believed it to be a summary of Tauler, whom he commends as a teacher unknown and despised in the schools, but having a 'more solid and sincere theology than is found in all the teachers of scholasticism in the universities'. Johann Eck and others of Luther's educated critics later protested that they had never heard of Tauler, a fact which points to the regional character not only of the *devotio moderna* but of the older mystical traditions stretching down to Luther's lifetime.

In broad terms, however, the theology of the Cross had been preached not only by Staupitz but by Wimpfeling and others who lived within less ascetic and mystical traditions. And when all is said and done, Luther's debt to mystical or contemplative teachings must be judged to remain strictly limited. By any normal usage of the word, Luther was not a mystic: he never became committed to any contemplative method, any ladder of spiritual experiences, such as those described by Meister Eckhardt in the fourteenth century or by St. Theresa of Ávila in the sixteenth. The suffering envisaged by the 'theology of the Cross' is not equivalent to the 'Dark Night of the Soul'. The young Luther who somehow ended by arousing the German nation was a professor of Biblical theology, searching for authentic Christianity, searching also for assuagement of his personal suffering, not in any sequence of ineffable psychological states presumed to emanate from the divine Being, but in the written sourcebook of Christianity, in the Scriptural record. His mature thought would appear to reject the anthropology implicit in Tauler and Gerson. And if he was connected but lightly with the northern mystics, he had far less in common with the Platonist mystical theory of Italians like Ficino and Pico della Mirandola. He took consolation not from any sort of cosmic euphoria but from the redemption of real human beings through the starkly historical event of the Crucifixion.[4] As for that more popular descendant of the mystics, the *devotio moderna*, Luther was well acquainted with its handbook, *The Imitation of Christ* (*c*. 1418). Amid his subsequent revulsion against monasticism he also continued to show respect for the main surviving institution of the *devotio*, the Brethren of the Common Life, whose school at Magdeburg was almost certainly the one which as a boy of fourteen he had attended in that city. And so far as concerns the 'theology of the Cross' one might well find it even in the *Imitation*, that most popular of all devotional books throughout Europe, a neglected source, or at least another proof of the wide diffusion of the concept a century before it comforted Luther.

Behold, in the Cross all doth consist and all lieth in our dying thereon; for there is no other way unto life, and into true inward peace, but the way of the Cross... Dispose and order all things according to thy will and judgment, yet thou shalt ever find that of necessity thou must suffer somewhat, either willingly or against thy will, and so thou shalt ever find the Cross. For either thou shalt feel pain in thy body, or in thy soul shalt thou suffer tribulation of spirit. Sometimes thou shalt be forsaken of God... but so long as it pleaseth God, thou oughtest to bear it. For God will have thee learn to suffer tribulation... and by tribulation become more humble. No man hath so cordial a feeling of the passion of Christ, as he who hath suffered the like himself.[5]

Yet as so often with these 'forerunners', a whole dimension is lacking. This one illustrates the relation of the *devotio* to Luther; and there can be few exercises better calculated to illuminate Luther's contribution to Christianity than a reading of his post-monastic writings alongside a reading of the *Imitation of Christ*.

[4] On Tauler and Luther, see E. G. Rupp in C. S. Meyer, *Luther for an Ecumenical Age*, pp. 71–2; and actual references for Tauler's lasting influence in E. G. Rupp, *Patterns of Reformation*, p. 255, n. 3. See also R. H. Fife, pp. 218–20; B. Moeller in *La Mystique Rhénane. Colloque de Strasbourg 16–19 mai 1961* (Paris, 1963). S. E. Ozment argues that Luther's mature theology developed as a polemical reaction against Tauler and Gerson.

[5] *Imitation of Christ*, bk. 2, ch. 12: 'Of the King's Highway of the Holy Cross'.

The popular appeal of the latter forms no small tribute to the spirituality of the fifteenth and sixteenth centuries, since it is in all senses a book of withdrawal from the world. A sequence of aphorisms, not a structure of argument, a distillation of the introspective and non-militant spirit, its hymns might suitably have begun with the line 'Inward Christian Pacifists'. It walks beside the still waters. It preaches restraint, silence, humility, self-denial, anti-intellectualism. Above all it demands a detachment from the love of creatures, including other men and women. It is wholly devoid of proper names and personalities. In effect it suggests that even when living and working in the world, the devotee should make a little monastery of himself. What a contrast is afforded by the mature Luther, whether as man or as writer! Paradoxically, having denied corrupt man any share in his own salvation, Luther abounds in warm affirmation, in a genial solicitude for people as individuals; conversely, he boils over into scabrous abuse of those whom he accuses of misleading the Christian world. He is involved, not withdrawn; mentally as well as physically, he has left the monastery and rejoined the human race.

In assessing the influence of the *devotio* upon the Lutheran Reformation in general, we are hence faced by a remarkable ambivalence. It had long become naturalized throughout large areas of Germany, and Professor Landeen has described its extension across the north-western regions and its merging with native devotional traditions.[6] Long before 1500 it had begun to modify the teaching of its own famous book: its schools formed centres of Christian humanism, its attitudes became more educational, less claustral. In parts of Germany as in its Netherlandish home, it continued to stimulate the urge toward a personal and experiential religion, the demand which Luther would answer more subtly upon his two levels, socially with positive reforms, but theologically with a more austere, more Biblical-historical, more Christocentric scheme of salvation. On the other hand it requires little study of the social and literary history of the Catholic Reformation to perceive that the *devotio*

---

[6] Cf. the three articles by W. A. Landeen; on the Catholic Bible-publishing of the Brethren's Rostock house, see K. A. Strand, *A Reformation Paradox* (Ann Arbor, 1960).

in general and the *Imitation* in particular contributed powerfully toward the revival of Catholic spirituality. Who doubts this should study the career of Jean Standonck, the writings of Abbot Blosius, and the place of the *Imitation* in the training of orthodox saints and reformers from Loyola downward throughout all Europe. And just as Luther made a special appeal to Germans, so the *devotio* continued its appeal to Netherlanders and their neighbours in the lower Rhineland, acting there as a prophylactic against the ready acceptance of Lutheranism.

From this point our chief concern will be to discuss two very different influences, familiar in some measure to all students of Luther: that of Occamism, the so-called *via moderna* in philosophy and theology, and that of Augustine, including his numerous disciples throughout the centuries. The former of these schools looked back to William of Occam (*c.* 1300–1349) as its founder, his work having been reinforced by several major thinkers like Jean Buridan, Peter d'Ailly and Jean Gerson. Its triumph over Thomism and other rival scholastic systems throughout the German universities was by no means total: even Luther's mentor Staupitz remained a Thomist. Nevertheless at Erfurt Occamism had long held a commanding position, especially since the days of its most renowned exponent Gabriel Biel (d. 1495), who taught Luther's own masters at that university, Jodocus Trutvetter and Bartholomäus Arnold von Usingen.[7] Biel also wrote the famous textbook on the Canon of the Mass much used by the young Luther. In contradistinction from Thomism, the *via moderna* denied reality to universals, i.e. general concepts representing the common elements belonging to individuals of the same species. These exist merely in the mind, while reality consists of single individuals related only by contiguity in time and space. This argument ended by placing

[7] On Luther's Occamist teachers and the Erfurt tradition, see R. H. Fife, pp. 49–52, 60–65; L. Meier in *Revue d'histoire ecclésiastique*, 1 (1955); texts in O. Scheel, pt. i. Concerning late medieval scholasticism and Luther, see the articles by G. Ritter, P. Vignaux, H. A. Oberman and S. E. Ozment in S. E. Ozment, *The Reformation in Medieval Perspective*. On Biel, I rely upon the standard work by H. A. Oberman, *The Harvest of Medieval Theology*. On Luther's early process of self-liberation from the *facere quod in se est* of the Occamists, see H. A. Oberman, 'Robert Holcot and the Beginnings of Luther's Theology' in *Harvard Theological Review*, lv (1962), reprinted in S. E. Ozment, *op. cit.*

the conclusions of human reason in stark distinction from the revealed truths of Catholic theology. According to logical analysis, argued some Occamists, both state and Church would be only the sum of their members. It might even be maintained that the Trinity must be three gods and not one God. But since revelation stood higher than reason, one must surrender to the former as expounded by the Church, even if it meant admitting to a double logic. Yet however submissive the Occamists might profess themselves, the outcome imperilled the Church's hierarchy, since its teachings would now depend upon plain Biblically-based revelation, or else—as in the theology of Indulgences—neither on Scripture nor on natural reason but on the mere fiat of the papacy or of some other ecclesiastical authority. The very being of God became even more mysterious and arbitrary, since Occamism maintained that the divine nature and attributes could not be analysed, nor the divine decrees questioned by man's puny instrument of reason. Here the *via moderna* tended to adopt extreme Augustinian or Scotist principles, maintaining that God did not will things because they were good, but that things were good merely because God had willed them. As we shall shortly observe, it remains a fallacy to suppose that sixteenth-century papalists regarded Occamism as heretical, or that in general they sensed its dangers. On the other hand, even during Luther's early career far-seeing conservatives were at work to rehabilitate Thomas Aquinas, the reconciler of reason and revelation. While Erfurt continued to embrace Occamism, Cologne not only resisted Luther but vigorously championed the Thomist revival. This process was to culminate in 1567, when Pius V declared Aquinas 'Doctor of the Church' and Thomism gained a firm hold upon the curricula of the new Catholic colleges and seminaries.

With the appearance of Professor Oberman's erudite work *The Harvest of Medieval Theology*, our knowledge of Biel and of late Occamism has greatly expanded. But the result may well be that in seeking to delineate the formation of Luther's thought we should now assign to Occamism a lesser part than it hitherto seemed to demand. Luther's long sojourn in this tradition doubtless developed his profound sense of the majesty, the omnipotence, the mysterious 'otherness' of God. He accepted the impotence of reason to fathom the nature and designs of God. Occamist thought formed at least the prototype of Luther's 'masked' God, who seems so often to say 'No', yet who for once in the person of Christ dropped the mask and replied to man's questioning with an affirmative. As for one who had started life in Occamist circles, it was also natural for Luther to develop his thought in terms of paradox, contradiction and dialectic tension. It is the beginning of wisdom to stress this recurrent characteristic of Luther's mind: Law *versus* Gospel; letter against Spirit; kingdom of God and kingdom of this world; God hidden and God revealed; the freedom and the servitude of a Christian. Yet at least equal contributors to Luther's dialectic are the writings of St. Augustine, to which we shall presently turn. A few other particular legacies Luther seems to have derived from Occam, d'Ailly and Biel: for example the omnipresence of the glorified Body of Christ, which we have already observed as an important element in his teaching on the eucharist. Modern scholars, including Boehmer, have also listed miscellaneous points in Luther's works which seem to echo passages in Occamist writers: his opinions on the inviolability of the confessional, on the admissibility of 'white lies' and on the relations of secular governments to the Natural Law. Yet even when all these ingredients large and small have been enumerated, Luther's debt to Occam and to Biel does not acquire overwhelming weight. Indeed, on certain essentials Luther actually recoiled from Biel. For example, the latter had found in St. Basil a warrant for investing the unwritten traditions of the Church with an apostolic authority comparable with that of the Scriptures. Again, Biel shows some distinctly Pelagian leanings. If, he says, a man really does his best, he can from his own natural powers love God above all else; spontaneously a man can generate the tiny spark which merits the infusion of divine grace. It would be hard to imagine two doctrines more important or more harshly opposed to the fundamental convictions of the mature Luther.

Yet only the more fanatical champions of Luther's originality will seek to show him as the unheralded author of this reversal. His reaction against the *via moderna* had been anticipated by, and in part derived from, Staupitz. While discussing the latter chiefly in his medieval setting, David Steinmetz nevertheless makes him, in Luther's own phrase, 'a preacher of Grace and of the Cross'. And in his last paragraph the modern theologian chooses as especially significant the deep conviction with which Staupitz turned from Nominalism to Augustine.

> Man is impotent, not only to earn merits apart from Grace (Thomas Aquinas is willing to assert that!) but even to act virtuously. Reliance on one's own natural powers is tantamount to a sentence of condemnation.

And in conclusion, Steinmetz selects as especially significant this rejection of Occamist anthropology. Before Luther, Staupitz had re-proclaimed Augustine's confession of the redemptive fidelity of God, who seeks out and preserves despairing men who did not even seek him.[8]

Regarding Luther's anti-papalism, we should be imprudent to attribute it to the influence of the *via moderna*, even though the latter had been cradled in an anti-papal setting and had placed papal authority in a dangerously exposed position. Indeed, Occam himself had joined Marsiglio of Padua in denying the pope all temporal authority, had conceded wide powers to lay rulers and had proposed a limited papal monarchy exercising a loose authority over a series of national Churches. The two famous rebels had teamed together in the service of the emperor Lewis IV, settled in Munich and supplied that aggrieved monarch with an arsenal of propaganda for use against the Avignonese papacy. Since those far-off days, later Occamists, and especially Gabriel Biel, had remained faithful to the philosophical and theological principles of the school, while yet suppressing its early anti-papal connotations. By this time it had become (whatever enthusiastic modern Thomists may suppose) one of the establishment systems: the works of Biel were to be praised by the Jesuit leader Laynez and included in a list of recommended books published by the diocese of Munich as late as 1569.[9] In short, Luther did not learn his anti-papal arguments

---

[8] D. C. Steinmetz, pp. 182–3; he has also a valuable bibliography covering this area. On Staupitz and Luther, see E. Wolf; H. A. Oberman in *Harvard Theological Review*, lix (1966).

[9] H. A. Oberman, *The Harvest of Medieval Theology*, pp. 426–7.

from Occamist teachers like Trutvetter and von Usingen, both of whom in the event refused to follow their former pupil into an anti-Roman schism.

One further differentiation between Biel and Luther has not hitherto been pressed; yet it is one which should at least appeal to historians, because it belongs to a category which, more surely than that of rational argument, determines the fate of ideas in society. Despite the political activism of some of its early founders, the *via moderna* had always been an intricate philosophical system, and as such hardly capable of forming a platform for mass-action. Its development by eminent theologians like Biel removed it still further from the public arena. One may scarcely call Occamism a devotional or a political movement, let alone a movement directed toward lay men and women. In the field of social-religious propaganda, manner and mode of appeal rank at least equally with subject-matter. From 1517 Luther began to speak directly to the masses, to select issues which they could understand and to simplify those issues by literary techniques amounting to an inspired journalism. One need only turn the pages of Gabriel Biel for half an hour to see that he had no such aim, no such style, indeed no such content. In our later chapters, as we pass through the doors dividing intellectual from social history, we shall find that Luther has gone ahead of us while Gabriel Biel is left behind.

Overshadowing all other post-Biblical influences upon the thought of Luther stood the figure of St. Augustine.[10] Yet this statement should instantly be followed by a reminder that Augustine's importance for Luther lay not solely within Augustine's own writings but in their impulse toward a reconsideration of their common master St. Paul. Moreover this dominant strain in Luther's ancestry remains hard to delineate with accuracy, since Augustine came to Luther not merely through direct reading but through a number of intermediaries, both early-medieval and late-medieval. Within whatever

[10] On the Augustine heritage there are some useful hints by J. Paquier in *DTC*, ix, cols. 1146–1335. Also relevant is G. Leff, *Gregory of Rimini* (Manchester, 1961). U. Saarnivaara centres upon Luther's emergence from the shadow of Augustine. Further references occur in E. G. Léonard, pp. 41, 370–71.

package it came, the basic message was that of a rigorous theological pessimism, tempered by somewhat pallid rays of hope. Natural man is a mass of perdition, hopelessly corrupt, morally helpless, unable to be justified or saved by his own determination, or by any other force save divine grace—and a grace vouchsafed by a wholly omnipotent Deity to those he elects, not on account of their merits but by his own inscrutable will. Here is summarized only one of the many disquieting aspects of a thoroughgoing belief in the divine omnipotence, a belief at the core of our legacies from Augustine, Luther and Calvin. It was indeed the last-named, citing Augustine incessantly throughout his *Institutes,* who put the matter most succinctly when he said that if God elects us for salvation 'ce n'est pas pour nos beaux yeux'.

Those who have slightingly said that the Augustinian Eremites of Luther's day had little of Augustine about them would seem to be in error, though a more intensive study of the German houses of the Order during the previous century would no doubt reveal a patchy spectacle. The likelihood remains that within his own Order the young Luther became exposed to oral and literary traditions of some strength. Its most famous author had been the former general, Gregory of Rimini (d. 1358) an Occamist in philosophy but a strenuous follower of Augustine in theology. Luther cites Gregory several times, but in every case after 1519, a fact suggesting to Boehmer and others that he had not read Gregory until that year.[11] Whatever the case for that deduction, Luther would have read passages from Gregory cited in Biel's commentary on the *Sentences* of Peter Lombard, and again in the works of Peter d'Ailly. The application of Augustine's teaching to personal religion Luther early encountered in the works of St. Bernard of Clairvaux, whose earnest teaching and ardent love of Christ he was later to proclaim. Again, Luther had to lecture as early as 1509 on the *Sentences,* and here he found Augustine's thought heavily represented. Even in the late *Table Talk* he is found still praising Peter Lombard in terms which suggest that his intensive studies within and around that still basic textbook had become more than an academic exercise.

[11] H. Boehmer, p. 140.

The most important questions still remain. When did Luther begin to study Augustine's great books in their original texts? More important, when did he pass beyond Augustine into his own concept of the Pauline doctrine of Justification?[12] Though the mature Luther revealed an intimate knowledge of several of Augustine's works, there remains too little evidence to authenticate any detailed programme of such studies during his early career. We shall shortly cite a passage in his *Autobiographical Fragment* of 1545, showing how a reading of Augustine *On the Spirit and the Letter* had seemed to confirm his new and epoch-making insight into the meaning of the righteousness (*justitia*) of God.[13] In due course, he relates, he went on to read 'nearly all of Augustine', finding a special interest in the group of writings against Pelagius, wherein Augustine had set forth his teaching on sin, grace and predestination. This study had shown that he, Luther, had been moving along the right lines, though for the time being he had felt restrained from publicizing his own more advanced concept of Justification. Unfortunately the date and even the exact nature of Luther's independent breakthrough remain subject to uncertainty and dispute. Here we approach some of the knottiest problems concerning Luther's early spiritual and theological development. We are dealing with his attainment of the concepts Justification by Faith Alone, Justification through the unearned imputation of Christ's merits to the sinner: the doctrine which formed the fly-wheel of Luther's teaching.

These involved issues are crucial enough for our assessment of Luther's originality and his relationship with Augustine, but it would require a whole book—and far more than the present writer's slender theology—to analyse the relevant texts in full detail. Our own brief glance may begin with certain sentences of the *Autobiographical Fragment* at the point where Luther has just brought his narrative up to the year 1519.

[12] On this highly controversial theme, while recognizing the weight of opinion on the other side, I have followed Saarnivaara, with his transitional date of 1518. This was supported by E. Bizer, *Fides ex auditu* (3rd edn., Neukirchen, 1966), but he in turn was criticized by E. G. Rupp in *Zeitschrift für Kirchengeschichte*, lxxi (1960) and by H. Bornkamm in *Archiv für Reformationsgeschichte*, lii (1961) and liii (1962).

[13] Full documents with scholarly apparatus in O. Scheel, pp. 191ff; crucial passages translated in E. G. Rupp and B. Drewery, pp. 6–7, 173–9.

Meanwhile in that year I had once more turned to the job of interpreting the Psalms, relying on the fact that I was better instructed for it because I had dealt in the schools with the Epistles of St. Paul to the Romans, the Galatians and the Hebrews. Certainly I had been inspired by a wonderful eagerness to understand *Romans*, but hitherto I had been held back, not by a 'lack of heat in the heart's blood'* but by one phrase in chapter one: 'The righteousness of God is revealed' in the Gospel. For I hated these words *justitia Dei*, which by the usual explanation of all my teachers, I had been taught to understand philosophically, as the so-called *formal* or *active righteousness* whereby God is just and punishes unjust sinners. My own situation was this: however blameless my life as a monk, I felt myself standing before God as a sinner with a most uneasy conscience; and I could not believe God would be appeased by any satisfaction I could offer. I did not love but hated this just God, who punishes sinners...

Luther here enlarges upon his burning grievance against God for thus confounding, both through the Law and the Gospel, the wretched human beings condemned already by original sin. Then, as he pounded against the iron gate of the Pauline text, he suddenly found it open.

As I meditated by day and night, God at last showed mercy when I turned my attention to these words: 'The righteousness of God is revealed; as it is written: the righteous shall live by faith'. And at that point I began to see that the righteousness of God is the righteousness in which a just man lives by God's gift, in other words by faith. [I understood] that what Paul means is this: that the righteousness of God revealed in the Gospel is *passive*; in other words, it is that by which a merciful God justifies us through faith...At this I felt myself immediately born anew, and entering through open gates into heaven itself...And now, to the same extent as I had hitherto hated the phrase 'righteousness of God', even so much did I begin to love and exalt it as the sweetest phrase of all: thus was this text of St. Paul for me the very gate of paradise.

Then he writes the sentences on Augustine: sentences which depict Augustine as confirmatory but nevertheless defective.

* Virgil, *Georgics*, ii. 484.

Later on I read Augustine *On the Spirit and the Letter*, where beyond all my hopes I found that he also interprets the righteousness of God in the same way...and although Augustine's statement on this matter is still open to criticism, and he is neither clear nor comprehensive on the subject of imputation, yet he is convinced that the righteousness of God should be taught as that by which we are justified.

The main difficulties lie in reconciling this late and somewhat cryptic narrative with the contemporary evidence stemming from three decades earlier, that is to say with the numerous passages suggesting theological development throughout Luther's lecture courses and other writings of the years 1512–19. From this attempt distinguished scholars have emerged with varying solutions. Boehmer, Vogelsang and Bornkamm suppose that Luther's new insight occurred substantially alongside his first course of lectures on *Psalms* (1513–14), despite his repeated association of the experience with the second course, written in 1518–19. They detect its effects already in the profounder lectures on *Romans*, dated 1515–16. On the other side Bizer and Aland place his theology of 1513–16 still within a Catholic framework, a conclusion supported by the step-by-step survey of these earlier writings made by the Finnish theologian Uuras Saarnivaara. This last detailed survey does indeed indicate some gradual advances in the earlier years: for example between 1516 and the early months of 1518 Luther is found upholding the literal interpretation of the Scriptures, abandoning the figurative, moral and anagogical interpretations of the schoolmen. Yet Saarnivaara seeks to demonstrate that the basic concept of Justification remains upon Augustine's level until we reach the sermon *Of the Threefold Righteousness*, published toward the end of 1518. Yet here, and also in another sermon which appeared not later than March 1519, Luther has detached his concept from that of his great predecessor. And as one would expect, the second course of Lectures on *Psalms* also appears in harmony with Luther's mature view.

Leaving the question of dates, we must attempt briefly to indicate in the light of Luther's later writings and their analysis by modern theologians something by no means fully explained in the *Autobiographical Fragment*: the actual terms of Luther's new insight into the Pauline texts, in other words the 'advances' he made upon Augustine's definition of Justification by Faith. Luther provides the key by his remark that Augustine's statement 'is neither clear nor comprehensive in the matter of imputation'. For Augustine, it is true, a man is justified—reconciled with God and put on the road to salvation—by grace alone, and through faith. Yet there occurs within his soul a gradual process of renovation and renewal, a process which cleanses him to the point where his own will can co-operate, however feebly, with divine grace. On the contrary, Luther interprets the New Testament to mean that when a man is chosen by God to receive the gift of faith, his guilt is instantly remitted, not through any gradual process of cleansing but through the imputation, the reckoning to his credit, of the righteousness earned simply and solely by Christ. The man is justified, says Luther, 'not by pieces but in a heap': or in another striking metaphor, the merits of Christ are suddenly hung about his nakedness like a garment, cloaking his sin from the awesome gaze of God. This act of imputation is 'extrinsic' or external, since it does not at once cleanse the soul within: the man remains at the same time justified and yet a sinner. Moreover his redemption will not depend at all upon any process of inward renewal, still less on the deeds of charity and devout observances arising from his increasingly co-operative will. Luther does acknowledge that Augustine's cleansing process must needs occur, once a man has been justified through God-given faith. This secondary process Luther identifies with the Pauline term 'sanctification', but he urges that it should not for a moment be confused with the primary process of Justification, of which it remains a mere consequence.

Today we mere historians may well ask awkward questions—and doubtless receive inconclusive answers—concerning the psychological and social results of this advance upon Augustine. How far were ordinary men and women, especially in the early years of the Reformation, led to understand and evaluate the difference between Augustine's gradual renovation and Luther's imputation-at-a-stroke? To such matters I propose to return at a later stage. Yet one need not attain a profound grasp of the theological issues in order to believe that some practical differences could follow an acceptance of the new teaching. Luther's message amounted to more than a subtle scholastic distinction. His doctrine can be claimed as even more Christocentric and theocentric than Augustine's, for there remains not even a lingering suggestion that a man is aided by grace to work his own passage. Yet once its full implications were grasped, Luther's concept might well have seemed to hold out a more solid comfort, since it bade the troubled soul—and there were many troubled souls in those days—to cast all its cares upon the Lord. The boundless inadequacy of man is balanced by a boundless sense of the divine mercy. Though any Christian must remain conscious of his bondage to sin so long as he lives, now he can rejoice in his faith and despite his lapses lay the burden on Christ, maintaining a joyous hope in his own destiny. The cheering can already begin since his battle has already been won by Another! As might have been expected, Luther soon had to face charges of antinomianism: the belief that by grace Christians are not only saved but set free from the daily fight to observe moral laws. Such was certainly not his intention. He repeatedly urges that faith cannot subsist without consequential works; it is 'always in action or else it is not faith'. Elsewhere he insists that good works must still be done, not to earn salvation but out of a love of God and a need to subdue the flesh. Even so, he continued to press the belief that neither the self-mortification of the monk, nor the alms-giving, the penances and Indulgence-buying of the layman contribute in the slightest degree to their reconciliation with God. Thus at the moment when, throughout European society, salvation by observances and other 'works' had reached its highest point of esteem, Luther produced an ultra-Augustinianism, a crushing blow against all merit-schemes of Christian life and salvation.

In regard to the foundations upon which Luther built this edifice, there still remain some critical questions unanswerable with dogmatic certainty. Among the most interesting is the relation of Luther with those fifteenth-century predecessors called rather unkindly by Philip Hughes the 'Augustinizers'. The chief of these had been Netherlanders or Rhinelanders involved not merely with Augustine's version of Justification by Faith but with the Brethren of the Common Life and with the *devotio moderna*, so pervasive in that region of Europe. Wessel Gansfort (d. 1489), John of Wesel (d. 1479), John Pupper of Goch (d. 1475) and some others were hailed in 1841–2 by Karl Heinrich Ullmann, who called his remarkable book *Reformers before the Reformation*.[14] Soon afterwards, this claim that Luther had real forerunners in a preceding generation underwent a heavy attack by the influential Protestant theologian Albrecht Ritschl, and it has never quite recovered. Apart from the genuine scholars, the whole nation of 'forerunners' has been displeasing both to the Luther-idolaters, who wanted to ascribe all Reformation origins to their hero, and again to some Catholic enthusiasts, who wanted along with Johannes Janssen to enjoy the spectacle of a devout Catholic Germany, fundamentally harmonious, suddenly and needlessly rent asunder by Luther's impatient revolt.

In an article of 1927, resolutely overlooked by the partisans, Gerhard Ritter showed that these 'forerunners' were not merely dominated by Augustine: they made their direct appeal to the Gospels and Epistles, sometimes against Augustine himself. Moreover Wesel, Gansfort and Pupper—the first with exceptional bluntness—did anticipate some of Luther's most concrete criticisms of a clerically, papally and legally orientated Church. Along with its hierarchic legalism, they denounced all reliance upon human authorities, even upon early ecclesiastical traditions, if they conflicted with the New Testament. Both Wesel and Gansfort disputed the right of the papal Church to burden Christians with regulations more onerous than those imposed by Christ. As examples, the former gave clerical celibacy, Indulgences, anointing with oil, the use of holy water, the extension of the prohibitions against marriage to distant degrees of relationship. Like Marsiglio before him, Wesel dismissed the priesthood as the mere administrators of God's mysteries, God alone holding the 'power of the keys'. Though they attached an importance to the perfecting of the human will which would have seemed Pelagian to Luther, these men

---

[14] On the 'Augustinizers' K. H. Ullmann is still useful, but see G. Ritter, 'Romantische und revolutionäre Elemente', translated in S. E. Ozment, *The Reformation in Medieval Perspective*; H. A. Oberman, *Forerunners*, pp. 18–19, 32–9; J. Mackinnon, *Luther and the Reformation*, ii, pp. 336ff.

proclaimed not only the omnipotence and glory of God but salvation by divine grace alone. From the Netherlandish and Rhineland theologians, there had arisen a school strongly opposed to the current Roman emphases, a school with some original, perhaps revolutionary implications. 'German life in the age of the Reformation', urged Ritter, 'was rich enough to allow a second original form of German piety rebelling against Rome to bloom beside the Lutheran Reformation.' Professor Oberman, in part following Reinhold Seeberg, has since examined this problem of the forerunners with an erudition and a semantic analysis which we do not propose to follow in detail. But amongst several helpful reminders he notes that the idea of the forerunner was contemporary; it did not begin with Ullmann or with modern historiography. Eck, Prierias, the universities of Louvain, Cologne and Paris all charged Luther as a lineal successor of earlier heretics: Waldo, Wycliffe, Huss and others. One might add that when in 1521 Erasmus was still according some guarded approval to Luther, he stated that the latter had taken his whole teaching from Augustine, Bernard, Gerson and Nicholas of Cusa. Later on Protestant controversialists were forced to become highly conscious of the question: where was your version of religion before Luther? In England the martyr-ologist John Foxe was to devote a vast amount of evidence to answering this question. Meanwhile in Germany Flacius Illyricus produced a *Catalogue of Witnesses to the Truth* (1556), which hails Luther as the heir of a very long succession of reformers.

It remains true that 'forerunners' need to be detected in a realistic spirit. In order to prove that Justification by Faith had always been an element in Catholic teaching—though not of course in Luther's definition—Denifle unearthed passages from numerous earlier theologians. This operation did not however prove very useful. For one thing, it could not have been other-wise, so long as theologians continued to read the Pauline Epistles or even textbooks discussing them. For another, there is no evidence that Luther knew or could have known the majority of the authors whom the learned Denifle cited. In the third place, whatever the alleged 'Augustinizers' had taught, it can scarcely be maintained that Justification by Faith had retained much practical influence in the religious life of the fifteenth century. In this case a real forerunner must surely perform one or both of two functions. He might qualify for the title, at least marginally, could he be identified as one of those who kept alive the great issues later raised by Luther. But with much more conviction he might be hailed as a forerunner, if from Luther's works or other hard documentary sources it could be proved that he either made Luther think, or at least confirmed him in certain recently-attained convictions. And obviously, the historical stature of a forerunner would be enlarged if his work were still being widely studied in Luther's day, if it were still contributing to the *mêlée* of the age. By these criteria some of the figures discussed by Ullmann, Ritter and Oberman remain rather impressive. All in all, as the present author has sought to affirm when discussing Luther's relations with humanism, historians of society and ideas cannot equate the history of ideas with the history of theology. A candidate for the role of forerunner does not necessarily suffer disqualification because on some central issue his theology diverges from Luther's, still less because he is not primarily involved in the favourite Luther themes of our own day. Such criteria might include those who wrote about Justification but exclude those whose main interest lay in the debate 'Scripture *versus* Tradition', a debate that even within the confines of theology retained an overwhelming importance. On a strictly theological basis, one could commit the historical absurdity of expelling both Reuchlin and Erasmus from among the forerunners of the Reformation. Finally, it would be almost as irrational to debar a writer from our list of forerunners just because he does not seem to have been known to Luther before 1520; as if at that point of time Luther stopped developing ideas or responding to the ideas of others; or as if, despite his repeated testimony to the reverse, confirmatory influences lacked importance in his mind.

What then of Luther's relation with the so-called 'Augustinizers' of the mid-fifteenth century? In 1520 Luther cited John of Wesel as the case of a typical persecuted scholar, and later on he made further friendly references to him as a former great man in his own university of Erfurt.[15] Thus situated he cannot have

[15] On John of Wesel see *ADB*, s.v. Rucherath; O. Clemen in *New*

been ignorant of John's anti-papal, indeed Marsiglian utterances, of his exaltation of the Scriptures above all other authority, of his notorious tract against the Indulgences issued during the papal Jubilee, of his enforced recantation in 1479. Again, when in 1522 Luther hailed Wessel Gansfort as being 'in accord with me in all things', he implied that he had only just realized the fact, yet the significant point remains that he did write the preface to the new printed edition of Gansfort's letters.

> If I had read this earlier, it could well have given my enemies the impression that I copied everything from Wessel, so much are our two minds at one.[16]

Similarly, he had just written the preface to the *Fragmenta* of Johann Pupper,[17] whose chief work was just being published by the Antwerper Cornelis Schryver, with the result that Schryver suffered imprisonment by the Inquisition. In his preface Luther discovers running through Tauler, Gansfort and Pupper a 'refined but hidden theological tradition', which 'has existed and still exists amongst the Germans'; and he looks forward to the day when not a single Thomist, Scotist or Occamist will remain throughout the world, 'but all will be simple children of God and true Christians'. Above all other, these 'Augustinizers' and their apparent predecessors suggested to Luther the notion of a pure

Schaff-Herzog; other standard works listed in *ODCC*, p. 741. Lau and Bizer cite a Münster dissertation (1955) by R. Samoray, *Johann von Wesel*. I have not yet secured this; or the article by J. F. G. Goeters, 'Johann Ruchrat von Wesel. Mittelalterlicher Ketzer oder Vorläufer der Reformation?' in *Monatsheft für evangelische Kirchengeschichte des Rheinlandes*, xvi (1967).

[16] 'Hic si mihi antea fuisset lectus, poterat hostibus meis videri Lutherus omnia ex Wesselo hausisse, adeo spiritus utriusque conspirat in unum' (*WA*, x (2 Abt.), p. 317). Cf. H. A. Oberman, *Forerunners*, pp. 18, 46 n. 33; A. Hyma, *The Christian Renaissance*, ch. 6. A major contribution is E. W. Miller, *Wessel Gansfort, Life and Writings* (2 vols., New York and London, 1917), which includes translations by J. W. Scudder of letters and treatises.

[17] *WA*, x (2 Abt.), pp. 327–30. The most comprehensive work on Pupper remains that by O. Clemen, who provides a full biography and description of his writings and doctrines. See also L. Abramowski, 'Die Lehre von Gesetz und Evangelium bei J. Pupper von Goch im Rahmen seines nominalistischen Augustinismus' in *Zeitschrift für Theologie und Kirche*, lxiv (1967). Cornelis Schryver is also called Grapheus or Scribonius: see *ADB* under the latter. A scholarly account with the prefaces is in O. Clemen, *op. cit.*, pp. 255–62, 269–75.

Germanic Church, known to God but largely driven underground by the tyrannical Roman hierarchy which had passed for the leadership of the Church during recent centuries. To him this tenacious survival brought a heartening message, since it indicated that the Church as a whole had not degenerated beyond all hope of reform.

What part in this scheme of history had been played by John Huss, and indeed by Huss's own forerunner, John Wycliffe? Here, despite the scandalous friendship between John of Wesel and a Hussite agent, Luther was surveying an essentially different field and in order to understand Huss, he had to throw off the nationalism and conciliarism of the German people, prejudices rationalized by the humanists, who had patriotically sought to depict their former Czech enemies as unlearned boors. Needless to state, Luther's revolt of 1517–18 was in no way inspired by the example of Huss, concerning whom he had at that time no balanced impression. The first turning point occurred at the Leipzig disputations of July 1519,[18] when his opponent Eck harped with remarkable persistence upon Luther's affinity with the Hussites. This manoeuvre had an obvious appeal to a Saxon audience. The university of Leipzig had been founded by Bohemian Germans fleeing from Czech nationalism in Prague, while later on the ducal lands had been harried by the victorious Hussites. In addition, if Luther showed even a slight sympathy with Huss, this automatically implied a heretical protest against the decisions of the Council of Constance, which had not merely burned Huss but acquired a lasting prestige in German public opinion. At first Luther granted the harmful character of the Hussite schism, but at a later stage he defied these prejudices by claiming that 'among the articles of John and the Bohemians there are many that are plainly very Christian and evangelical, and which it is impossible for the universal Church to condemn'. At this point Duke George, who had organized the disputations in an almost sporting spirit, is recorded to have roared out 'Plague take it'. Luther nevertheless went on to explain that

---

[18] Described in detail by R. H. Fife, chs. 18, 19; see especially pp. 360–65. On the broad problem consult the articles by J. Pelikan, 'Luther's Attitude toward John Huss' and S. H. Thomson, 'Luther and Bohemia'. Note also M. Spinka, *John Hus' Concept of the Church* (Princeton, 1966), p. 385.

amongst these acceptable Hussite articles was the denial that salvation depended upon a belief in the superior authority of the Church of Rome. He added: 'Whether it be of Wycliffe or Huss I do not care', and he cited the early Greek Fathers, who had likewise rejected the primacy of Rome. The later abusive exchanges with Eck, who maintained that this repudiation of Constance made Luther a plain heretic, did not much advance the issue, while Luther saw the obvious dangers involved in any enlargement of his thesis.

During the following year, however, he not only read and applauded the *De Ecclesia* of Huss but had it printed, announcing that it was high time Bohemians and Germans forgot their old enmity and worked together for the furtherance of the Gospel. Even in *Christian Nobility* he risked a backlash from his German audience by proposing a sympathetic re-examination of the Bohemian heresy. He began to realize that Huss had not only propounded some acceptable religious ideas, but had done what he, Luther, was now doing: he had aroused a whole nation to throw off the papal yoke. That this proposed brotherhood in the Gospel made only limited progress should be attributed to the Czechs rather than to Luther. With more than his wonted share of liberalism he stood prepared to accept the conservative majority of the Hussites as fellow Evangelicals, and did in fact arouse the admiration of the German population within Bohemia. But broadly speaking the Czechs, still divided among themselves, retained their traditional affinities, though in due course many of them went over to Anabaptism or to Calvinism.

Luther cannot be shown to have subjected the Bohemian heresy to any detailed historical analysis. He appears to have had little direct knowledge of Wycliffe as one of its inspirers, less still of Huss's Czech predecessors. On the other hand, regarding the English heresiarch there remains a little to add to the outburst at Leipzig. In the first place, though Luther did not know it, Wycliffe was the true author of the *De Ecclesia* of Huss which moved Luther so deeply.[19] In the *Babylonian Captivity* he repeatedly ridicules the notion that a doctrine is heretical simply because it can be dubbed Wycliffite.[20] Once more, in *De*

[19] H. Boehmer, p. 295.
[20] J. Dillenberger, pp. 265–6.

Servo Arbitrio, he declares 'that Wycliffe's tenet "all things come to pass by necessity" was falsely condemned by the Council— or rather the Cabal and Conspiracy—of Constance.'[21] Moreover, while the English Lutherans reinforced their claims by printing Lollard tracts, Luther actually forestalled them in 1528 by printing such a tract at Wittenberg. This was the *Commentary on the Apocalypse*, written by an imprisoned English heretic, apparently one of Wycliffe's Oxford followers. Though sent to Luther by his friend Dr. Johann Brismann, this work had formerly exercised a lively influence among the Hussites.[22] Luther's preface shows him to have been attracted not merely by its assault upon the misdeeds of the papacy but by its relative antiquity. Sensitive as usual to the question of precedents, he remarks that 'we are not the first to interpret the Papacy for the reign of Antichrist', and he refers to the author as 'a witness preordained by God, so many years before us, for the confirmation of our doctrine'. Again, though Luther would not have realized the fact, Wycliffe was the true begetter of the antithesis represented in such a work as the pictorial *Passion of Christ and Antichrist*, produced in 1521 in collaboration with Cranach and Melanchthon. Despite the undeniable interest of these references, too much should not be made of them, since the works of Wycliffe and even those of his followers were not available to Luther in the quantity or in the literary shape required to form a major buttress for the Evangelical Church.

In reclaiming a modest though not a primary role for the 'forerunners', we seem to be on the perfectly safe ground of Luther's own attitude. Nevertheless the claim may still fail to commend itself both to theological rigorists and to denominational enthusiasts, especially insofar as it is applied to the Netherlandish and German 'Augustinizers' of the mid-fifteenth century. Here, however, a just perspective may well have been threatened both by those who claimed the Augustine tradition as proto-Protestant

[21] *Martin Luther on the Bondage of the Will*, ed. J. I. Packer and O. R. Johnson (1957), p. 189; cf. *WA*, xviii, p. 699. Earlier in the work (p. 109; cf. *WA*, xviii, p. 689) Luther notes that Erasmus had dismissed his (Luther's) supporters as consisting of Wycliffe and Valla, failing to add Augustine to the list.

[22] M. E. Aston, 'Lollardy and the Reformation' in *History*, xlix (1964), pp. 156–7.

and conversely by Tridentine conservatives who, armed by an *a priori* verdict in favour of the decisions taken at Trent, dismissed all 'Augustinizers' as potentially or actually non-Catholic. But the emphasis upon Augustine was far from being destined to a purely Protestant survival, for it could no more be exorcized from any major Christian school of thought than could the Pauline Epistles upon which it based its claims. As early as 1511 the future Cardinal Contarini had undergone a spiritual crisis not wholly unlike Luther's,[23] and in later life he became the centre of a distinguished group of Catholic reforming prelates, including Morone, Pole, Giberti and Seripando, who placed a strong emphasis upon Pauline-Augustinian Justification by Faith. In the thirties some members of the loosely-knit group undoubtedly went ahead into the works of Luther and Calvin. But while a few fled to embrace the new creed, the main group merely sought to contain the growing Protestantism of the north Italian cities and dioceses, not by repression but by conciliatory teaching along Pauline and Augustinian lines. In 1541, even then writing his *Letter on Justification*, Contarini was allowed to conduct serious negotiations with Melanchthon at Regensburg, but his failure and discredit in Rome were swiftly followed by his death in 1542. Thence developed a papalist reaction, later to be embodied in the decisions of the Council of Trent, which flatly discouraged both Contarini's theology of Justification and his whole effort to find common ground with the Lutherans. An 'orthodoxy' was thus established which had not existed in the Middle Ages. Emasculated by the Catholic establishment, the Augustine tradition nevertheless survived in a few theologians like Michel Baius (d. 1589) and finally took root again in the suspect and persecuted Jansenism of the seventeenth century. In recent times some liberal Catholic theologians like Hans Küng have sympathetically studied even Luther's theology of Justification,[24] while others, at least reluctant to dismiss so powerful a Christian tradition, have drawn a delicate line between the gradualist, 'intrinsic' doctrine of Augustine, and

[23] H. Jedin, 'Ein Turmerlebnis des jungen Contarini' in *Historisches Jahrbuch*, lxx (1951); see also the two Contarini articles by J. B. Ross in *Studies in the Renaissance*, xvii (1970) and in *Church History*, xli (1972).

[24] English translation: *Justification*, trans. T. Collins and others, 1964.

the 'extrinsic' imputation doctrine of Luther. Modern ecumenical possibilities arising from this distinction can be studied, for example, in the survey by Louis Bouyer, *The Spirit and Forms of Protestantism*. Upon these later developments the present work cannot enlarge, but it has seemed desirable to observe that the Augustine tradition did not simply pass over into Protestant Europe, and that certain aspects of its interpretation create to this day meaningful issues among and between Catholic and Protestant scholars.

The mention of rival Catholic traditions has reminded the present writer to conclude his sketch of Luther's intellectual background by stressing a gigantic but too often overlooked feature of that background. To a greater extent than the other major Reformers, Luther continued both to react and to construct within a Catholic framework. On the negative side a vast proportion of his writing takes the form of response to Catholic criticism. He was a pugilist with remarkably fast reflexes, and the hard counter-punch was his most formidable weapon. Yet through this very fact his immense and ebullient output might be judged to contain too many (and too hasty) counter-attacks and, in view of his proved genius for religious and social thinking, too few sustained and creative treatises. On the other hand, his works also reveal many positive debts to his Catholic origins: they should by no means be discussed merely in terms of reaction against those origins. The distinguished Protestant theologian Wilhelm Pauck remarks that Luther set up a revised creedalism which never seriously entertained the possibility that 'pure doctrine' was debatable.[25] Notwithstanding some concepts which appeared radical in the Church of his day, Luther continued to relate his understanding of Christian doctrine to the understanding of the old Church. 'Whenever a dogmatic view of his was seriously challenged', continues Pauck, 'he therefore fell back upon a literalistic Biblicism, in spite of the fact that he himself had overcome it.' Even in his disputes with other Protestants he remained unwilling to allow them full exercise of the principles of Biblical interpretation which he had personally developed early in his career. 'He could not cope with dissent.'

[25] W. Pauck, pp. 42–59.

Judging his utterances outside their desperate historical context, even people who admire Luther's prayerful study and value his real—if not always fully intentional—contributions to spiritual liberty, may nevertheless find too often a tendency to equate his own passionate convictions with the voice of God. Modern ecumenism has sometimes found in him a dogmatism as repugnant as that of Tridentine orthodoxy. Nowadays few Lutherans would exclude the possibility of reasonable variants of Luther's theology of Justification or of the eucharist. The Evangelical tendency—happily never universal in that Church— to impose Wittenberg doctrine can all too easily be explained by reference to the practical needs of the sect-torn sixteenth century, to the threatened chaos of beliefs, worship and social behaviour. It is a platitude to say that the age was not prepared for theological liberalism, a commodity rarely detectable even within the sects which advocated toleration. Only a few sanguine eccentrics could then believe in the possibility of a social and political order based upon a multiplicity of religious and philosophical systems. To our own day such a belief remains effectually limited to certain countries in the western liberal tradition. With all these thoughts in mind, few realistic students of history would blame Luther for accepting territorial and national churches exercising controls over society similar to those wielded by the national and territorial hierarchies of the Catholic Church. The criticisms uttered by the sectarians and by their modern admirers should likewise be set alongside the pastoral needs of the people and seen in their full limitations. While proclaiming freedom of conscience, the Radicals of Luther's day expended immense energies upon divisive conflict which profited only the Reformation's adversaries. The sects were not content to await the Last Judgment and so did not cater for whole populations. Instead each sect tended to envisage itself as a small minority of the redeemed amongst the great majority of the condemned. Moreover, issues of political survival were at stake. Luther was bound to listen to the princes when they argued a basic need for ecclesiastical unity and order, since it seemed all too probable that they would have to rally together and organize their subjects to withstand in arms a Habsburg-papal onslaught. Amid our admiration for the genuine liberals, who were far less numerous than many historians of religion would like to suppose, we should not lack all sympathy for leaders who undertook the prosaic task of managing sixteenth-century men facing sixteenth-century problems in a sixteenth-century setting. The princes and cities might have done far worse, for in the event the problems set by Luther's revolt were not solved by measures of conspicuous intolerance or inhumanity—at all events until the Peace of Augsburg was upset by the Thirty Years War.

Yet when we have listed all these practical reasons for Luther's return to something not unlike the old creedalism, the old ecclesiastical structures and disciplines, the heart of his position still remains concealed. Both his greatness and his naïvety lay in the fact that he could not regard his movement as a dissenting movement, a minority which should remain content to practise its beliefs in holes and corners. He was doubtless guilty of gross simplification, yet innocent of conscious paradox and posturing, when he declared that Rome formed the very centre of dissent from the true Gospel of Christ. This he believed with an ever-increasing acerbity to the day of his death. The apparent negation which modern ecumenists would sweep under the carpet should surely be taken as his most fundamental affirmation. We may bewail the establishment of a Lutheran orthodoxy, but Luther really believed that the movement he had started was orthodox, that the papacy stood condemned as heretical. Consequently he did not for a moment suppose himself to be erecting a new Church, let alone a sect: he believed he had been chosen as a humble mouthpiece of the Almighty Word, the instrument of a miracle by which God was cleansing the whole Catholic Church of both false doctrine and misconduct. In his eyes Catholics were not evil heretics but rather fellow Church-members, as yet foolishly resisting the irresistible. With absolute conviction Luther sought to convey the inevitability of this divinely-ordained change in a sermon of March 1522.

Take an example from me. I strove against the Indulgence and all the papists, yet without using force. I merely preached and wrote God's Word: otherwise I did nothing. Even if I had slept or sat drinking with my Philip and Amsdorf in Wittenberg, the papacy would still have been made weak, weaker than any prince or emperor has ever made it. I did nothing: the Word did it all. If I had wanted to go ahead the hard way, I could have led Germany into great bloodshed. Yes, I could have started such a game at Worms that the emperor himself would have been in danger. But what would that have been? A fool's game. So I did nothing: I just let the Word manage things.[26]

During the 1520s and 1530s changes so unprecedented were befalling the German nation that even men far less sanguine had ample reason for supposing that some extraordinary action of God was afoot. Armed with hindsight and with methods of historical analysis purporting to replace such notions of divine providence, we shall now study the mass media which altered the tenor of religious and social life for millions of Europeans and their descendants throughout the world.

[26] *WA*, x (3 Abt.), pp. 18–19.

5

The Printers and Luther

Throughout the remaining chapters of this survey we shall be chiefly concerned with the spread and popularization of Protestant beliefs. Our main attention will be demanded by the nine critical years 1517–25, since no comparable period of German history—with the possible exception of those tragic years which saw the rise of National Socialism—has proved so fateful in European and world affairs. Even while the revolts of the knights and the peasants collapsed, the Lutheran Reformation established a firm grip and thus prepared the way for a 'final' division of western Christendom. At this stage the expansion of the new creed was in large measure indebted to the pamphlets, the *fliegende Blätter* or *Flugschriften*, which poured forth from the German presses in millions of copies.[1] Most of them ranged

---

[1] In this and the following chapter I am especially indebed to H. Gravier, a guide too little used by Luther scholars. Also valuable in this field are the articles by G. Blochwitz; L. Holborn and E. L. Eisenstein. For general guidance on printing, see O. C. Clemen, *Die lutherische Reformation und der Buchdruck*; L. Febvre and H.-J. Martin; K. Schottenloher, *Flugblatt und Zeitung* and *Flugschriften zur Ritterschaftsbewegung*; S. H. Steinberg; H. Volz. Documentation will be found in *Archiv für Geschichte des Buchwesens*, listed below under Works of Reference. On the role of women, see R. H. Bainton; M. Heinsius; R. Stupperich; on that of the peasantry, the survey by K. Uhrig; on the 'common man' in general, P. Böckmann. For reprints of pamphlets see A. E. Berger; O. C. Clemen; O. Schade. On the printers themselves, see J. Benzing; A. Götze, who describes (pp. 1–59) some fifty-seven Reformation printing firms and subsequently reproduces a large selection of title-pages. There are some regional and local surveys, such as those of M. Grossmann on Wittenberg, M. von Hase on Erfurt, and T. Legge on Westphalia.

from fourteen to forty pages in length: the vast majority were in German and in many the argument was reinforced by accompanying engravings or woodcuts. Through them there occurred the first mass movement of religious change backed by a new technology, by the factor most clearly differentiating Luther's enterprise from its predecessors. Waldensianism, Wycliffism, Hussitism had made, or failed to make, their several ways without the mechanical standardization and reproduction of their manifestos. A century later Francis Bacon was to remark that recent history had been moulded by three great inventions: gunpowder, the mariner's compass and printing. If he had added that the greatest of these three was printing, few modern historians would feel disposed to cavil.

This admission does not, of course, necessitate a simple mechanistic theory of the Reformation: a doctrine of Justification by Print Alone.[2] The themes, the quality and style of the appeal also mattered. Thirsty people are interested in pure water as well as in water-pipes, and in fact more than one system of pipes conveyed the doctrinal fluid. When we come to investigate the advent of the Lutheran Reformation into the cities—unquestionably its most vital recipients—we shall find that the issue was most frequently clinched in the pulpits, sometimes by organized disputations between rival preachers. No agency of change could replace the Protestant preachers, who in these early stages received so few challenges from competent champions of orthodoxy. Yet on further analysis the two agencies, press and pulpit, seem inextricably fused. The triumph of the orator was won over minds pre-conditioned by the pamphlet and the vernacular Bible; it was a victory confirmed and consolidated by those same mighty allies. On the other hand many tracts, including some of the most effective items in Luther's repertoire, were printed sermons and frankly so entitled. Everywhere we find printed passages bearing obvious debts to the modes of persuasion gradually developed by the preachers of late medieval Europe.

[2] That printing constituted a major causal factor as well as a mere vehicle is forcefully indicated by my friend Elizabeth L. Eisenstein. Naturally, in regard to the Reformation the picture must be balanced by (a) a strong emphasis on the continued importance of preaching and (b) reference to the intrinsic force of Luther's religious and social arguments within the context of the period.

Geiler von Kaisersberg had been merely an eminent figure amid the host of those who had long exploited the marked susceptibility of urban proletariats to the spoken word. Old habits died hard. From these early years onward Wittenberg was no mere publishing centre but also a training-school for preaching missionaries. From Wittenberg both Luther and Melanchthon strove manfully to prevent the collapse of teaching and ministration throughout the towns and villages of Saxony and Thuringia. In those days a special power lay with the orator, who could not only produce a string of ostensibly relevant Bible texts, but knew also how to translate the Gospel into a contemporary idiom, to garnish theology with folk-wisdom, to illustrate abstractions by concrete metaphors drawn from workaday life. Nevertheless the pamphlet had capacities lacked by the preachers and by those lesser yet still interesting agents, the little dramatic companies which enacted propaganda plays in favour of the Reformation. In communities where rulers and magistrates opposed them, preachers and actors could function only amid difficulty and danger. By contrast the silent, unobtrusive pamphlet could go to work in any society: it was as insidious as plague bacilli in an age unprovided with antibiotics. Throughout Europe several stories illustrate its elusive quality: not least that of the Catholic English bishop who was induced by a go-between to purchase dearly a stock of William Tyndale's proscribed pamphlets. The bishop duly destroyed them, yet his money was swiftly transferred to Tyndale and used to finance a larger edition![3] Meanwhile in Germany the multiplicity of states rendered government control and censorship even less effective than in the centralized kingdoms to the west.

Of course, printing had interacted with ideological movements earlier than the one led by Martin Luther. By 1500 some 200 presses were functioning in the German lands, though those of six cities—Cologne, Nuremberg, Augsburg, Strassburg, Basle and Leipzig still produced nearly two-thirds of the total output. Already printing had become a large industry in terms of both labour-force and invested capital. Profoundly involved with humanist scholarship, it influenced as well as reflected the major cultural advances and controversies. Thanks to printing,

[3] Edward Hall, *Henry VIII*, ed. C. Whibley (1904), ii, pp. 160–62.

Erasmus had become an international legend, while on the eve of Luther's appearance the world of humanism seemed to have achieved through printing a new cohesion, a strange hold upon Europe's lay and ecclesiastical leaders. Whistling in the dark, Erasmus and other optimists wanted to believe they were leading society toward a new age of universal peace and enlightenment. The change in the pattern of publication at Strassburg, for example, had been dramatic. Before 1500 over half the books published there were concerned with religion, while under ten per cent had been those of the ancient authors beloved of humanism. Yet between 1500 and 1520 no less than one-third of Strassburg's output consisted of classical texts or modern humanist books, while only twenty-seven per cent could be classified as religious.[4] Then, however, Luther's revolt brought a swift and radical change both in Strassburg and in the other major centres. This took the form of a movement away from aristocratic book-production, away from both the classical and the liturgical folios. Instead the printers hastened to commission and publish cheap little pamphlets, treating of serious themes yet clearly aimed at all classes, not at a moneyed and cultivated élite.

This poor man's press was not in all respects a novelty. For many decades single broadsheets and then small pamphlets of anonymous authorship had been sold in the fairs and markets: little books of devotion, lists of saints to be invoked, newssheets with sensational reports of earthquakes, meteorites, monstrous births and similar portents. In addition, popular pamphlets by named authors discussing more serious issues were not wholly unknown even before 1500. From about 1485 the Augsburg *Meistersinger* Jörg Preining issued about thirty devotional leaflets. A second known author of pamphlet literature was none other than Sebastian Brant, the true father of the *Flugschriften*. When in November 1492 a meteor fell at Ensisheim, Brant published a pamphlet in both Latin and German, following his account with an appeal to Maximilian to take this as a portent of victory and so attack the French. 'Nimm wahr, der Stein ist dir gesandt.' The next year he issued another on the

[4] L. Febvre and H.-J. Martin, p. 265. On Alsatian literary life see C. Schmidt; P. Adam; M. U. Chrisman, ch. 4.

German victory at Salins, and in 1495 a third interpreting a birth of 'Siamese' twins near Worms as a prophecy of political union. Others followed, mostly adjurations to the Habsburgs and prophecies of their coming rule over the world. Brant was forward-looking in his illustrative use of woodcuts. On some occasions he did not disdain to produce Latin versions, doubtless aiming these at the large readership among the lower clergy.[5] Another development in the history of pamphleteering came with the Reuchlin quarrel, which between 1515 and 1521 directly produced at least forty-four writings. Here, however, the issues do not seem to have aroused the general public. As we have observed, Reuchlin failed to become a hero for the whole humanist community, let alone a hero in the eyes of the masses.[6] Numerically, moreover, this shower of *Flugschriften* does not even begin to compare with that soon to swirl around the figure of Martin Luther. The years 1518–24 saw the output of the German presses multiply by a factor of six or more, and without question this portentous growth arose in very large measure from the religious cataclysm.

Despite the facts that the famous Brant had been a German pamphleteer and that the even more eminent Erasmus had—albeit in Latin—written brief works for a wide public, some scholars and ecclesiastics felt the need to explain to patrons their descent into the common arena, and their choice of a genre at once miniature and vernacular. Luther, who rarely apologized to anyone except God, did in fact become one of these apologists. Dedicating his *Sermon on Good Works* to Duke John of Saxony in 1520, he remarks that he could write large and learned tomes, but that God's purposes would be better served at this juncture by little sermons directed to the common man.[7] His convictions categorically demanded this broad appeal. In his view the Christian faith remained dead unless individual lay men and women could be made to experience directly and afresh the claims of the Gospel, instead of accepting a processed version from a priesthood which had falsely claimed a divine commission.

[5] On Brant, see p. 25, n. 2 above.
[6] On Reuchlin, see p. 30, n. 7 above.
[7] 'Ich acht aber, szo ich lust het, yhrer kunst nach gros bucher zumachen, es solt villeicht mit gotlicher hulff mir schleuniger folgen, aan yhnen nach meiner art einen kleynen sermon zumachenn.' (*WA*, vi, p. 203).

His whole project depended on his ability to interest and to involve unintellectual people in theological matters by no means closely related to everyday life, in spiritual demands which could not be met by a physical act of charity or penance, least of all by a donation to Church funds.

It seems no wonder that most modern writers in the field have become dominated, often too exclusively so, by Martin Luther the publicist. He was the best-seller, the most voluminous and versatile author, the one indubitably great German writer of these pamphleteering years. Outstanding gifts as a popularizer are rare enough in the genuine man of religion, perhaps even rarer in the original thinker about religion. Equally arresting are the antinomies between Luther's massive commonsense and his hasty injustices, between his brutal invective and his delicate spiritual perceptions. We have already observed forces at work upon the German mind which induced the nation to accept both the positive and the negative features of his message. Above the other writers of his day he had two remarkable advantages. One was an affirmative Biblical evangel which lifted him above the cold tide of anticlericalism threatening to engulf German society. The other was a talent for simplification, direct statements, concrete analogy, which brought at least some aspects of his positive thinking within the reach of uneducated laymen. Of course, the term 'Luther the journalist' does scant justice to his popular appeal. Had the masses merely read him because of his sensational repute, they would doubtless have abandoned him after the first few years. Yet on the contrary, as the surge of pamphleteering subsided after 1525, his literary reputation merely became consolidated. He had written so many of that small minority of pamphlets which deserved to survive.

The breadth of Luther's appeal derived from a host of factors, some carefully calculated, others arising naturally from a personality of exceptional force. Deliberately he used linguistic forms intelligible to the Germanic peoples from Austria to the borders of the Low Countries: by so doing he standardized the literary language. He admitted that he listened for and employed the phraseology of the household and the marketplace. Aided by Cranach and lesser artists, he also made use of crude and tendentious cartoons, especially to display by visual means the antithesis between primitive and papal Christianity.[8] But on a far higher level he understood and could demonstrate the social implications of religious belief. He tried hard to sort out that muddled intermixture of secular and religious ideals which beset the minds of his generation. No publicist, not even Erasmus, perceived so clearly the potential outcome of a firm personal faith in terms of a more just, rational, ordered and educated society. Finally, from 1522 onward, Luther's authority as a master of apologetics was reinforced by that masterly translation of the Bible which he accomplished in gradual phases to its conclusion in 1534. This crowning achievement, together with pamphlets less radical than those of 1520, helped to stabilise the atmosphere after the tragedy of the Peasants' Revolt. After 1525 states and cities continued to enter the Lutheran camp, yet the threatened war between the Catholic and the Protestant powers was somehow deferred until 1547. Even then it was mercifully not fought to a finish and it ended in the tolerable compromise made in 1555 at Augsburg. Thus by the later phases of the pamphlet war Luther was already taking a prominent stand with the forces of law and order. Luther accepted this choice as clearly commanded by the Scriptures, but it remains hard to see what other choice he could have made on grounds of commonsense. The knights and the peasants seem to us foredoomed to failure, and even had either rebellion succeeded, it could not conceivably have provided a stable basis for ecclesiastical or social reforms.

At this point we do not propose to supply what can be found with great ease in scores of competent books: a detailed account of the literary work of Luther as pamphleteer, theologian and translator. Observing the scene in broader perspective, we intend to glance at certain less familiar figures and aspects of the pamphleteering world. Nevertheless it should be frankly stated that so brief a survey will be more meaningful for readers with some little knowledge of Luther's own works. And no modern commentaries can fully replace a reading of the actual texts, now for the most part available in good translations. A sound basis

---

[8] On visual aids see S. Scharfe; other references in F. Lau and E. Bizer, p. 26. The article by F. Betten has points, but is marred by denominational anger.

could be laid in a very few hours of reading: perhaps the *Ninety-five Theses*, with their deadly calm, their ominous refrain *docendi sunt Christiani*; *To the Christian Nobility of the German Nation*, that most succinct and devastating of all programmes of social reform; the *Babylonian Captivity* in all its theological radicalism; the *Freedom of a Christian* with its echoing paradoxes between service and liberty, its telling apotheosis of a creative faith. Such a selection would, it is true, unduly flatter Luther as a literary artist, perhaps even as a man of religion; yet it would convince even a disbeliever in heroes that, given the mental climate of 1517–20, Luther alone could have generated enough light and heat to disturb the outlook of a nation. Between these years he discovered that the millions could be moved by the same gifts and arguments as those he had so often directed toward a congregation or toward the troubled conscience of an individual. Nevertheless, alongside the tributes one should enter a caveat: that Luther's literary achievement cannot be properly measured outside the context of that whirlwind of propaganda which he did so much to set in motion. Luther read as well as wrote, and it was the pamphleteering of the lesser men which kept him in touch with the public mind. Unlike most of his opponents he took great pains to sense the trends of opinion. Having studied the conservative critics, the moderate deviators and the wild men, he so often sat down and wrote a reply on the spot. His workroom became a silent forum of debate, and a large part of his creation consists of his reactions to stimuli. When the sententious Bucer said that the Wittenberg theologians should more often leave their Saxon citadel and go around preaching to the people, Luther cut him short with a simple but pregnant phrase: 'We do that with our books'.

Francis Bacon was far from being the first observer to stress the historical changes wrought by the art of printing. Throughout Europe Luther and his followers expressed the sentiment in less secular terms, for they saw the press as quite literally a godsend. Luther wrote that printing was 'God's highest and extremest act of grace, whereby the business of the Gospel is driven forward.'[9] He did but anticipate that equally

[9] Cited by M. H. Black in S. L. Greenslade (ed.), *The Cambridge History of the Bible*, iii (Cambridge, 1963), p. 432.

famous sentence of the English martyrologist John Foxe, who gave thanks 'to the high providence of almighty God, for the excellent art of printing, most happily of late found out, and now commonly practised everywhere to the singular benefit of Christ's Church'.[10] Thanks to this invention, an obscure professor suddenly became a national figure, and not by defying the emperor at Worms in 1521 but from the issue of his *Theses* in 1517. The recent intensive debate as to whether the *Theses* were actually posted up in Wittenberg lacks major historical importance. Their significance arose from the rapidity of their circulation. Within a few weeks the *Theses* were being printed and distributed not merely from Wittenberg but from Nuremberg, Leipzig and Basle, then soon afterwards from many other places throughout central Europe. In the printers' shops and with the book-pedlars at the country fairs they outsold the ephemeral broadsheets, the almanacks and prophecies, the news of the Turkish menace. Luther soon followed them by a range of explanatory essays, as it were serializing his theology. During the four years 1517–20 he published some thirty popular writings on penance, Indulgences, the commandments and the Psalms, the Lord's Prayer, the sacraments, the Passion, preparation for death. Already unauthorized reprints flowed from numerous presses: one pamphlet reached twenty-four editions, while by the end of 1520 about 370 editions of his output had passed into the market. Taking the normal estimate of a thousand copies as an average edition, we may accept Dr. Holborn's cautious assumption that even before Luther made his dramatic stand at Worms, there were abroad some third of a million pamphlets, specially designed to convey his version of Christianity to the masses.[11]

The *Sermon of Indulgence and Grace*, which best popularized the *Theses*, had thirteen reprints in High German and one in Low German during the year 1518, five more in 1519 and four in 1520, its main publishing centres being Wittenberg, Leipzig, Nuremberg, Augsburg, Basle and Breslau. Thanks to Luther, little Wittenberg (which had about 2,000 residents, and which

---

[10] J. Foxe, *Preface to the Whole Workes of W. Tyndall, John Frith and Doct[or] Barnes* (London, 1572–3), sigs. Aiir–Aiiir.

[11] These and the succeeding figures are largely drawn from L. Holborn.

Luther himself described as on the frontiers of civilization)
became a major publishing town, even before its ill-endowed
university attracted students from all parts of Germany and
most countries of Europe. Meanwhile, in August 1520 Melchior
Lotther of Wittenberg printed and distributed 4,000 copies of
Christian Nobility, but within a week Luther began preparing
the second edition. Including the pirated ones, which Luther
welcomed because he wanted publicity and not royalties, no less
than fifteen editions appeared in rapid succession. Though having
a far less secular appeal, *The Freedom of a Christian* ran into
eighteen editions and was also plagiarized by other devotional
writers. Even greater sales were enjoyed by Luther's translation
of the New Testament. The first edition of 3,000 copies came
out in the autumn of 1522, and a second issue in the December.
High-pressure salesmanship and favourable opinion from both
humanist circles and the general literate public reinforced
Luther's own exertions. In July 1519 Beatus Rhenanus wrote to
Zwingli recommending a certain colporteur, who went from
town to town, village to village, door to door, offering nothing
else than Luther's writings. 'This', added the humanist, 'will
virtually compel the people to buy them, which would not be the
case if he allowed them a wide choice.' Not everyone rejoiced in
this situation. In 1523 Erasmus protested to Henry VIII that in
Basle nobody dared print a word against Luther, while anybody
could write whatever he desired against the pope. The next
year he again bewailed this narrow canalizing of the stream of
publication, which ran outside the field of his own endeavours
and ideals. 'Among the Germans one can hardly sell anything
except the writings of Luther and those of his adversaries.'

It is certain that the great majority of the printers violently
favoured Luther and his allies. Again, one cannot doubt that
many of them were heavily motivated by financial incentives.
In that day as in this, the rationalization of self-interest proceeded apace, and in all likelihood many were just as convinced
of their Protestant idealism as were the Augsburg bankers—
financially tied hand and foot to the Habsburgs—of their own
deep Catholic fidelity. Some publishers seem to have been open-
minded to the point of indifference. Knoblouch of Strassburg,
a generous benefactor of Catholic institutions, nevertheless

published Lutheran writings. Farckall of Hagenau was a close associate of Grieninger, the loyal publisher of Luther's adversary Murner, yet he also published both Karlstadt and Luther. With an even greater impartiality Schoeffer of Mainz printed the works of Luther, the pamphlets of Luther's libellous arch-enemy Cochlaeus, and for good measure the famous 'Twelve Articles' of the rebellious peasants.[12]

After the decisions taken at Worms in 1521, people setting forth heretical pamphlets were exposed to dire penalties under imperial law. The execution of this latter depended upon the zeal of princes and magistrates: in due course some sporadic prosecutions are recorded, together with at least one death-sentence for printing Anabaptist propaganda. Perhaps the most clearly convinced men among the printers were those who worked for the unpopular Radical groups, since they at least ran increasing perils during the 1520s. The Catholic publishers must also have needed all their religious convictions to sustain them. Of two printers ordered to persevere with Catholic books by the highly conservative Duke George, Thanner ended in prison for debt, while Stöckel finally quitted ducal Saxony in order to continue publishing Luther. But the risks depended on the generally predictable attitudes of local magistrates; and from the first many of these interpreted heresy according to their own prejudices or fears of disorder. For several years in towns such as Strassburg, Rothenburg and Worms even publishers of scan-dalously radical pamphlets appear to have escaped prosecution. In his biographies of the printers, Götze also cites the case of Setzer, who worked from 1522 in the predominantly Catholic town of Hagenau, yet nevertheless continued unmolested to issue some fifty works by leading Reformers, including Luther, Melanchthon, Bugenhagen, Brenz and Johann Agricola. In liberal Strassburg the Anabaptists flourished awhile: on the other side Grieninger bravely published Catholic propaganda by Eck and Murner, though in the end the magistrates suppressed both his activities and those of the Radicals. Of the other printers recorded as active at Strassburg from 1521, six were Lutherans and one ostensibly indifferent. In Augsburg during the early

[12] L. Holborn, pp. 134–5. H. Gravier, pp. 73–4, 251, gives facts, partly taken from A. Götze, on opportunist printers.

1520s Catholicism remained more influential; yet there were nine Protestant printers as opposed to three Catholics, while of the latter only one produced fighting pamphlets. Needless to add, all the six Wittenberg printers around this date were Lutherans.

By and large, the profits seem to have been big enough to warrant the risks taken by the Lutheran faction among the printers. Several times Luther grumbled about the greed of these 'sordid mercenaries' and on one occasion was told that Lotther made profits of 100 to 200 per cent. Elsewhere Adam Petri of Basle is said to have acquired a great fortune by selling Lutheran books. Luther himself made no money by writing and most authors doubtless felt they received only the crumbs. In 1524 Eberlin von Günzburg published an amusing dialogue between three journeymen, who agree that 'God's word must also serve the idolatrous greed of the printers…but God will not laugh for long at this: he will have no mercy on the grasping printer.' On the Catholic side the going remained hard for authors and printers alike, and the difficulties of Thanner and Grieninger are far from being the only ones recorded. Even while Luther was coming for trial at Worms, the papal legate Aleander had to bribe the local printers to execute his own work. In that same year Hieronymus Emser complained that he had to finance a book against Luther out of his own pocket. Later on Georg Witzel said that had he been a Lutheran, his publisher would not be putting him off with vague promises and keeping his manuscript unprinted for a whole year. As we shall see, Luther's gifted adversary Thomas Murner, having been virtually driven into exile, tried to print his own work.

The available statistics speak eloquently on two points: the vast total expansion of printing between 1517 and 1525, and the immense numerical preponderance of Lutheran over Catholic publications. During the year 1518 German publication numbered only about 150 recorded books. By 1520 the total had risen to 570; in 1522, 1523 and 1524, to 680, 935 and 990 respectively. During this time the hitherto minor centre of Wittenberg rose to the top of the league with a grand total of 600 published from 1518 to 1523.[13] As observed, the national

[13] Detail on Wittenberg printing in M. Grossmann. On the whole Wittenberg background, the works of E. G. Schwiebert are exceptionally valuable.

figures declined from 1525, yet it would be risky to deduce, as some historians have done, that this decline marked the end of the Reformation as a folk-movement, or that Luther's harshness toward the peasant rebels had brought about such an untoward result. Other explanations would not be difficult to conjecture, and in any event, the peasants were the one class which seldom produced pamphleteers, while the actual pamphleteers did not depend upon a peasant readership. After all, the boom of polemical tracts could scarcely continue for ever: by 1525 the Lutheran champions had said their say, while some were defecting either to Catholicism or to sectarianism. Whatever the case after 1525, the Lutheran predominance before and indeed for some time after that date has long been apparent. On the basis of the pioneer lists made in G. W. Panzer's *Annalen der alteren deutschen Literatur* (1788–1805), Ranke calculated that the publications of the single year 1523 included no less than 183 editions of works by Luther or in some cases falsely attributed to him. In addition 215 editions appeared by writers favourable to Luther's cause.[14] But on the Catholic side there could be found a mere score of works. The present writer is not aware of the existence of any full and up-to-date analysis covering the earlier 1520s, but he sees no reason to suppose that such a revision would display anything other than an enormous imbalance toward the Protestant side. Very gradually after 1525, the proportion of Catholic treatises began to rise as the total output fell, and this development doubtless owes not a little to the known pressures exerted by Duke George and other Catholic rulers, under whose patronage champions of the old Church began to recover confidence. The statistical approach to publication needs developing further, yet only within limits can it be held to reflect the tenor or fluctuations of popular opinion on the Reformation struggle. More accurately does it reveal the state of affairs among publicists and printers, who both accepted and influenced—but did not wholly dictate—the feeling of the masses. As will appear when attention is focused on the religious

[14] L. Ranke, *History of the Reformation in Germany* (English translation, 1905), pp. 284–5. This chapter 'Diffusion of the New Doctrines, 1522–1524' shows Ranke thinking in the social dimension. Further extended calculations from modern bibliographical data seem now badly needed. For tables on Strassburg books, see M. U. Chrisman, pp. 301–2.

history of the cities, considerable variations of pace developed between one community and another. Again, as in all countries at the Reformation, large uncommitted elements proved ready to accept a lead on religion from their rulers, to hear propaganda from both sides, occasionally to favour liturgies based on compromise or local measures of mutual toleration. Nevertheless before I leave the media in order to examine the public reactions, other matters demand discussion, since hitherto I have considered publishing largely from the viewpoint of the unusual writer Martin Luther. What about the other authors of the *Flugschriften*? Who were they? From what backgrounds did they come? For what public did they write? How far did they actually adhere to Luther's message? With what success did they communicate complex religious and social ideas to an unintellectual but opinionated public? With such problems our next chapter will be concerned.

6

Polemicists and People

Though the *Flugschriften* of the early Reformation are most commonly unsigned, a probable authorship can often be deduced, so that at least fifty personalities emerge from the throng.[1] They belong to several strata of society: indeed, a rigid occupational grouping would throw little light upon either writers or readers. 'I am the son of a peasant', wrote Martin Luther, but in middle life his father became a mining lessee of some substance. Hans Sachs, a shoemaker by trade, attained wide literary fame and showed no small ability as a popularizer in verse of Luther's theology. Hans Schwalb, an obscure lay citizen of Erfurt, raged in 1521 against the excommunication of Luther, whom he eloquently hailed as a God-given prophet. The glass-painter David Joris lived incognito as a cultured aristocrat in Basle, while in fact managing a wide sectarian network. Both in Germany and in Switzerland a few of the known Protestant pamphleteers were craftsmen: the furrier Sebastian Lotzer, the baker Hans Staygmayer, the weaver Ulrich Richsen, the gunsmith Georg Motschidler. A very few were women, like Katharine Zell, wife of the Strassburg preacher; and Argula von Grumbach, who staggered this male world by publishing pamphlets in 1523–4, corresponded with Luther and Osiander, and alienated her own embarrassed family.[2]

[1] The general bibliography coincides largely with that in the first note to ch. 5.
[2] On David Joris, see numerous references in G. H. Williams. On Hans Schwalb, see H. Gravier, p. 58. On Katherine Zell and Argula von Grumbach see R. H. Bainton, *Women of the Reformation*, chs. 3 and 5: he gives their publications and the main secondary works, pp. 74–6, 109.

At the upper social extreme stood a handful of aristocrats, including not only Hutten but Hartmut von Cronberg, a country gentleman of the Taunus, and again that anonymous nobleman from Augsburg who in three dialogues denounced Luther's clerical enemies and even reproached his own class for its failure to assume the religious and social duties imposed by Luther's teaching. Such men did not necessarily accept the harsh secular anticlericalism of Hutten. Before becoming involved with Franz von Sickingen and the rebellious knights, Cronberg began his series of pious, Biblical, non-humanist tracts in support of Luther. After the collapse of the knights he fled to Bohemia, then came to Basle, whence he won over Duke Ulrich of Württemberg to the Reformation. Ultimately in 1541 Martin Bucer was to reconcile him with Philip of Hesse, who restored his forfeited lands.[3] But when all these unusual figures have been listed, the majority of the important Lutheran pamphleteers were men of thorough humanist training, such as Eberlin von Günzburg, Johann Brenz, Andreas Osiander, Nikolaus von Amsdorf, Justus Jonas, Johann Lang, Urbanus Rhegius and Martin Bucer. Alongside them were men who might be described as educated preacher-pamphleteers, like the leading Strassburg Reformer Matthäus Zell or the peasant leader Christoph Schappeler. Among the best-equipped and most influential of all were the famous *Ratschreiber* of Nuremberg, Lazarus Spengler,[4] and the cosmopolitan Vadianus, whom we have already met as a Germanic historian. In short the humanists, hitherto with rare exceptions communicating horizontally with each other, were now communicating vertically with other social strata.

By no means all these men preached in a devout spirit. Dürer's close friend Willibald Pirckheimer, whose sexual morals were less fastidious than his taste in Greek literature, has been credited with *The Purified Eck* (1520), a pamphlet also attributed to Nikolaus Gerbel. A piece of black humour, it describes the removal of Eck's intellectual vices by means of a series of

[3] A full account of Hartmut occupies W. R. Hitchcock, ch. 5. Further references in *NDB*, s.v. Cronberg, and in H. Gravier, p. 303; for an edition of his writings, see E. Kück.

[4] Standard account by H. von Schubert; see also H. J. Grimm in C. S. Meyer, *Luther for an Ecumenical Age*, pp. 108–19.

surgical operations. Detesting such anti-Lutheran zealots, Pirckheimer nevertheless emerged in the end as a member of the Catholic Church.[5] A more significant publicist was Eberlin von Günzburg (c. 1470–1533), a popular Franciscan preacher at Tübingen, Ulm and Freiburg until in 1521 Luther's writings converted him to the Evangelical faith.[6] Leaving the cloister, he preached the new beliefs throughout southern Germany and published *Fifteen Allies*, a set of tracts supposedly contributed by fifteen would-be reformers of the nation's social, political and religious grievances. Influenced both by Hutten and by Luther's *Christian Nobility*, Eberlin attacked monasticism and celibacy on the one hand and Eck upon the other. He was among those who noted Eck's defence of interest-taking, and so dubbed him the pet theologian of the Fuggers, a family disliked both as Catholics and bankers. In one tract he invents a Utopia called Wolfaria, where the lesser nobility are the leaders of an agrarian society inspired by simple Germanic morality. Here they reorganize the Church, safeguard public morality and insist that priests should marry. Eberlin's translation of Tacitus' *Germania* was but one symptom of this archaic but ardent patriotism. Elsewhere he calls upon the rulers to restore the shining virtues of the national spirit. The emperor should forthwith protect the preachers, while the rulers should expel the mendicant Orders and ensure that no future emperor should receive his crown from the Antichrist of Rome. Like Luther, Eberlin both got married and denounced the peasant rebels in the year 1524: he was then assigned a pastorate at Leutershausen, where his life ended amid disillusioning struggles against opponents of the Reformation.

Along with Eberlin many other writers helped to exalt the name of Luther while yet enunciating quite varied individual views upon the struggle. In 1520 there appeared at Strassburg

---

[5] L. W. Spitz, *Religious Renaissance*, ch. 8. The important article by H. Rupprich in *Schweizer Beiträge*, xv (1957) is now translated in G. Strauss, *Pre-Reformation Germany*, pp. 380–435. On the authorship of *The Purified Eck* see P. Mercker, *Der Verfasser des Eccius Dedolatus* (Halle, 1923). A reprint is in A. E. Berger, *Sturmtruppen*.

[6] Account in W. R. Hitchcock, ch. 4; see also H. Gravier, pp. 52–4, 303; references in K. Schottenloher, i, nos. 5144–67; *NDB*, s.v. Eberlin. On Eberlin's *Wolfaria* see S. G. Bell in *Church History*, xxvi (1967).

the dialogue *Karsthans*, attributed to Vadian.[7] Whereas most of the popular authors wrote with too much haste and passion to achieve first-rate literary structure and style, *Karsthans* is adjudged a graceful exception, and worthy to be ranked alongside the best pieces by Luther and Murner. The fictitious character Karsthans, 'Jack Hoe', is a German equivalent of the English Piers Plowman: the honest son of toil, the foe of humbug, the embodiment of sound religious and social aspirations among the poor. Vadian's dialogue appeared in answer to a recent attack on the peasants by the Catholic satirist Thomas Murner, who had expressed the fear—later shared by both parties—that all stability would vanish if these rude yokels were encouraged to play a part in the religious struggle. Vadian makes Karsthans attack not only Murner's private failings but his acknowledgment of the pope as the highest authority of Christendom. Karsthans, the layman who has read the Scriptures, replies that this authority is Christ, not the pope. The dialogue has five speakers, including the referee Mercury, who appropriately speaks Latin. In the one corner is Karsthans, seconded by Luther in person: in the other, clumsily aided by Murner, is Studens, the son of Karsthans. An evident pupil of the 'Obscure Men', Studens proudly displays the scholastic learning he has recently acquired at the university, and he is ashamed to see his parent lacking respect for Duns Scotus and Nicholas of Lyra. On his side Karsthans commits some malapropisms but is astounded by the bizarre gibberish talked by Studens. This he opposes with his robust good sense and Scriptural reading. In this antithesis Vadian owes obvious debts to the abrasive *Letters of Obscure Men*; yet he depicts Luther as a man of peace, for when Karsthans menacingly pulls his flail from his bag, Luther restores his good humour, saying that a man of faith does not appeal to force but relies only on the weapon of the Gospel.

Four years later, even this mild idealization of the poor was to become suspect when viewed alongside the Peasants' Revolt and

[7] Leading authorities are C. Bonorand; W. Näf, *Vadian und seine Stadt St Gallen* (2 vols., St. Gallen, 1944, 1957). See also *ADB*, s.v. Watt; H. O. Burger, pp. 377ff; E. G. Rupp, *Patterns of Reformation*, pt. iv; H. Gravier, pt. i, ch. 3, and pp. 222, 307–8. *Karsthans* (reprinted in O. Schade, iii and in A. E. Berger, *Sturmtruppen*) was edited by H. Burckhardt (Leipzig, 1910).

the manifestos of Karlstadt, Müntzer and other prophets of radical religion and social upheaval. In real life the man with the hoe refused to play the idealized role invented by liberal humanists: he tried to resist the growth of economic exploitation and refused to become the willing tool of other classes. For a few desperate months he did not merely quote the Bible but used his flail in earnest. Finally he capitulated and sullenly returned to the soil, yet only after a bloodbath which tended to dissociate him still further from humanism and possibly from the two religions which had united to ensure his suppression. Henceforth the Lutherans who had written the best popular pamphlets also became obsessed with the fear of social anarchy. Even in the religious sphere they had too much to say about abuses coming from Rome, and despite some exceptions too little to say about those arising from the aristocratic and secular-minded prince-bishops. These latter, as guilty as anyone, managed to remain standing as pillars of the empire. For the moment, the fictitious Karsthans survived Vadian's publication: he even suffered the indignity of enlistment to the cause of Sickingen and the knights. The pamphlet *Neu-Karsthans* (1520), attributed to Sickingen's chaplain Martin Bucer, depicts the famous knight as converted by his associate Hutten to a pious Lutheranism, in which he then tries to interest Karsthans.[8] With rich if perhaps unconscious humour, the author makes the peasant show astonishment at the godly learning suddenly displayed by his overlord, especially when Sickingen relates how at mealtimes he daily hears readings from the Bible and the Fathers. As Gravier has suggested, Sickingen is shown as deriving three ideas from Luther: the title Antichrist for the pope; the phrase Luther applied to the bishops, 'idols anointed by oil'; and the more serious if more abused doctrine of the priesthood of all Christians. We shall see that during these confused years, a similarly selective treatment was applied to Luther's teaching by other men, other social groups.

The foregoing analysis should doubtless conclude upon a cautious note, lest it give the impression that the Protestant pamphleteers were generally or primarily concerned to make

[8] On *Neu-Karsthans* see H. Gravier, pp. 56–7; reprinted in O. Schade, ii and in A. E. Berger, *Sturmtruppen*.

selective appeals to particular classes or social groups. Whatever its title, Luther's own famous tract of 1520 is in its substance very far from being aimed exclusively at the German aristocrats. Following this lead, and at least equally the much older tradition of the *gravamina germanicae nationis*, many minor authors showed themselves intent to stress the nationwide and multi-class character of the grievances they laid at the door of the Church. Any bibliography of the pamphlets published in the early 1520s has numerous items, mostly anonymous, with such titles as *Beclagung Tütscher Nation* (Strassburg and Augsburg, 1521); *Lamentationes germanicae nationis* (Schlettstadt, ?1521); *Teütscher nation beschwerd von den Geistlichen* (Strassburg, 1523); *Eyn Klaggeschrift an alle Stende Teütscher Nation* (Nuremberg, 1523). Throughout the story, Protestantism thus balanced its sectional appeals by a strong and true instinct to hold the nation together by casting it in its favourite role of victim. This instinct is clearly related to another: the stubborn effort to find salvation in the venerable shibboleths of the Holy Roman Empire.

The initial response of the Catholic champions proved inadequate not merely in quantity but in popular appeal. With few exceptions, their best minds were as yet those of professional theologians concerned to write point-by-point refutations of Luther rather than to speak about religion to the common people or even to clothe the old Church in new and shining garments. It would be entirely mistaken to dismiss these men as mere scholastics, since most of them had undergone humanist training and were far from ignorant of Erasmian scholarship. Both Emser and Eck even translated the Bible in rivalry with Luther's famous version. Their relative failure arose rather from the paucity of their polemical and devotional writing in the German language; again from their inability to rekindle a personal Catholic religion, as their predecessors of the *devotio moderna* had done and as their successors of the Counter Reformation were to do in later years. Such criticisms apply most markedly to the three academic leaders, Johannes Eck (1486–1533), Hieronymus Emser (1478–1527) and Konrad Koch Wimpina (*c.* 1460–1531).

The first of these must be granted a heroic and monumental

quality.[9] Armed with an immense range of studies, a formidable
memory and a stentorian voice, Eck cut a good figure in the
public disputations of Leipzig and elsewhere. With remorseless
skill, he drove Luther's revolutionary thoughts into the open,
and then from 1520 he produced an able series of treatises—but
mostly in Latin—defending the papal supremacy and the
traditional doctrines of penance, purgatory and the Mass. His
Enchiridion locorum communium adversus Ludderanos (1525)
provided a detailed attack upon Melanchthon's *Loci Communes*,
and during the rest of the century it was to attain over ninety
editions in various languages. In the long run it thus provided a
valuable armoury for the Catholic priesthood and became one of
the basic writings of the Counter Reformation. Yet in the short
run this and the rest of Eck's writings cannot have made much
direct impact upon lay opinion: only to a limited extent did they
belong to the world of the *Flugschriften*. So far as concerns the
educated classes of his own generation, his appeal also proved
limited. He heaped up his 'authorities' with formal skill rather
than with critical discrimination. His intellect and personality
were too obviously those of the uncompromising gladiator. To
endorse the Roman viewpoint on almost every issue was to
invite opposition from many educated German Catholics of the
period before Trent. Like Luther, Eck did not mellow with age.
Sincerely enough, he blamed Luther both for the Peasants'
Revolt and for Anabaptism. He spurred on the hesitant Dukes of
Bavaria to persecute, and his efforts were crowned with success
in 1527-8, when at last they burned numerous heretics. Again,
during the negotiations of 1541 with Melanchthon he showed
his usual rigidity of outlook, detaching himself from the moderate
Catholic theologians Gropper and Pflug.

Between 1520 and 1527 Emser, secretary to Duke George,
wrote eight vigorous polemical tracts in German against

[9] Guidance on Eck is in H. Jedin, i, p. 394, n. 3; other references in
NCE; ODCC; *Lexikon für Theologie und Kirche*. Much relevant information
also appears in J. Lortz; R. H. Fife; H. Grisar, *Luther*, trans. E. M.
Lamond (6 vols., 1913–17), i, pp. 262ff; iv, pp. 377ff. On the relations of
Eck and other theologians with Albertine Saxony, much material occurs
in F. Gess, *Akten und Briefe zur Kirchenpolitik Herzog Georgs von Sachsen*
(2 vols., Leipzig, 1905). On Eck's important role in the Bavarian Counter
Reformation, see G. Strauss, 'The Religious Policies of Dukes Wilhelm
and Ludwig'.

Luther, Karlstadt and Zwingli: he also tried to undercut the Reformers by publishing a German New Testament, based upon Luther's yet armed with anti-Lutheran annotations.[10] In Johannes Cochlaeus, successively in the service of Albrecht of Mainz and of Duke George, we observe an equally zealous but lesser controversialist.[11] Of peasant origins, he was not without ability to reach the common man, while in course of time the sheer number of his publications appear to outnumber those of any contemporary author save Luther. On the other hand his lack of intellectual quality and erudition was not repaired by his talent for invective and slanderous anecdote. Luther treated him with contempt and replied only once to his arguments, but after Luther's death Cochlaeus took his revenge in the mendacious *Commentary on the Acts and Writings of Martin Luther* (1549). At the famous Augsburg Conference of 1530 Eck and Cochlaeus were accompanied by the older theologian Wimpina, whose writings illustrate other basic shortcomings among the defence.[12] A true scholastic, Wimpina strove to amass patristic and medieval opinions rather than to evaluate the Biblical sources. Modern Catholic theologians have criticized his tendency, shown in the theses he compiled for the use of the Indulgence-seller Tetzel, to present debatable opinions as established dogma. His work *Anacephalaeosis* sought to expose Luther's theology as a farrago of all the errors current in every age of Christianity, but this technique was obviously too cumbersome to attract either the humanists or the simpler readers of the new age.

On the Catholic side there remains the very different figure of Thomas Murner (1475–1537), the one with more than a touch of imagination and literary flair.[13] Brought up in Strassburg, he

[10] Cf. E. L. Enders, *Luther und Emser, Ihre Streitschriften aus dem Jahre 1521* (2 vols., Halle, 1890–92); K. A. Strand, *Reformation Bibles in the Crossfire. The Story of Jerome Emser, his anti-Lutheran Critique and his Catholic Bible Version* (Ann Arbor, 1961).

[11] M. Spahn, *Johannes Cochlaeus, ein Lebensbild aus der Zeit der Kirchenspaltung* (Berlin, 1898) catalogues 200 of his works (pp. 341–72). See also H. Grisar, *Luther*, iv. pp. 380ff, and useful references in J. Lortz; H. Jedin.

[12] Articles by E. Iserloh in *NCE* and by L. Cristiani in *DTC*. The standard biography is J. Negwer, *Conrad Wimpina, ein katholischer Theologe aus der Reformationszeit 1460–1531* (Breslau, 1909).

[13] A full account of Murner is in C. Schmidt, vol. ii, bk. 5; H. Gravier is also valuable: cf. pp. 61–71, 206–16, 305–7. Further important materials are in A. E. Berger, *Satirische Feldzüge*. On Murner as printer, see A. Götze, p. 32.

had entered the Franciscan Order at the age of fifteen and had studied the humanities, law, theology and medicine at a variety of universities from Paris to Cracow. Crowned laureate by Maximilian as early as 1506, Murner tilted against the proposals of Wimpfeling to laicize German education and then in 1514 turned to vernacular poetry. A popular preacher, he managed to hold important offices within his Order despite his bold denunciation of ecclesiastical abuses. A moralist rather than a religious reformer, he perceived and began to attack Luther's radical tendencies by the end of 1520. He also translated Henry VIII's *Assertion of the Seven Sacraments*, which attracted German attention on account of its royal authorship. More effectively than the rest, Murner asked that ever-embarrassing question: with so many divergent theologians now claiming to interpret the Scriptures, what authority had Luther above that of his rivals? Nevertheless, his most elaborate and spirited attack misfired. This was *The Great Lutheran Fool* of 1522, a shapeless, allusive, but often entertaining mass of buffoonery and invective aimed against all his Protestant detractors. The latter included Martin Bucer and Katharine Zell, who had taken up the pen in defence of her husband. In his prologue Murner announces: 'As they have done to me, so I have done to them.' Unfortunately the Strassburg magistrates were now misusing the Worms prohibition against scandalous writings in order to suppress Catholic authors and publishers, while leaving the Protestants to write much as they pleased. Murner fled to Lucerne and in 1525 set up a press there for the publication of his own pamphlets, of which some fourteen are known. Not far away he found another target in Zwingli, and when in 1529 the Protestant cantons tried to extradite him for trial, he fled to the Palatinate, at last returning to die in his native Alsatian village. Murner was thus denied a fair trial of strength in the leading city of the Reformation, yet even had *The Great Lutheran Fool* circulated freely there, it might have proved too complex, even too frivolous to have disturbed the Protestant zealots. The latter, now in stolid and pious mood, found the earnest sermons of Bucer and Zell more to their taste than an extravaganza in the tradition of Erasmus' *Praise of Folly*.

Before Thomas Murner had finished struggling against the Strassburg authorities, there opened up a new front in the war of the pamphlets. Having been dismissed by the Diet of Worms in April 1521, Luther spent his lonely but fruitful sabbatical year on the Wartburg. During this period his mercurial colleague Andreas Karlstadt (c. 1480–1541) took control of the Wittenberg Reformation and carried along the city council against the feeble resistance of moderates like Melanchthon and Jonas. In a spirit of fundamentalism Karlstadt set forth a shortened and partially German Mass with communion for the laity in both kinds: he also brought the monks and nuns out of their cloisters and made strong propaganda for clerical marriage. Denouncing his university degrees, walking about in bare feet and calling himself Brother Andreas, he displayed some of the more alarming traits of extremist academic liberalism. This rapid acceleration of the pace at Wittenberg coincided with the arrival in town of the prophets from Zwickau, who had inherited Hussite millenarian ideas from nearby Bohemia. They also came as emissaries of the Zwickau priest Thomas Müntzer (c. 1468–1525), heir to the prophecies and the mysticism of Joachim, the Fraticelli and Tauler. Despite Karlstadt's involvement with these people and his emphasis on the claims of 'Spirit', he and Müntzer represent divergent tendencies in sixteenth-century Radicalism.[14] Whereas Karlstadt now seems one of the more striking forerunners of puritan and congregational principles, Müntzer provides a far more genuine example of that Spiritualism which exalted the inner light at the expense of the Biblical sources. A former admirer of Luther, he had now begun to denounce him as a bibliolater and a prince-worshipper, as one who had put both those authorities before the promptings of the Spirit.

Both Karlstadt and Müntzer now became pamphleteers in their own right: they vied in the revolutionary courses which were ultimately to draw them both into the vortex of the Peasants' Revolt of 1524–5. While Karlstadt professed a sentimental regard for peasant wisdom, the original and unaffected Müntzer developed a more profound and luridly expressed belief in the necessity of social revolution. He has

---

[14] For valuable discussion and references on both Karlstadt and Müntzer see E. G. Rupp, *Patterns of Reformation*, pts. ii and iii.

attracted Marxists as an apostle of modern class-war, but in reality his concerns were religious and pastoral. He believed that extreme poverty, the need to scratch ceaselessly for subsistence, weighed so heavily upon many people as to debar them from religious thinking and hence from salvation. He therefore felt that the religious Reformation could only proceed on a basis of rapid social and political change, a programme of liberation from material want and even from the oppressive fear of authority. He clung to every scrap of liberalism he could find in German law and history, as well as to every prophecy which foretold the coming of a glorious new era of Christianity.

On his return from the Wartburg in March 1522 Luther soon recovered local control in Wittenberg, but the wider struggle with Radicalism remained to be fought. In 1523, having left the city, Karlstadt passed still further beyond Luther's teaching. He abandoned the sacrament of baptism and professed to see in the Lord's Supper only a sign or symbol of the union between God and the soul. Moreover he condemned all religious pictures and images, encouraging townsmen and students to violent iconoclasm. Instead of distinguishing between use and abuse in traditions, he wanted forthwith to eradicate every non-Biblical element in the life of the Church. At least more worldlywise than the Radicals, Luther saw the need to move at a gentler pace, which would carry along the large uncommitted elements in all classes, the slow-thinking men of goodwill and prudence who could easily be alienated and so relapse into the old beliefs. Denouncing Karlstadt to his face, Luther also sought to deter Müntzer by private letters, and to put the princes on their guard against the doctrines taught by Müntzer at Zwickau and from 1523 at Allstedt. By this stage Luther realized he must pamphleteer afresh and redefine some of the sweeping and resonant phrases he had applied to Christian liberty back in 1520. Quite consistently, he detested Karlstadt's romantic notion that scholarship and formal teaching had become liabilities in the brave new world of revelation, and in January 1524 he published the splendid tract urging magistrates to erect Christian schools. In addition he issued two pamphlets which to radical opinion seemed downright reactionary. *Of Secular Authority* (1523) drew a clear distinction between inward faith, to which no man can be constrained, and outer obedience to the secular powers. True Christians need no law, any more than a good tree needs teaching to bear good fruit; yet they are in a minority, and the wicked world as a whole cannot be governed by the Gospel. A ruler who tried to accomplish this feat

> would be like a shepherd who should place in one fold wolves, lions, eagles and sheep together...and say, Help yourselves, and be good and peaceful among yourselves; the fold is open, there is plenty of food; have no fear of dogs and clubs. The sheep, forsooth, would keep the peace and would allow themselves to be fed and governed in peace, but they would not live long...For this reason, these two kingdoms must be sharply distinguished, and both be permitted to remain; the one to produce piety, the other to bring about external peace and prevent evil deeds; neither is sufficient in the world without the other.[15]

Not long afterwards (January 1525) Luther pulverized the Radicals unmercifully in his tract *Against the Heavenly Prophets*:

> But should you ask how one gains access to this same lofty spirit, they do not refer you to the outward gospel but to some imaginary realm, saying: Remain in 'self-abstraction' where I now am and you will have the same experience. A heavenly voice will come, and God himself will speak to you. If you enquire further as to the nature of this 'self-abstraction', you will find that they know as much about it as Dr. Karlstadt knows of Greek and Hebrew...With all his mouthing of the words 'Spirit, Spirit, Spirit', he tears down the bridge, the path, the way, the ladder and all the means by which the Spirit might come to you...he wants to teach you, not how the Spirit comes to you, but how you come to the Spirit. They would have you learn how to journey on the clouds and ride on the wind.[16]

These three pamphlets are masterpieces of their kind: in clarity, style and the use of metaphor they outclass almost everything

[15] J. Dillenberger, p. 371, from the translation by Schindel in *Works of Martin Luther* (Philadelphia, 1930), iii.

[16] E. G. Rupp and B. Drewery, pp. 118–19, from *Luther's Works* (American Edn., ed. J. Pelikan and H. J. Lehmann, Philadelphia, 1943–), xl, pp. 146ff.

among the *Flugschriften* except Luther's earlier batch of 1520. Thus on the eve of the Peasants' Revolt it would have been easy to forecast the line Luther would take if any such emergency arose. He did indeed try to allay the rebellion by a preaching tour, and on more than one occasion his voice was raised in favour of reconciliation and mercy. Yet when the great explosion occurred, he penned his notorious and unretracted pamphlet bidding the princes to kill ruthlessly. It cannot justly be excused as a hysterical aberration; rather was it based upon a firm belief in the death-deserving nature of rebellion, a belief widely shared by his contemporaries throughout Europe.

Examining his reactions throughout these troubled years, we should flatter Luther by arguing that he displayed a wholly consistent scheme of thought in the matters of religious liberty and public coercion. On the one hand he bade the authorities put down the Catholic Mass as a public blasphemy. On the other, he continued to doubt whether sectarian heresies could be repressed by material weapons, and he was inclined to believe that the chaotic forces would nullify one another. Even so, the Radical pamphleteers had begun to defy Luther, while Martin Bucer and many others in south-western Germany were leaning toward Zwingli or seeking to mediate between Zürich and Wittenberg. While organizing missions, Luther might well announce that the Word had done more against the papacy than all the kings, emperors and armies of former ages. But he had now been made aware that, whether in print or in the pulpit, the Word did not seem to be saying the same thing to all men. The first phase of the German Reformation thus ended in an atmosphere dramatically different from that of its inception with the *Ninety-five Theses*. A heroic and generally-applauded gesture had led not to united religious revolt but to a seething cauldron of ideas which left Luther little choice between surrender to the pope of Rome and becoming a dogmatic leader in such a manner as to attract the gibe 'pope of Wittenberg.' It would be hard to find eight years more pregnant with the future dilemma of western history.

So far this account of the pamphleteering years has left untouched a good many problems important to social and intellectual historians. The most interesting questions may well seem the least precise and the most obviously unanswerable in quantitative terms. Given this immense outflow of tracts and sermons, how deeply are the masses likely to have understood Luther's religious teaching? What was his relationship with the millions who lacked the theological equipment to follow closely in his wake, let alone to make independent assessment of his claim? Did he do more than supply a vague but positive rationale for the old negative anticlericalism of the masses? To such questions we shall presently revert, but from the first a distinction needs to be made between these early years and the decades after 1540, when throughout the Lutheran lands a settled and increasingly educated pastorate was teaching a more or less agreed body of doctrine. Our present enquiry concerns the period and the nature of the revolution rather than its ultimate sequels. Despite the conservatives and the Radicals, Luther was never more popular than during the stage when he seemed to be leading the nation toward a new freedom and self-respect, to be transferring to a religious plane the aspirations of people, prophets and humanists alike. Yet this early wave of popularity, so clearly attested even by his enemies Aleander, Murner, Eck, the Archduke Ferdinand and numerous others, was attended by an unclarity not wholly dissimilar to the *Unklarheit* said by certain modern theologians to have afflicted the late medieval Church.

Considerable evidence for the popular understanding and response could be gathered by a closer study of the average or inferior popular pamphlets, of the anonymous writers standing nearer to the common people than did the scholarly theologians and humanists. Even with the aid supplied by so many editors and commentators, this task still demands several years of work by a number of scholars. Here I propose merely to glance at an example recently selected as significant of the type by the late Carl S. Meyer. It is a *Dialogue or Conversation between a Father and his Son*, published at Erfurt in 1523.[17] Unsophisticated from a literary standpoint, it represents a reversal of the roles laid down in Vadian's *Karsthans*. The son, recently returned from Evangelical study at Wittenberg, converts his already wavering father to a full acceptance of Lutheranism. As with so many

---

[17] *A Dialog*, translated by C. S. Meyer in his *Luther for an Ecumenical Age*, pp. 82–107.

tracts, its most striking characteristic is a virulent anticlericalism. This is first applied without discrimination to bishops and abbots: 'dogs, as the Holy Ghost calls them in Isaiah 56, who can no longer bark, who in good days have filled their bellies with the blood and sweat of the poor sheep'. Throughout, the disinterested Luther is contrasted with these money-making clerics. Even the father, whose conservative resistance is most perfunctory, remarks that the priests 'do not read and understand the Scriptures, and they are such uncouth clods that they can scarce sing a requiem. They oppress and fleece the poor sheep.' A related feature is the extreme alacrity with which these would-be theologians fix upon Luther's teaching of the priest-hood of all believers. The son exclaims

> 'Oho, father, I too am a priest and consecrated. Christ says so, Matthew 5: You are the salt of the earth. He does not say "The priests are"; no, "you are". I also can absolve as well as any priest or monk.'

And when the father feebly interrupts that 'nevertheless we must follow the old custom, which our forefathers observed', his offspring adroitly replies, 'Ah father, isn't that the old custom, which God and the Apostles taught?' Later on he reverts to the same theme. 'Haven't you heard, that we are priests and may absolve? After all, God can just as easily spread his Gospel through a poor ploughboy as through monks and priests.'

As one would expect, the subtler aspects of Luther's teaching on faith, grace and works are avoided, yet the straightforward replacement of Indulgences by a firm personal faith is urged with force. The scholastic authors, Aristotle, Scotus, Aquinas and Occam are dismissed in the same breath as 'permits to eat butter, Indulgence-myths and Romish grace, lying un-Evan-gelical matters'. Aroused by the young man's tirade, the father goes to find his own letter of Indulgence and throws it on the fire with the valedictory cry, 'There you lie in the name of Eck, Emser and Murner. We praise thee O Lord!' He then accepts the advice to 'buy yourself a Bible, since it has now been put into German by Martin'. This remark underscores one of the effective elements in a performance of mediocre insight. Its author is well versed in the Scriptures, which he cites with remarkable frequency—though not always with discrimination—to substantiate every claim. Again, though without any searching analysis of the distinctions between Augustine and Luther, he roughly grasps and expounds with some eloquence Luther's basic notions of a trusting faith, a truly omnipotent God and an imputed righteousness.

> 'If you believe that you are forgiven, then you are already forgiven. If you now believe that you have a benevolent, gracious, wholly merciful God, and follow him, then you are saved... You or your natural self cannot accomplish it. And therefore faith is nothing else but to trust and to believe in all the words of God... Now if you have such a faith, then love to God and your neighbour will flow out of it.'

Needless to add, this passage comes very near to Luther's own words: so does the succeeding denial of Justification through good works.

It would seem dangerous for social historians to explore the educated minds, let alone the popular minds, of the early Reformation in the light of those deep interpretations and extensions of Luther's theology put forward by the theologians of our twentieth-century 'Luther Renaissance'. Even if a historian happens to become interested in this modern thought, must he not divest himself of its many-splendoured garments and be prepared to rub shoulders with the unsophisticated, once he has climbed down into the workshop of the sixteenth century? At all events he will find the early years filled by puzzled non-theologians, like those commercial travellers who early in 1522 stayed at the Black Bear in Jena, and happened to meet up with Luther, then returning incognito from the Wartburg. There, along with the Swiss John Kessler, they all talked about religion, but failed at first to recognize this bearded stranger wearing a sword.

> Then the two merchants spoke their mind and the old one said, 'I am a plain simple layman and I don't understand much about this business. But this I do say. Either this Luther is an angel from heaven, or he is a devil from hell. I wouldn't mind giving ten guilders if I might make my confession to him, for I think he knows about quietening consciences'.

Meanwhile—so continues the reminiscence of Kessler—the landlord came up and said, '"Don't worry about the bill. Martin paid for you!" And this really thrilled us, not the money or the food, but to have been the guests of such a man.'[18]

One thing is certain: that in the 1520s Luther's doctrine was not, and could not have been, viewed by the people with nearly the same balance as we can attain today. To us his system centres upon that original doctrine of Justification by Faith Alone, with its subtle but theologically fundamental differences from the parallel in Augustine. Yet in Luther's early mass-selling tracts meagre space is allotted to explaining this distinction: several of the most famous do not mention it at all. We should also beware of any tendency to believe that the whole structure of Luther's theology was clearly set forth in print by the early 1520s. What is likely to have been the impression drawn by a careful reader from these primary writings? Hans Hillerbrand asks himself this question in a recent article, and replies:

> The writings available conveyed certain basic religious notions—an emphatically christological orientation, the repudiation of so-called human traditions, the affirmation of the primacy of Scripture in the formulation of religious truth, the open rejection of the Catholic Church and the pope where-ever the new religious insights clashed with ecclesiastical tradition. To these notions must be added an intense stress on personal religion and a disregard of external rites and ceremonies.[19]

To this just and penetrating summary one might perhaps add—if the popular tracts are helpful guides—the priesthood of all believers. Doubtless also one should lay stress upon Luther's 'liberal' phraseology of 1520, notoriously wrenched out of context by the peasant rebels and unstressed in later years by its author.

> Therefore I declare that neither pope nor bishop nor any other person has the right to impose a syllable of law upon a Christian man without his own consent.

[18] E. G. Rupp and B. Drewery, pp. 82–6, translate the passage from Kessler's *Sabbata*.
[19] H. J. Hillerbrand, 'The Spread of the Protestant Reformation'.

Taken alone, this and other sentences in the *Babylonian Captivity* were among the most staggering things said to mass audiences for many centuries! Once sounded, this trumpet could not be unsounded, not even by Luther himself, and it served as a summons to prophets, *illuminati* and sectarians of various types. Nevertheless one could not substantiate any claim that the German public rapidly attained an accurate grasp of Luther's doctrine of Justification, let alone of his still more difficult doctrine of the Eucharist. One could indeed cite a few passages in other men's pamphlets where the former is reasonably grasped and summarized, but it remains hard to avoid the impression that the years of pamphleteering must have left some blurred and simplified impressions of Luther's central doctrine.

Faced by this likelihood, the natural reaction is to add, 'Obviously so, since in any case only the theologians could have grasped the deeper and more difficult teachings of Luther.' But historical fact does not always neatly support commonsense assumption. The odd fact remains that even professional theologians outside Luther's immediate circle often did misinterpret Luther. While even some of his own distinguished supporters soon wanted to modify his teachings, his Catholic adversaries were hampered by their very learning, their knowledge of older heresies, which stopped them from understanding Luther's new propositions. They stereotyped his alleged heresies according to the patterns and issues with which they were already familiar. Eck, Prierias, the condemnations of Louvain and Cologne, the *Determinatio* from Paris, all fitted his teachings into historical pigeonholes. Again, even at a later date, when the nuncio Van der Vorst went around Germany asking people what they believed to be the main controversial issues, he came back with nine points, amongst which Justification by Faith did not appear at all![20] Such confusion may well seem ludicrous to us, yet despite it all there nevertheless occurred a great religious, political and social revolution, one which did not

[20] H. Jedin, i, p. 408. It is fair to add that a number of widely-read Lutheran writings, as well as the *Dialog*, do briefly discuss Imputation: e.g. J. Bugenhagen, *Epistola ad Anglos* (1525); Olavus Petri, *Answer to the Twelve Questions* (1526); W. Tyndale, *Prefaces to N. T.* (1526); R. Barnes, *Essay on Justification* (1531).

remain simply anticlerical or anti-papal, one which truly engaged the soul of a great nation.

By a strange yet explicable paradox, many of those learned in theology and Church history grasped some essentials of Evangelical teaching far less firmly than did the simple men and women who at least obeyed Luther's basic command: to read the Bible. While that great scholar Hubert Jedin rightly illustrates the public unawareness of theological issues—an unawareness which the work of Erasmus had in some measure helped to create—there can be no doubts regarding the Biblical knowledge attained by so many of the common people.[21] And any student of the English Reformation will here find his own evidence striking a common chord. Desirably or otherwise, the Bible tended to bypass philosophical theology. The reading of the Scriptures was the very heartbeat of the popular Reformation, insofar as the latter won through to the status of a positive religious movement. Nevertheless, for this very reason the Reformation was not to be wholly Luther's Reformation. The assiduous Bible student could so easily become a sectarian, or some other sort of non-Lutheran Protestant. An extensive menu *à la carte* succeeded the Lutheran *table d'hôte*. And which of us today would prefer a monolithic Reformation to have emerged from the pamphleteering years? In the German Bible lay Luther's glory and achievement. In the German Bible lay the major limitation and the division of his movement. In all the vernacular Bibles lay one of the many roots of that complex turmoil, the 'free' western world. Inevitably, we now concentrate a special attention on Luther and on his fellow-writers, the messengers to a nation; yet even as we do so, should we not observe how the vernacular Bible triggered off vast forces which passed far beyond the control of any one group of publicists, any one Church? The effects willed even by publicists of genius have seldom corresponded with the effects meted out by history. This realization should by now have become a commonplace, but it remains the beginning of wisdom for historians, most of all for social historians.

[21] H. Jedin, i, pp. 187–92; but J. Lortz, i, pp. 216, 329, stresses the pervasive character of Luther's Bible, as indeed Cochlaeus and so many contemporary opponents had done.

7

Nuremberg and Strassburg

The ultimate aim of the next three chapters is to examine very broadly the mental and social processes which led so many German cities into the Protestant Reformation. If we seek any degree of realism an abrupt change of scale is now demanded. By any reckoning, there existed many hundreds of urban communities in Germany; and it would seem advantageous to obtain our bearings by first examining in some detail two famous and well-documented places: Nuremberg and Strassburg. What conditions helped to predispose these cities to the reception of Protestant ideas? Which people initiated the movement and which sections of society first accepted it? How far were the deeper implications understood by the citizens? What considerations seem to have governed the attitudes and decisions of the city councils? In regard to this last question we need to remember that, within the loose framework of the Holy Roman Empire, the councils of the larger and more powerful imperial cities faced issues and took decisions resembling those of sovereign governments rather than those of mere municipalities.

Nuremberg, perhaps the most widely admired and imitated of the imperial cities, had in Luther's day a population of some 20,000, plus another 20,000 within its unusually large extramural territory.[1] Splendidly walled and towered, it stood almost

---

[1] On Nuremberg my chief debt is to G. Strauss, *Nuremberg in the Sixteenth Century*. I have consulted the recent substantial city history by G. Pfeiffer; also the comparative article by H. Baron and that by H. J.

impregnable to the military forces of that age. Its wealth owed little to the rather poor agriculture of Franconia, but it stood at the convergence of a dozen major trade routes. Its network of direct commerce extended from Spain to Poland, from the Baltic to the Adriatic. It boasted reciprocal customs treaties with scores of German, Netherlandish and Swiss cities. In river barges and in covered wagons reminiscent of the American West, Nuremberg merchants took its renowned manufactures throughout most of Europe: they returned with metal ore from Hungary, cloth from England and skins from the North. Even in the field of extra-European commerce the contacts of the Nurembergers were extending, and among the many offices maintained by the city's great business houses was one in Lisbon to handle the African trade. How far did this breadth of outlook pass beyond the economic sphere? We may well dramatize Nuremberg as the home of Albrecht Dürer, just as Dürer dramatized the solid Nurembergers who commissioned his portraits. Yet by and large, the city could claim distinction for superb craftsmanship rather than for creative literature or for political and social ideas. If we would sense her characteristic role in European civilization we should visit the Germanische Nationalmuseum and examine the marvellous collection of guns, armour, globes, armillary spheres, astrolabes, travelling sundials, clocks of all sizes, even Peter Henlein's new pocket watches, known as 'Nuremberg living eggs'. It was around 1500 that Nuremberg reached its zenith as the metropolis of precision work and accomplished technical feats which a modern historian might relate to the scientific revolution of the seventeenth century as much as to the art of the High Renaissance.[2]

Grimm on Spengler. Concerning the last, and the Nuremberg Reformation in general, see especially H. von Schubert, which also provides a valuable bibliography. Other standard works are F. Roth, *Die Einführung der Reformation in Nürnberg, 1517–1528* (Würzburg, 1885); P. Kalkoff, *Die Reformation in der Reichsstadt Nürnberg nach den Flugschriften ihres Ratschriebers Lazarus Spengler* (Halle, 1926); A. Engelhardt, *Die Reformation in Nürnberg* in *Mitteilungen des Vereins für Geschichte der Stadt Nürnberg*, xxxiii–iv–vi (3 vols., Nuremberg, 1936–9). On the city's foreign policy, see E. Franz, *Nürnberg, Kaiser und Reich* (Munich, 1930). Schottenloher, ii, nos. 20362–72, gives further items on Spengler, and *ibid.*, ii, nos. 26154–64, on the Nuremberg Reformation generally.

[2] G. Strauss, *Nuremberg in the Sixteenth Century*, pp. 134–45.

Alongside the merchants and industrial masters there lived indeed some able lawyers and humanists, yet in general the worshipful and wealthy city fathers treated them as employees or technical advisers and allowed them little share in the decision-making. Not only by custom but also by law, sovereignty lay with the forty-three patrician families admitted to the Inner Council. Indeed, day-to-day control lay with a smaller caucus: a committee of seven elders drawn from the so-called 'first old families' settled in Nuremberg since the thirteenth century. We tend to envisage the German city politics of the period in terms of a struggle between such oligarchs and, on the other side, the mass of small guildsmen and the unprivileged populace. Of some this remained true, but in Nuremberg, as in many others, this old constitutional struggle had been largely settled before 1500. The next chapter will study the considerable influence of class struggles on the Reformation in the Baltic cities; and parallels could be drawn from places nearer Nuremberg: for example, Goslar, Regensburg, Schweinfurt and Mühlhausen. But had class tensions continued to dominate life in Nuremberg, the fact would undoubtedly emerge from the voluminous records. Instead, year in and year out, we observe a spirit of acceptance on the side of the people, a real sense of duty and a solicitude for public welfare on the side of the patricians. Later passages will discuss the important role of the unprivileged in demanding Protestant preachers and Bible-Christianity. Yet this popular element does not render the Reformation the by-product of a class war, because in so many places which accepted it no recognizable class war was being conducted. Under patrician rule the life of the unprivileged in cities like Nuremberg seems to have been distinctly more tolerable than elsewhere in Germany, and more tolerable than the lives of most European underdogs. Nuremberg and the great imperial cities were not in fact the picturesque haunts of filth and overcrowding depicted by some writers on the late medieval city. The public baths and saunas were used weekly by people of all classes, municipal employees being given an hour off for this purpose every Saturday. Health regulations were minute and in general observed, while even the poor artisans lived one family to one house.

Here in fact was something as near good government as one would find in Europe around 1500; yet certainly one would be misguided to use the term liberal in any of its senses. Neither the merchant patricians nor the guild-members had any use either for democratic controls or for *laissez-faire* economics. Every act, every commodity, every service that could be prescribed, regulated, weighed and measured was duly prescribed, regulated, weighed and measured. By law at least, people could not part their hair except by rules. Until our own day, no state could boast closer-meshed industrial and social legislation. And the evidence suggests that, unlike so much medieval law, it was well enforced. Compared with the demarcations between and within the Nuremberg crafts, the brotherly differences of our modern trade unions seem almost wildly liberal. Such places exemplify in full what Henri Pirenne called 'municipal socialism'. And if we speak of the paternalism of the city fathers, this must be understood as the paternalism of austere, disapproving, distrustful stepfathers. Long before Luther added his rationale of theological pessimism, the government of the German cities took a dark view of human waywardness, profligacy, depravity. Their puritanism seems particularly ill-matched with the genial Middle Ages of romantic legend. They not only meted out harsh punishments but made use of torture to extract information, at least from those presumed to be criminals. The patrician members of the *Rat* might sit together in their fur-lined capes looking blandly Holbeinesque, yet below their feet there passed through the floor a speaking-tube giving them direct communication with the lavishly-equipped torture chamber beneath. Here the very sight of the hardware usually produced a gush of evidence. Not without reason, Gerald Strauss has suggested that the tragic view of human frailty may have predisposed people like the Nuremberg councillors to accept the equally tragic anthropology of Martin Luther.[3]

Indeed, some years before Luther burst upon the scene, these attitudes were already being reinforced by an invasion of formal Augustinian theology. In 1516, when Luther was still an obscure professor, his better-known mentor Johannes Staupitz, General

[3] *Past & Present*, xxxvi (1967), pp. 56–7.

of the Observant Augustinians, preached in Nuremberg a series of Advent sermons on predestination and the impotence of the human will.[4] His preaching led immediately to the foundation of a holy club consisting of several members of the patriciate, plus Albrecht Dürer and Lazarus Spengler, secretary to the council. Accepting the cult of personality, these converts called themselves the Staupitz Society—*Sodalitas Staupitziana*. One of their number, the jurist Christoph Scheurl, translated the sermons of Staupitz into German and published them in 1517. In fact Scheurl started corresponding with Luther in that same year, while Wenceslaus Link, another Augustinian friar and a colleague of Luther's in the university of Wittenberg, was sent to Nuremberg by Staupitz to preach the Advent sermons for 1518. Not only did Link perform this task; he also took the opportunity to introduce the Nurembergers to Luther's unprinted theology. Only months afterwards, as we again find in Scheurl's correspondence, the Nuremberg group received a copy of Luther's *Ninety-five Theses*. That they approved was only natural, because in fact the Nuremberg council had already refused to permit the sale within their jurisdiction of the notorious Indulgences for the building of St. Peter's. Finally in October 1518, on his way to meet Cajetan at Augsburg, and again on the return journey, Luther himself visited Nuremberg, met the *Sodalitas Staupitziana* and made a deep impression on its members.

This gradual introduction to a 'new' theology by Augustinian friars preaching St. Augustine's Christianity has an obvious relevance to the Reformation. 'Staupitz', wrote Luther, was 'a preacher of Grace and of the Cross'; and elsewhere he adds, 'Staupitz began the doctrine.' The recent theological assessment of Staupitz by David C. Steinmetz has very rightly encouraged us to study this remarkable man in his own right, not merely as a pendant to Luther. But other theologians who tell us that Staupitz was not a forerunner of Luther are thinking in abstract terms, unresponsive to the social dimension within which ideas—even religious ideas—must operate. Even so, these interesting events of 1517–18 were emphatically not the crucial phase of the Nuremberg Reformation. They concerned a mainly lay upper-class group, one much easier to convert than, say, the

4 On Staupitz see p. 82, n. 8 above.

clerical academics in a big university like Erfurt, which always contained a strong faction of Aristotelians preconditioned to dislike not only humanism but also Augustinianism, and *a fortiori* the teaching of that ultra-Augustinian, Martin Luther. Undoubtedly some of the lay soil proved shallow, and Luther's doctrine did not long prosper in the mind of every humanist and jurist. Scheurl himself was one of the many who began to turn against Luther about the time of Luther's dispute with Eck in the summer of 1519. From this point Nuremberg's council secretary Lazarus Spengler became the best known and most enthusiastic of the Nuremberg disciples. That Spengler and his friends won over some of their fellow councillors seems likely enough. Spengler openly argued Luther's case in 1521 and in response the Nuremberg authorities refused to take even nominal action to enforce the Edict of Worms against Luther and his followers. On the contrary they elected several known Lutheran sympathizers, including Andreas Osiander, to offices in the two main city churches of St. Lorenz and St. Sebaldus.

Osiander is known in England as the uncle of Archbishop Cranmer's wife. Far more important, he converted the future ruler of Prussia, Albrecht of Hohenzollern, when the latter was visiting Nuremberg in 1522. Osiander stood among the most rigorous of the Lutheran theologians, and Melanchthon thought he overstressed some aspects of original sin. Immediately after Luther's condemnation at Worms he and his associates began to worry the Nuremberg council by openly preaching the new doctrines.[5] Nevertheless this energetic group soon found a ready response from the middle and lower populace, and this—as will appear—commonly proved the crucial stage of a city Reformation. In general it meant that all except the more extreme conservatives on a city council would follow the popular trend for fear of disrupting the internal life of the city. In Nuremberg things moved rapidly toward such a climax as Luther's following grew apace during the years 1522–3, while the half-hearted restraints imposed by the council scarcely presented a façade of Catholic respectability toward the emperor and the princes.

[5] On Osiander see *ADB*; *ODCC*; Schottenloher, ii, nos. 26154–64. H. von Schubert and K. Schornbaum (note 1 above) are also useful. A former Wittenberg student, Osiander also belonged to the *Sodalitas Staupitziana*.

Nevertheless, Nuremberg's traditions were more warmly imperialist than those of most cities. Proud to recall the frequent residence of former emperors, the council had also several realistic motives.[6] Most obviously, a city with a big extramural territory and one which depended upon long-distance trade needed a stable imperial structure. Over and beyond these needs, the emperor seemed a natural ally against the rising power of the territorial princes. Ranke was long ago proved wrong in his contention that in earlier years Berthold von Henneberg and the princely reform party had intended to grant weightier imperial functions to the cities. The latter owed little to the princes but much more to the emperor. It was the government of Charles V which at the outset of his reign (1519) granted the imperial cities two seats on the Council of Regency. Again, when in 1521-3 the princes made persistent efforts to erect customs barriers along the frontiers of the empire, it was the imperial court—by this time in Spain—which quashed the plan, one doubly obnoxious to Nuremberg with its far-flung trade across these frontiers. When from 1524 to 1529 the Reformation had taken root, the Nuremberg council argued with the imperial government that the popular pressure had been so strong that they simply could not enforce legislation against Protestantism. On the other hand, Nuremberg and many other cities refrained from joining the Protestant militants led by Philip of Hesse. In other words, the internal pressures favoured the Reformation, while external pressures on the whole opposed its course. Italian governments were not the only ones confronted by intricate political chess-boards, and Guicciardini would have found a worthy subject for his powers of analysis had he sat alongside the patricians of Nuremberg. This situation persisted until 1529-30, when the emperor, having concluded peace with the pope and France, ceased making religious concessions and appeared all too likely to start enforcing Catholicism inside as well as outside the walls of the cities. Even the politically conservative Luther now began to see that the Protestants might have to resist in arms, yet Augsburg, Frankfurt, Regensburg and many others, in varying degrees and for varying periods, still sought to co-operate with the emperor. In Augsburg the Fuggers and other great

[6] H. Baron, especially pp. 415-23.

financiers inevitably became pillars of religious and political conservatism, if only on account of their loans to, and their mining concessions from, the Habsburgs. And while Nuremberg and the rest of the Franconian and Swabian cities were not faced by these banker's problems, they also began for different reasons to forfeit leadership in the Protestant movement. While they continued their refusal to eradicate that movement within their walls, their conciliatory attitudes toward the emperor nevertheless meant that the leadership of the Protestant Reformation would pass to a city capable—through both tradition and geography—of a much more vigorous defiance. This successor was Strassburg.

The Evangelical teaching accepted by so many Nuremberg citizens, and even councillors, seems exemplified by the cobbler-poet Hans Sachs, especially by his poem *The Wittenberg Nightingale*, written in 1523 when Sachs owned 40 of Luther's sermons and tracts in print. With admirable clarity, if in somewhat superficial terms, the poem stresses the complete impotence of the human will to obtain salvation, and in contrast the total omnipotence of God and the unique saving might of Christ.

> First Luther tells us that we all
> Inherit sin from Adam's fall,
> In evil lust and foul intent
> And avid pride our lives are spent;
> Our hearts are black and unrefined
> Our wills to horrid sins inclined,
> And God, who judges soul and mind
> Has cursed and damned all human kind.
> Within our hearts we know this state,
> Feel burdened with a dreadful weight
> Of anguish, fear, bewilderment
> That we should be so impotent.
> Sure of man's inability
> We change pride to humility
> And then, and only then, we see
> The Gospel, sent to make us free,
> For in it we find Christ, God's son
> Who for us men so much has done,
> Fulfilled the law, wiped clean the stain
> And won God's grace for us again.

There follows a catalogue of the low and depraved thoughts of mankind and a harsh caricature of Catholicism, which according to Sachs pretends to put you on the right track by observances, by candles and pilgrimages:

> Feasts by day and fasts by night,
> Confessions to your heart's delight.[7]

With equal propriety one might cite the diary of another Nuremberger far more famous, and yet like Sachs no professional theologian. 'There is nothing good in us', writes Albrecht Dürer, 'except it become good in Christ. Whosoever therefore wants to justify himself is unjust. If we will what is good, Christ wills it in us.' These laymen are only summarizing the message of the Lutheran preachers. To them we could add several others, including secretary Lazarus Spengler, whose writings show a fair understanding of Luther's central doctrines as early as 1520, before the popular preaching had taken effect. Everywhere the new Evangelical idea of salvation is superimposed upon a generation brought up in the fear of hell-fire and perhaps yearning for release from Catholicism's unbearable appeal to human choice and human willpower.

A social historian naturally looks for evidence showing that the social and economic aspirations of the poor were somehow a force behind the conversion, but unlike so many other places Nuremberg yields hardly any facts to support such a notion. Likewise it appears certain that the city council did not connive at the spread of Lutheran doctrines in order to secularize Church properties. In Nuremberg the city council and not the bishop of Bamberg already controlled benefices, schools, orphanages, hospitals, the collection and distribution of alms. Indeed, clean contrary to the popular impression, it was the medieval city which put social welfare into lay hands, while the Reformers sought to exercise it through ecclesiastical authority. As for religious houses, in 1524–5 the monks and friars of Nuremberg proved all too ready to accept pensions, but two nunneries chose

[7] G. Strauss, *Nuremberg in the Sixteenth Century*, p. 167. A general account is in G. Kawerau, *Hans Sachs und die Reformation* (*Schriften des Vereins für Reformationsgeschichte*, xxvi, Halle, 1889).

continuance and were permitted to survive until late in the century, dying out gradually through a prohibition against new entrants. While the learned abbess Charitas Pirckheimer beheld her life's work in ruins, her unsympathetic fellow-citizens avoided violent social-religious changes and experiments. Satisfied to remove clerical privileges, the council did not proceed—like the Zwinglians in Switzerland and the Bucerians in south-western Germany—to attempt that closer integration of clerics and lay governors which became the hallmark of Reformed as distinct from Evangelical societies.

Despite the need to avoid the hostility of the imperial government, the Lutheranizing of Nuremberg approached completion in the years 1524–5, while the pressure was still coming from below. At Easter 1524 thousands of citizens took communion in both kinds. The people openly satirized monks in general and the Dominicans in particular. Caricatures of the pope and the papal legate were passed from house to house. On the council Osiander and his colleagues pressed powerful Lutheran memoranda. Early in 1525 the city fathers became more closely involved as sponsors of the Carthusian monastery, the monks there having accused their own prior of heresy and demanded a public disputation. Accordingly in February the council ordered all the city's preachers, including those still faithful to Catholicism, to list what they deemed to be the essentials of Christian belief. These lists the council reduced to twelve main issues, and appointed 3 March as the day when the debate would be initiated. In the event this affair was manipulated in favour of the Protestant preachers. Of the four presiding officers, three were still nominally monks, but actually Lutherans or crypto-Lutherans. Again, besides the council, a prejudiced crowd of burghers packed itself into the Rathaus. On their side the Catholic priests made the mistake of talking to the laity *de haut en bas*, while the Lutherans found less difficulty in simplifying the complex religious issues. Needless to add, the council stipulated that all speeches should be in German and carefully recorded.

The minutes which precede this record show that the main concern of the council was to preserve local religious unity. Like most European rulers, they believed chaos would develop if two or more rival religions were disseminated from the pulpits. They already perceived that internal concord could now only be attained under a substantially Lutheran system; they hoped that by staging a public debate they would convince the waverers and cause them to join the Lutheran majority. In terms of sheer length and exhaustion this preach-in exceeded even its secular equivalents in our own day. Extending from 3 to 14 March, it traversed the burning issues of good works, Justification by Faith and the theology of the eucharist. At the finish Osiander appealed to the city fathers not to wait for a national council of the Church, but to establish there and then in Nuremberg the Scriptural religion enunciated by Luther. With characteristic aplomb, self-confidence and deliberation the councillors neither rushed matters nor consulted Luther prior to their decision. But three days later they suddenly expelled the chief Catholic preachers, ordered the rest to stop preaching, outlawed the Roman Mass, and soon afterwards published an Evangelical Mass of their own. They also abolished as unscriptural the veneration of saints, reduced the number of religious holidays, assumed an even more complete control of all ecclesiastical appointments, founded a training school for ministers and brought in Philip Melanchthon to advise on its curriculum.

With impressive swiftness and self-sufficiency—once its mind was made up—a body of patrician laymen thus erected nothing less than a territorial Church. As we shall see, many features of this revolution became widely characteristic in Germany: the pressure from a populace stirred by Lutheran sermons; the refusal of the council to permit rival pulpits; the emphasis upon appointing, controlling and training preachers. It remains a most impressive fact that these money-minded Nurembergers allocated no less than 1,000 gulden per annum to the instruction of ministers. Coming from this source, the figure indicates a certain measure of genuine religious conviction! Doubtless so early, so rapid, so decisive a break was exceptional among the German cities: it suggests not merely this element of conviction among the inner ring of councillors but a degree of political and military confidence which bade them place the internal unity of the city before the ancient respect of Nuremberg for the emperor's authority. In the last resort they were not deterred by the fear that the Catholic emperor would take reprisals. Yet in regard to this possibility, one should recall that from 1522 to 1529 the emperor remained in distant Spain, and that, despite his former dramatic stand against Luther at Worms, all men thought his future relations with the papacy were cloudy in the extreme.

We now move westward to Strassburg,[8] now a day's drive from Nuremberg but in the sixteenth century distant by a week's journey for a merchant with his wagon or pack-horses. At first sight a knowledgeable subject of Charles V might have been struck by the contrasts rather than the similarities between the two great imperial cities. Indeed such a contrast forms a major theme of Hans Baron's penetrating article, 'Religion and Politics in the German Cities during the Reformation'. Unlike Nuremberg, Strassburg had long stood at the head of urban militancy within the empire. Decades earlier it had sought to refuse imperial taxation and felt no very warm allegiance either to the imperial constitution or to the persons of the successive emperors. Geographically situated on the frontiers, Strassburg needed to temporize with the king of France and had found natural allies in her neighbours the Swiss. Alsatians could not remain oblivious to the fact that the Swiss had, not so long ago, cast off the Habsburg link. And while Nuremberg depended upon long-distance trade, profited from the integrity and unity of the empire and demanded a liberal imperial customs policy, Strassburg's economy allowed her to adopt more independent, more provincial attitudes. Her prosperity was closely bound up with the rich towns, the fertile fields and vineyards of Alsace and the Rhine valley.

On the other hand, it would not have proved difficult to list some positive comparisons. The two cities were approximately of the same size and population. In 1520 they still lacked universities and were thus free from at least one important type of internal instability. Though their internal struggles had pursued differing courses, by the year 1500 their governmental and social structures did not radically differ. Strassburg was likewise ruled by a small group of patricians, alert to curb the restiveness of the common people, the intrigues of bishops and

[8] On Strassburg I am deeply indebted to my friend Miriam U. Chrisman, whose admirable work embraces and extends those of Schmidt, Wendel, Rott and others.

ecclesiastics, the machinations of unsympathetic neighbouring states. Beginning in 1263, soon after it had expelled its bishop, the Strassburg council had ever-increasingly undertaken the appointment of parish clergy, the management of churches and hospitals, the relief of the poor. These processes had been facilitated, as at Nuremberg, by divisions among the clergy. There were constant feuds between the bishop and the so-called 'five chapters'—those of the cathedral and the main monastic houses—which were led by clerics of patrician background, and sided with the municipality against their ecclesiastical superiors. One may here recall that it was the cathedral chapter of Strassburg that Erasmus ridiculed when he said it was so exclusive that Christ himself would never have been elected to membership.

Examining early Reformation events in Strassburg, one senses in comparison with Nuremberg more liveliness and independence among the guilds and the lower orders in general. And so far as concerns the educated classes, there appears a certain parallel liveliness of spirit. Indeed, the records of human-ism and of social criticism had certainly been more interesting and distinguished in Strassburg than in Nuremberg. It was a proud moment when in 1514 the literary society headed by Wimpfeling greeted Erasmus, for amongst its members were Jakob Sturm, Thomas Vogler, Matthias Schurer, Hieronymus Gebwiler, Sebastian Brant. If one were parodying a stilted Renaissance dialogue between the two cities, one might feel a little tempted to personify Nuremberg as Vulcan, Strassburg as Mercury. But Nuremberg was not without its men of letters, while Strassburg's intellectual distinction was shared with other places in Alsace, especially with Schlettstadt, which also stood for a time among the leading half-dozen centres of German humanism.[9] Here in Alsace, indeed almost anywhere along the Rhine valley, we move recognizably along the track of Erasmus, a track prepared for him by forerunners. Even so, these men lacked that quality so often praised by the less reflective ad-mirers of Erasmus as internationalism, but which one might well prefer to call statelessness. At the Reformation, some of the literary Strassburgers had been educated at Basle; the rest were all alumni of German universities, and while they were prepared

[9] Pp. 25–8, 105 above. On Schlettstadt see the concise survey by P. Adam.

to haggle over imperial taxation and even to play off the king of France against the emperor, they had no doubt whatever that they were Germans. Wimpfeling's *Germany, in Honour of Strassburg* had typified Alsatian humanism by dwelling at length on the German inheritance of imperial power, on the Germanism of the early emperors, and in particular on the Germanic origins of Alsace. Of course, the emperors had needed to respond in kind: a famous letter of Maximilian I calls Strassburg the bulwark of the empire and commends its good old German honesty and courage.

What of the religious background on the eve of the Reformation? At Strassburg did anyone play the forerunner as Staupitz had done in Nuremberg? Surely there was an equivalent of sorts. That most renowned of late medieval German preachers Geiler von Kaisersberg thundered continuously from the pulpits of Strassburg from 1478 until his death in 1510, and thenceforward he continued as a best-seller in print, two or three editions of his sermons appearing annually from 1511 to 1522.[10] As we shall soon observe, the chief Protestant preacher of the early Strassburg Reformation was Matthäus Zell, and we find Zell fully acknowledging the great weight of Geiler's influence.[11] For his denunciation of ecclesiastical abuses Geiler has been compared with his contemporary Savonarola. If he remains anecdotal and moralistic in true medieval pulpiteering style, in another sense he is already looking forward, because at every stage of his argument he calls upon the Scriptures. Before Luther, even before Erasmus, Geiler von Kaisersberg strove to make the Bible meaningful to ordinary men and women. To the social historian he may well matter more than Staupitz, for he did not merely found a *sodalitas* among an educated minority: he also stirred the hearts of ordinary citizens by methods not so very different from those of the first Lutheran preachers, who reached Strassburg only a decade after his death.

None of the earliest recorded preachers of Luther's doctrines in Strassburg became a great local figure, but in the following year Matthäus Zell made his first impact. From his pulpit in the

[10] On Geiler see E. J. D. Douglas; E. C. Kiessling; C. Schmidt, vol. i, bk. iii. A summary account is in M. U. Chrisman, ch. 5.
[11] M. U. Chrisman, p. 78.

St. Laurence Chapel of the cathedral Zell defended Luther and denounced as rogues the antagonists who had raised the cry of heresy. In the early autumn he announced that he would preach the pure gospel of Jesus Christ, beginning with the *Epistle to the Romans*. Such vast crowds then poured into the cathedral that Zell asked leave to move into the nave and use the great stone pulpit built for Geiler in earlier years and standing intact to this day. When the canons refused and kept the entrance door locked, some of the neighbouring carpenters constructed a wooden pulpit which they carried into the cathedral for each sermon, and then removed to a private house later in the day. Could any local episode be more meaningful for Reformation history? Quite as characteristic was the sequel. When the bishop instituted proceedings against Zell, the canons denounced his action as an episcopal infringement of their ancient privileges, and they allowed Zell to continue preaching from his portable pulpit.

In 1522-3 a pamphlet war raged around Zell, but the council let him continue, adding a firm admonition to stick to the Word of God. Then two newcomers of the first rank arrived; Martin Bucer in March and Wolfgang Capito in May 1523. The former, who had already tasted adventure as chaplain to Franz von Sickingen, leader of the rebellious imperial knights, was already far from subservient toward Luther's theology. In these years Bucer seems also a far more militant figure than Bucer the ecumenical patriarch who died in Cambridge nearly thirty years later. Of equal immediate interest is the conversion by Zell of Capito, a leading Hebraist and a friend of Erasmus. Hitherto very much the cool humanist, Capito had recently served as court chancellor to Archbishop Albrecht of Mainz, that mundane beneficiary of the notorious Indulgence-campaign attacked by Luther. The Reformation owed much of its initial success to university-trained but lowly-placed clerics; yet this formula scarcely applies to Capito, who as provost of St. Thomas stood third in the Strassburg hierarchy after the bishop and the cathedral provost. At first the polished scholar was startled by the Evangelical bluntness of his former fellow-student Matthäus Zell, who in one of the most significant recorded conversations of these years drew a sharp line between the humanist and the preacher of the Word. The humanist, urged Zell, was distinguished by his desire for mere glory and worldly wisdom, by the narrowness of his contacts, so largely restricted to his brother-humanists. By contrast the preacher felt himself to belong to the whole community of men, and responsible to Christ for its salvation. 'We preachers', he added, 'are concerned alone for the common simple meaning of [the Scriptures], which we can communicate to the whole people.'[12] These arguments, which represent yet another democratic aspect of the urban Reformation, certainly won over Capito and so brought a superior style and scholarship to the cause. Not every humanist accepted these priorities. As we have seen, Eobanus Hessus certainly favoured Luther's cause, yet already in 1523 he showed himself alarmed by the tendency of preachers to despise humanism and secular knowledge; he feared that such men were the heralds of a new barbarism. And it may be added that the council of Strassburg, like those of some other cities, found Protestant preachers less tractable than it expected.

When both Zell and Capito incurred dismissal from their benefices, the citizens vociferously demanded that Capito be retained as one of the city preachers. Meanwhile the cathedral chapter encountered trouble when it tried to find a successor to Zell, since in turn each appointee amid popular applause declared himself a Reformer. The third of these hydra-heads was Capito's well-known follower Caspar Hedio, whom the chapter, sick of the struggle, finally left in the benefice despite his obvious Protestant sympathies. A further interesting case of popular intervention occurred in 1523 in the parish of St. Aurelie, which was dominated by a body with a reputation for secular militancy: the guild of gardeners. In their parish a minor Reformer called Altbiesser had briefly preached, but on his death the chapter of St. Thomas, proprietors of this parish church, appointed an elderly conservative. The gardeners then arose and demanded what they called 'a learned Christian man'. They already had their eyes upon the recently-arrived Martin Bucer: they sent a deputation to the city council and asked leave to demand his appointment. On this occasion they said they wanted 'a preacher who preached like others in the city. If the chapter was going to give them one who fiddled on the same

12 M. U. Chrisman, p. 110.

old note, they wanted to install a preacher at their own expense'. The council had no legal powers to appoint, and the notorious fact that Bucer had married before coming to Strassburg did not help his backers. But when, early in 1524, the chapter refused to compromise, the parishioners illegally installed Bucer.

At this stage no less than five of the nine Strassburg city parishes spontaneouly drew up a petition to the council which forms something of a landmark. It is a rather fumbling document but it vividly reflects the attitudes of laymen stimulated by Protestant sermonizing. These parishioners draw a sharp anti-thesis between the ignorant old priest and the educated preacher. They say they must have such preachers because they them-selves, their wives and children cannot otherwise attain the Word of God. Well endowed by their forefathers, the parishes can already boast a supply of university-trained clerics and should be taken over by the city. Then, in alarmingly secular terms, the parishioners grumble that they have to work hard every weekday and do not want their Sunday quiet to be disturbed by ecclesiastical pageantry, or by what they call 'the unnecessary howling of choirs'. *Bürgerlich* peace and unity, they add, would be restored by the appointment of godly preachers, who could be supported by a careful management of the old parish endowments, and would not necessitate new taxation. In sum, the common people of Strassburg wanted Bible-Christianity handed out by educated teachers and managed without undue financial outlay by their own city council.

Thus encouraged by pressure from below, the council now assumed the right of appointing to parish incumbencies on the grounds that the old patrons—in fact, the ecclesiastical chapters—had not done their duty, that disorder had developed, and that the parishioners themselves were forcibly installing preachers. The magistrates also ruled that, on appointment, new incumbents must swear loyalty to the city and the council. Characteristically their official edict says nothing about doctrine, not even about the 'pure Word of God'. Nevertheless, there could be no doubt as to the doctrines now favoured. One of the vital changes had occurred: a cautious and still divided city council had placated Protestant parishioners and, without tarrying overmuch for theology, had taken steps to establish Protestant teaching in the parishes. The council had indeed became an accomplice of the Reformers; it has assumed ecclesiastical functions which its members or their successors would never be likely to renounce in favour of any bishop or chapter. Whatever steps Protestant theology had failed to inspire had been suggested by the instinct of laymen to enlarge state-sovereignty at the expense of the Church. As events were soon to show, that instinct had become endemic throughout Europe.

In sum, one might make four observations on the Strassburg Reform. Among its personalities Matthäus Zell was no mean revolutionary: he had that sort of mind which cuts through the web of social and political tradition. Cautious in theology but radical in action, he shows the marks of Reformed rather than of Lutheran leadership.[13] Again, as an opposition local Catholicism was hamstrung by the internal feuds, by the narrow-minded, legalist corporate loyalties which had so long bedevilled Church life in medieval Europe. In the third place it may be doubted whether at any time before 1528 an actual majority of fully convinced Protestants existed on the Strassburg city council. Despite the early support given by that able statesman Jakob Sturm, we do not observe a coherent, organized Protestant party working consistently to execute major religious changes. One is reminded of Dutch city politics half a century later, of the so-called 'Erasmian' regent class dealing uneasily with the lower world of fiery Calvinist preachers and their aroused congregations. Between the 1520s and the 1570s the dogmas have been clarified and the political heat has mounted, yet the social and psychological patterns remain curiously similar. These patterns correspond in some measure with the power-structures evolved during the later Middle Ages. Yet the dichotomy within Strassburg lay not only between the politically responsible and the politically unprivileged, nor between rich merchant and poor craftsman. It was concerned also with education; it lay between the heirs of what we loosely label the Renaissance and, on the other hand, those excluded from that heritage, the less educated who had skipped the Renaissance but run full-tilt into that more classless phenomenon—the Reformation. The humanist might or might not stand by the cause of Protestant Reform, but his view

[13] M. U. Chrisman, *passim.*

of its possibilities and functions was bound to differ from the view of popular enthusiasts, clerical or lay.

A fourth and final observation concerns the sectarian or Radical branches of the Reformation, since one cannot leave Strassburg of all places without a glance in this direction. Anabaptist preachers were at work in the city as early as 1523, while in the following year the gardener Clement Ziegler founded a radical Christian brotherhood in an attempt to replace the beer-drinking and card-playing company in the gardeners' guildhall. In 1525 came the more famous Anabaptist Balthazar Hubmaier, and in 1526 a swelling stream of sectarian immigration. Up to this stage, nearly a decade before Europe supped on the horrors of Anabaptist Münster, Reformers like Zell retained a certain amount of sympathy with the sectarians, while Strassburg, unlike Nuremberg, prided itself upon the mild humanity of its laws. Even so, in the late 1520s and early 1530s the council began to lose patience. From 1529 many of the Radicals were expelled, yet as many continued to flood in. At one time or another most of the major sectarian Anabaptists and Spiritualists stayed in Strassburg; Reublin, Sattler, Hetzer, Denck, Marbeck, Hoffmann, Franck, even Servetus.[14] Both Bucer and Capito charitably concealed the extremism of Servetus, while Katharine Zell was not only a pamphleteer but a great social worker and protectress of all sorts of refugees, respectable and non-respectable.[15]

Yet when all is said and done, sectarianism was not the child of Strassburg, or in any special sense the offspring of big cities. The court records show that the great majority of its adherents were working-class people from all parts of Germany. Dr. Clasen's recent analysis of Swabian Anabaptism shows it as essentially a rural phenomenon, though the fact that persecuted Radicals fled to the more liberal cities like Strassburg doubtless forms a social comment of real interest. Though a few native Strassburgers

---

[14] M. U. Chrisman, ch. 11; R. Kreider, 'Anabaptists and the Civil Authority of Strasbourg 1526–1548' in *Church History*, xxiv (1955). The documents are in M. Krebs and H. G. Rott, *Elsass I and Elsass II, Quellen zur Geschichte der Täufer*, vols. vii–viii (Gütersloh, 1959–60). Bibliographical aid on Radicals is in G. H. Williams, *passim*; H. J. Hillerbrand, *Christendom Divided* (London and New York, 1971), pp. 332–3; F. Lau and E. Bizer, pp. 36–9, 64–7, 99–103.

[15] R. H. Bainton, *Women of the Reformation in Germany and Italy*, ch. 3.

associated with the sectarians, these links seem in general to have been ephemeral. Movement and flux dominate our picture of sectarianism, and it remains impossible even roughly to estimate how many of its devotees were residing in Strassburg at any one time. One observer says that 400 Anabaptists belonged to a cell which met near the Dominican convent; another, that 100 had arrived from Augsburg alone. But such figures can be misleading in the context of sixteenth-century religious evidence. And while for many years the sectarians had good reason to regard Strassburg as their main city of refuge, a more meaningful fact remains: that the great mass of Strassburg citizens loyally adhered to their own Reformed leaders Zell, Bucer, Capito and Hedio.

So much for this brief tale of two cities, which has at least introduced some leading social and religious agencies operating within German urban life during the early stages of the Reformation. There appear some divergences of outlook and of experience as between Nuremberg and Strassburg; yet striking similarities emerge as we trace the earlier backgrounds and the essential relations between council, preachers and citizens. Without further evidence, however, we cannot assume such common features to have been dominant throughout all Germany. We have already noticed, for example, that in Augsburg the parallel middle-class and popular support for the Reformation was complicated by the Catholicism and the Habsburg financial ties of the bankers, who had no parallels in either Nuremberg or Strassburg.[16] A much more basic deviation occurred in Cologne, where a good relation persisted between the municipality, the Catholic theologians, the prince-bishop Hermann von Wied and the ecclesiastical corporations. Cologne avoided sizeable Protestant movements and stayed Catholic even in the face of Hermann's own lapse in later years.[17] One crucial factor behind

---

[16] H. Baron, pp. 628ff.

[17] The detailed narrative is in L. Ennen, *Geschichte der Stadt Coeln* (5 vols., Cologne and Neuss, 1863–80), vol. iv. On the preceding events there, see the article by G. Eckertz. E. Keyser, *Deutsches Städtebuch-Rheinisches Städtebuch* (Stuttgart, 1956) has a long entry on Cologne. On church life and secular complications in the whole archdiocese of Cologne (which contained some twenty states) see L. Ennen, *Geschichte der Reformation im Bereiche der alten Erzdiözese Köln* (Cologne and Neuss, 1849).

this conservatism must have been economic, since the trade of Cologne depended very largely upon the Emperor's city of Antwerp, and to a lesser extent upon peaceful relations with the several Rhenish ecclesiastical states. If one merely selected these four cities, Nuremberg, Strassburg, Augsburg, Cologne, one might well hesitate to make any bold generalizations. Yet presently, as we move northward, more homogeneous patterns will become discernible.

8

Some Hanseatic Cities— and Erfurt

The secular complications which marked the course of the Reformation in some southern cities cannot be regarded as peculiar to that region. Even more markedly, the Lutheran Reformation found many northern places suffering economic decline and failing to resolve their old internal struggles. During the last years of the fifteenth century the far-flung Hanseatic world began to fall into disarray. From 1494 Ivan III closed its depot at Novgorod, which reopened ten years later but never regained its former importance. Soon afterwards the trading privileges of the Hansa suffered curtailment in Norway and at Bruges. More chaotically than ever, the cities competed with one another, and several in effect allowed their membership of the League to lapse. Meanwhile, acting insidiously through northern agents, the Fuggers of Augsburg established during the first two decades of the sixteenth century a considerable measure of financial control over the Baltic trade.[1]

The Reformation, preached in so many north German towns in or soon after the year 1522, added not a little to the disruption begun by political and economic factors. Almost everywhere the guilds and the populace accepted the Lutheran missionaries,

---

[1] For general background see P. Dollinger, especially pt. iii. Apart from the references below and those given by B. Moeller, *Reichsstadt und Reformation*, several important books and articles on northern cities occur in F. Lau and E. Bizer, p. 60 and in the bibliographies of recent numbers of *Archiv für Reformationsgeschichte*. A notable account of a complex case is that by H. Müller, *Die Réformation in Essen* (*Beiträge zur Geschichte von Stadt und Stift Essen*, lxxxiv (1969)).

though for some years both the ruling patriciates and the neighbouring princes tended to support the old beliefs. And while in 1525 the Hanseatic Diet made a belated attempt to impose order by denouncing what it called the Martinist sect, no strong or co-ordinated action followed within the towns themselves since, irrespective of his religious beliefs, no citizen wanted internal affairs to be regulated either by the League or by any ecclesiastical authority. In general Lutheranism deepened or revived the rifts between the ruling councils and the rest of the citizenry, yet the latter, beset by conflicting social and economic partisanships, failed on the whole to make Lutheranism a path toward permanent urban democracy. In the case of the Baltic cities of Stralsund, Rostock and Wismar, Dr. Schildhauer has made a detailed study of this interaction between religious, social and political dissent. He is a Marxist, but not unduly given to ideological simplification or to ignoring the religious motive.[2]

Engaging in Europe-wide commerce, these three places had never attained the political status of imperial cities, yet they had been granted by the medieval rulers of Mecklenburg and Pomerania a high degree of internal self-government. This stable situation changed from the late fifteenth century, when the dukes of both states began to centralize administration and to increase their tax revenues from cities, clergy and nobles, the last-named being the most powerful group within their provincial estates. While for the time being these cities retained most of their liberties as against both princes and local bishops, the weight of taxation became a disruptive force within their walls. The ruling oligarchies used much of the money to finance the frequent maritime campaigns which benefited themselves rather than their subjects. Municipal taxes bore most heavily upon the middle groups, the smaller merchants and mastercraftsmen, while below them about half the town populations consisted of almost propertyless artisans. In other words, the mass of the population had either something to gain or nothing to lose by a redistribution of power. They were increasingly

[2] In my consideration of these three cities I rely almost solely upon Dr. Schildhauer's work, but (as will appear) similar patterns occur in other places—as described by non-Marxists.

disposed to use forcible tactics, the more so when they saw their councillors mismanaging municipal finances, distributing offices to favourites, and even intriguing with the dukes in order to preserve a monopoly of power.

On the other side, these middle and lower classes disliked the ecclesiastical establishment quite as heartily as they disliked its secular counterpart. In all three cities the number of parish clergy, monks and friars was large, and in order to survive many had to grasp in an uncharitable fashion at every petty source of revenue. The natural resentment of poor people against rich and blue-blooded bishops and canons was thus not counterbalanced by any affection for the lower clergy. Here, and in German cities everywhere, innumerable popular slogans and rhymes—later exploited by Protestant propaganda—bewail the burden imposed by ecclesiastics who will not share the duties and taxes of the urban community.

> The parsons, monks and nuns
> Are only a burden upon the earth...
> They will not become burghers.

Making the most of every clerical scandal, the laity deeply resented the power of churchmen to cite them in the ecclesiastical courts. Even more did they detest that onerous and soulimperilling punishment, the ban of the Church imposed upon sinners, notorious anticlericals or people who haggled unduly over ecclesiastical taxation. Even had Leo X, Albrecht of Mainz and their agents the Fuggers not abused the Indulgence system, the Church had already allowed to develop in the cities formidable groups of hostile or lukewarm people, all too ready to see clerical religion as a forced affair, a burden both to their souls and their purses. On the eve of Luther's advent, Stralsund, Rostock and Wismar exemplified such combustible situations, threatening Church and city governments alike.

Throughout the Baltic lands and indeed most of the north, humanism had by 1520 made relatively little impact upon public opinion, and one should not equate the mental atmosphere of these mercantile Hanseatic communities with that of Strassburg or even Nuremberg.[3] On the other hand, ideas of religious

---

[3] J. Schildhauer, pp. 83–6.

reform did not suddenly burst upon an unprepared northern world. If has recently been shown that Hussite doctrines— probably mixed with Wycliffite teaching from the outset—had attained considerable strength in the Baltic towns.[4] Again, it is clear that the Franciscan and Augustinian friaries in these places had already inclined to radical reformism, and when the Lutheran movement appeared, these houses did not merely furnish it with individual preachers but with active centres of organization. Even more notoriously, this became true of the Premonstratensian house at Belbuck in Pomerania where Johann Bugenhagen, the future apostle of northern Lutheranism, had been appointed teacher in the monastic school.

Before the end of 1521 Luther's pupil Antonius von Preen and other known favourers of the new doctrines were holding clerical appointments in Rostock and probably influencing local opinion. In Stralsund the first preachers appear to have been active by the autumn of 1522 or at latest by the spring of 1523, while two sermons by Lutherans are known to have been delivered at Wismar at the Easter of 1524, one of them before Duke Albrecht of Mecklenburg. Ample evidence shows that Luther's ideas immediately attracted support from the middle and lower strata of the three town populations, the first audiences consisting largely of master-craftsmen, artisans and harbour-workers. On some occasions the churches would not hold the crowds, and sermons had to be preached in the open air. It would seem wholly unrealistic to imagine that these 'common men' stood listening for hours, while yet uninterested in the new religious message; or that their attraction toward the Reformation sprang merely from malice toward their complacent secular and spiritual overlords. Nevertheless it remains apparent that the popular Reformation and the fight to democratize urban constitutions ran parallel and connected courses within the Hanseatic cities: in some considerable measure, the two movements overlapped and afforded each other mutual support. Where we can trace their social origins, nearly all the early preachers themselves can be shown to come from the ranks of the dynamic lower and middle urban groups. Obviously, the degree of overlap between the secular and the religious movement

[4] *Ibid.*, p. 107.

cannot be stated with precision. Yet leaving aside the known personalities, within such relatively small citizen groups the two movements cannot possibly have proceeded in psychological and social isolation from each other. Needless to add, it was not long before Anabaptism also reached these northern coasts, where it appealed to the most militant spirits and perhaps absorbed those enthusiasms aroused not many years earlier by left-wing Hussite contacts.

During the later 1520s the secular and religious struggles developed along similar lines in all three cities. In each place the opposition comprised the lesser merchants, the master-craftsmen and all the plebeian groups: it soon set up large citizen committees which forced the councils to accept their guidance. During this stage Lutheran preachers were placed in charge of the churches, while the religious houses passed into more or less voluntary liquidation. In Stralsund, however, the mob staged an attack on churches and monasteries, thus demonstrating its strength both to the hierarchy and to the propertied classes in general. From the lower end of the opposition there emerged a left wing of artisans, labourers, boatmen and servants, who together with the paupers and beggars threatened to constitute a permanent revolutionary force. But with this element the leaders of the opposition saw no reason to identify themselves, once they had grasped through the citizen committees a firm hold upon municipal policy. Except in Rostock, these leaders, mostly prosperous men, won some places on the councils themselves, and thenceforth their attitudes soon began to resemble those of the conservative patricians. They did not merely enter city government; they accepted its exclusiveness and unaccountability. No longer supported by the mass of the townspeople, the citizen committees lingered on with declining influence and were ultimately dissolved in 1536–7. The plebeians meanwhile attempted to create new committees, or even demanded that council decisions be voted upon by the whole citizen community; yet they lacked leadership, cohesion and a clear sense of their own objectives. As the burgher opposition thus split apart, the Lutheran pastors, disturbed by religious radicalism among the democrats, sided with the forces of conservatism. And since it proved possible to contain the radical sectarians, the Lutheran Reformation thus found itself the fortunate beneficiary, once the secular struggle died down and power remained with the enlarged yet by no means demo-cratized councils. Not long afterwards the whole Lutheran church organization fell increasingly under the management of the dukes of Mecklenburg and Pomerania. With this process the Reformation ended by weakening the control hitherto exerted by these particular councils over the churches within their respective cities.

A comparable pattern has been traced—though in less depth and detail—in the towns of Westphalia. Theodor Legge's researches into their sermons, pamphlets and municipal records convinced him that the Reformation movement was rather loosely linked with Luther's religious propaganda, and that its chief strength arose from a remarkably powerful fund of anti-clericalism. Many Westphalians displayed a cautious yet hard-headed, critical and materialistic outlook. Some indeed came to a conservative standpoint, acknowledging the serious nature of Luther's case, while yet arguing that many issues at stake—especially those *Bagatellen* concerning saints and images—supplied no grounds for rending the Church asunder. On the whole, this proved a slow-moving area. In places like Lippstadt and Herford, where there were influential houses of Augustinian friars, Luther rapidly found agents and the Reforma-tion was preached early in the 1520s. But in almost all other places, it began late and made slow progress; moreover, it seems to have been less a religious than a democratic and social movement. For this latter the stage had been set well before Luther's advent. During several decades of economic decline and growing fiscal burdens, the tax exemptions secured by the religious foundations had inflamed all classes of lay society. Moreover, many clerical corporations had vigorously under-taken trading and manufacturing on their own account, their enterprise and unfair privileges becoming notorious through their large purchases of property hitherto in lay hands.

Such charges against grasping churchmen are made in the pamphlet *Claws Bur* (1523) and in other popular manifestos of the period. The tension became especially chronic in Paderborn, a city striving to recover from a major attack of the plague and a destructive fire. At length, during the annual May Day festivities of 1528, a bloody riot developed between the young workmen and the retainers of the cathedral chapter. Several of the participants were left dead upon the square, while the residences of the canons underwent looting. The bishop punished the city with a fine, while the text of the concord signed between him and the council strongly suggests that the grievances of the burghers against the clergy were at bottom economic, not religious. The document mentions the Reformation in only one clause. This secular analysis of the trouble was in fact maintained by writers at Paderborn later in the century. Likewise at Soest in autumn 1531, satirical verses against the clergy were set up on the pillory and measures were taken by the council to arrest the decline of trade and industry by protecting the burghers against ecclesiastical competition. In short, the Westphalian evidence shows little public indignation against superstition and doctrinal error, little partisanship for the Protestant gospel. On the other hand it attests not only criticism against clerical privilege but a sharp sense of the disproportion between the wealth of the monasteries and the small number of their religious inmates. Nevertheless, toward this crisis Protestant preaching appears to have made a distinct contribution. Though a large reservoir of economic resentment had built up, the dam held so long as the people accepted the papal, episcopal, sacerdotal and monastic hierarchy as God-given. When, however, it seemed to many that the Reformers had exposed the falsity of this assumption, the frail barrier broke and the clergy were inundated by a flood of unpopularity.[5]

The experiences of these cities resembled in many respects the experience of the richer and more powerful city of Lübeck, where we need not rely on historians of Marxist inclination. Here the interplay of political and religious causes merged with an aggressive foreign policy to produce events of a more sensational character. Several leading members of the old patrician council had relatives who held lucrative prebends

---

[5] T. Legge, especially pp. 118–22, 152. He claims that this social interpretation had been substantially maintained by another regional historian thirty years earlier: F. Landmann, *Das Predigtwesen in Westfalen* (Münster, 1900).

and other emoluments in the Church. Their natural hostility
to the Lutheran Reformation was increased by their anxiety
to avoid the emperor's displeasure, which might redound
to the disadvantage of a city with international ambitions.
On the other hand the council members largely belonged to
old established *rentier* families, opposed not merely by the
guilds and the populace, but by a powerful middle group of
virile and enterprising merchants. These latter included the
future popular leader Jurgen Wullenwever, formerly of
Hamburg, where his brother was in fact to become a leader of the
local Reformation party.

The Lübeck story during the decisive years 1528–30 has been
related in minute detail by Jannasch from the voluminous
documentary sources, and it shows some obvious parallels with
the experiences of the Wendish cities described by Schildhauer.
For some years the heavy strains upon Lübeck's finances had
caused the council to make ever-increasing demands for taxes,
and between 1528 and 1530 it negotiated with a succession of
citizen committees, which were gradually enlarged from a
membership of 36 to one of 100. With rising emphasis these
committees demanded concessions in return for their compliance
with the council. They insisted upon the imposition of heavier
taxes upon the clergy, churches and monasteries. Still more
vociferously did they demand that the ecclesiastical authorities
and the council should secure the appointment of 'good preachers'
to the city pulpits. The community was only prepared to come to
terms in matters of taxation if the council did likewise in Church
matters. Though doubtless stimulated by the intermittent visits
of Lutheran missionaries and by news of Evangelical preaching
in neighbouring towns, the demand did not in 1528 arise from
anything like a solidly Protestant citizen body. As yet the convinced Lutherans still formed a minority, while even at the end
of 1528 the bishop and cathedral chapter remained influential
enough to secure the expulsion of prominent Lutheran preachers.
On the other hand the orthodox ecclesiastics, though to some
extent aware of their peril, signally failed to find and appoint
Catholic preachers. Had such been forthcoming, and had they
made some intelligent concessions to the confused clamour for
Christianity according to the Gospel, the Lübeck Reformation

could at least have been weakened and postponed. In the event victory passed to the Lutherans largely by default of their opponents.[6]

By the summer of 1530 the citizen committee, now led by the powerful Wullenwever, had realized its objectives. While obtaining virtual control of the municipal finances, it attacked the former anti-Lutheran measures with such force that the council recalled the preachers and allowed them free utterance in the churches. Within a few months Bugenhagen, now Luther's chief agent in the northern lands, arrived to organize an Evangelical Church and to preside over the abolition of the Mass and the religious houses. The valuable plate of the monasteries was melted down and used to pay for the Danish war. Since the fourteenth century—when alongside the Rathaus the Lübeckers had built their Marienkirche far bigger than the bishop's cathedral—episcopal power had been weak, and the churchmen offered little resistance. Nevertheless, before long the enthusiasts for Reformation ran into difficulties of another sort.

Wullenwever now ruled Lübeck through the citizen committee, and having driven out his chief rivals he obtained by 1533 legal election as burgomaster. Considering the strength of his position and many circumstances favourable to his activist foreign policy, the nemesis came with surprising speed. In order to dominate the Sound and thus exclude their Dutch rivals from the Baltic, the Lübeckers sought to make a pawn of King Frederick of Denmark, who was not only fighting his nephew Christian for the succession but also confronting a division between his Catholic nobles and his Protestant townsmen and peasants. Wullenwever tried to seize upon Danish weakness by arousing all the Hanseatic cities, but apart from Rostock and Wismar these 'natural' allies gave him little or no support. And while he obtained an encouraging subsidy from Henry VIII of England, he managed to quarrel with a figure of more weight in the Baltic world: Gustavus Vasa of Sweden, then laying the foundations of a great dynasty and executing a royal Reformation

---

[6] W. Jannasch, bk. iv, chs. 1–3, especially pp. 211–31, 251–71; he ends in 1530, after which the Wullenwever story is told by several others, e.g. P. Dollinger. On another instructive Hanseatic story, see K. Beckey, *Die Reformation in Hamburg* (Hamburg, 1929).

somewhat similar to the one in England. Wullenwever also offended his own Protestant supporters by continuing to back the Danish claimant Christian II, even when the latter professed Catholicism in order to secure Habsburg support. Even so, for a brief space events favoured the plan. In alliance with the Count of Oldenburg, the Lübeck forces brilliantly captured Copenhagen and the Sound in the summer of 1534. Yet on King Frederick's death the new claimant, Duke Christian of Schleswig (Christian III) united the Danish leaders and concluded alliances with the Elector of Brandenburg and the dukes of Pomerania and Brunswick. Forced into a truce by November of that year and then losing his hold upon Copenhagen, Wullenwever tried gallantly to maintain the struggle. At length, imprudently crossing the lands of the Catholic archbishop of Bremen, he found himself delivered to his enemy the duke of Brunswick, who extorted confessions from him by torture and after a prolonged trial had him executed in 1537. In Lübeck itself, the patrician council recovered power, yet it now found itself quite unable to eradicate Lutheranism, which had established a strong hold over the population during Wullenwever's period of ascendancy. Apart from all this warlike foreign policy, the social and religious developments at Lübeck hence resembled those of the smaller Baltic cities.

Much further east lay the Prussian provinces including Ermeland, and in these a comparable basic pattern was associated with secular factors of a somewhat different kind.[7] In 1466 the Teutonic Order had been forced to return West Prussia and Ermeland to their rightful rulers, the kings of Poland. Even before this date the prevalence of Hussite beliefs had caused much concern to the Grand Master of the Order and to the local hierarchy. Again, so far from retaining a primitive simplicity, the Church had its full quota of immoral priests, sinecure pluralists and lay anticlericalism: throughout this German-Slav frontier it faced a crisis of confidence similar to that apparent elsewhere in Europe. The low morale of the regular clergy is suggested by a precipitate flight from their houses in Braunsberg and Elbing at the first breath of the Protestant Reformation.

[7] Here I draw upon the erudite but somewhat compressed article by the distinguished Polish scholar H. Zins.

Even so, the bishops and chapters remained influential. They were exceptionally large landowners, while the towns remained small and, apart from Braunsberg, where the citizens overthrew the council in 1525, they lacked economic weight. Nevertheless the councils and people waged internal strife similar to that we have just observed further west, while the Reformation was likewise closely related to the popular pressure for constitutional change. Following the activities of Lutheran preachers and the conversion in 1525 of the Grand Master of the Order, Albrecht of Hohenzollern, the struggle in Ermeland lay between two main parties. The conservatives were headed by Moritz Ferber, bishop of Ermeland from 1523 to 1537, who sprang of a family of Danzig patricians, enjoyed membership of the Polish senate and received backing from the Catholic king of Poland. On the other side were ranged the town populations, mainly German by race and getting support from Albrecht, who secularized the lands of the Order, making himself duke of Prussia under nominal Polish suzerainty. He thus stood among the earliest princes to carry through a sweeping Reformation.[8] In the pro-Polish view of bishop Ferber, 'the larger Prussian towns, and especially Danzig, were inclined to revolt as a result of Lutheran separatism and in the event of renewed hostilities to go over to the side of the Grand Master, who is the chief supporter of this sect'. In the end the Polish monarchy, while seeking without marked success to discourage Lutheranism in those towns under its direct sovereignty, could not seriously hamper the state-aided Reformation in the ducal lands.

Far to the west in the North Sea port of Bremen, a relatively liberal constitution allowed new wealth to enter the magic circle of the council. Nevertheless, on the sidelines there stood an archbishop with strong Catholic views and ambitions to regain whatever he could of the powers lost by his predecessors, who centuries earlier had been effective overlords of Bremen. In other respects Christoph of Brunswick-Wolfenbüttel exemplified the worst type of aristocratic German prelate: immoral, extravagant, untrustworthy, subject to violent impulses. Allowing his soldiers freedom to despoil the peasantry, he incurred the cordial hatred of city and countryside alike. Such a figure was

[8] See W. Hubatsch.

hardly the one to defend the old Church within a commune so strong and independent as Bremen. By way of melodramatic contrast, the Bremen Reformation soon came to be led by an authentic hero, Heinrich of Zütphen, a member of the Augustinian Order and one of Luther's earliest friends at Wittenberg.[9] Returning to his native Netherlands in 1522, Heinrich was arrested when preaching on the banks of the Scheldt near Antwerp. The night before his intended removal to Brussels and a certain death, a crowd led by women broke into his gaol and allowed him to escape from the Netherlands, where the Habsburgs could, and did, persecute with vigour. Heading for Wittenberg, he made a detour through Bremen, but was encouraged to stay there by enthusiastic supporters. Though the council gave him no positive assistance it tolerated his preaching, presumably because this was popular among the common people. The citizens refused to allow his attendance at a provincial council summoned to Buxtehude by the archbishop. Aggressively they sallied forth and destroyed the neighbouring abbey of St. Paul; then called two additional Lutheran preachers to their churches.

Soon afterwards Heinrich embarked upon a more hazardous mission to convert the peasant farmers of the district of Dithmarschen across the Elbe, and among them he found some sponsors. Yet these communities, which had so proudly upheld their rights against local princes, did not as yet favour religious innovations, and in December 1522 they were incited by the Dominican prior of Meldorf to seize Heinrich and summarily to execute him by burning. Luther himself published a moving account of this early martyr, while the episode contributed not a little to the advance of the Evangelical cause in Bremen, and even in Dithmarschen. After some vicissitudes Lutheranism found complete acceptance at Bremen in 1528, though the city had to wage a running fight with the obnoxious archbishop for the remaining thirty years of his life. Finally it dashed his hopes by withstanding two imperialist sieges during the Schmalkaldic War. By the year 1529 several north-western towns stood alongside Bremen: Hamburg, Flensburg, Husum, which were joined far to the south by that ancient home of emperors, Goslar. And when

[9] *ADB*, s.v. Heinrich von Zütphen; Christoph, Erzbischof von Bremen.

in February 1531 six princes and ten leading cities signed the charter of the Schmalkaldic League, Bremen and Magdeburg were among them, while Brunswick, Göttingen, Goslar and other northern places joined not many months later.

In the face of these facts and many others, it cannot be argued that the solid northern burghers were tardy supporters of the Reformation. It is true that humanist criticism and intellectual curiosity could not boast a long or distinguished record in the north, yet the crucial decisions to accept Lutheranism did not in the main depend upon the local record of such differing and sometimes dubious contributors. In each case we have just observed, the effective pressure to join the cause came neither from scholars nor from patricians within the cities but from the eager adherence of the restive middle and lower citizen groups to a small but determined band of missionaries. Again, the dramatic scene in Dithmarschen suggests that cool social analysis, vital as it is for modern historiography, does less than justice to the occasional acts of heroism or emotion, the glowing personalities, which could affect the issue in a given place. Westphalia alone provides a number of such high dramas. At Soest the council gave way to the people and allowed some Lutheran preaching. Nevertheless in July 1533 it arrested a Protestant tanner named Schlachtorp who, flushed by wine, had abused the council and could thus be condemned for sedition. In the event the manoeuvre failed, since he adopted the posture of a religious martyr, and at the place of execution led the sympathetic crowd in singing the hymn *In peace and joy I journey hence*. The headsman, perhaps unnerved by this turn of events, missed his aim and wounded Schlachtorp in the back, upon which the victim arose, snatched the sword and was carried amid public acclamation to his home. Sad to say, he died later and was buried in pomp with the sword on his coffin. Yet these events led to the fall of the old council at Soest and the adoption of Lutheranism by its successor.[10]

Not long beforehand a similarly affecting scene had occurred thirty miles away at Paderborn, where a popular tumult had

[10] K. R. Hagenbach, trans. E. Moore, *History of the Reformation in Germany and Switzerland* (Edinburgh, 1878), pp. 211–12. On the Reformation at Soest, see A. E. Berger, *Satirische Feldzüge*, pp. 146–93.

brought about the assignment of certain churches to the Lutherans. On the occasion of an official visit by the Elector Hermann von Wied of Cologne, the council was encouraged by the canons to arrest, imprison, torture and condemn the leaders of the democratic faction. Nevertheless at the final moment the executioner refused to despatch innocent men, while the crowd, headed by weeping women, besought the Elector's mercy. Though not yet converted to the new doctrines, Hermann himself shed tears and pardoned the offenders. In this case, however, Lutheranism continued under repression and Paderborn has remained a predominantly Catholic city.[11] Again not far distant, the unique story of Münster has been too often told to detain us here, yet it bears a certain relevance to the urban norms, since it indicates the explosive result which might have followed more often, had rulers made no concession to 'moderate' reforming demands.[12] At Münster the snatching of leadership by Anabaptists, both native and Netherlandish, led with a horrible inevitability to the prolonged siege, the excesses of crazed demagogues, the bloody retribution by the forces of the prince-bishop and his allies. Yet in general this notorious episode did not convey lessons of tolerance to contemporary observers. Catholics and Lutherans alike regarded it as an appalling glimpse of that abyss of chaos into which society threatened to relapse.

When, however, all the sensational episodes have been given their due, it must be acknowledged that this first generation conducted the struggle without gigantic religious persecutions and crusades, even without a period of civil war so prolonged and widespread as the formidable massing of forces seemed to prophesy. In not a few places, both northern and southern, abusive polemics were followed by a fair measure of common-sense and tolerance. Cities like Erfurt, Augsburg and Frankfurt-am-Main were among the first in Europe to affirm and prove what almost everyone else disbelieved: that the rival religions could coexist within one political community.

Amongst all the central and northern places none affords a more complex and interesting spectacle than Erfurt, the great

[11] K. R. Hagenbach, *op. cit.*, pp. 212–13.
[12] A referenced account of the Münster episode will be found in G. H. Williams, ch. 13.

university city of Thuringia, academically famous a century before it became the scene of Luther's early career.[13] The many-towered city stood at a great crossroads, and it grew rich by levying heavy transit dues rather than through industrial enterprise. 'The university of Erfurt', says Luther in the *Table Talk*, 'used to be of such standing and repute that all others in comparison might be looked upon as high schools.' Yet he also genially refers to it as 'a bawdy house and a beer house', and he remarks that the 'courses' given in such places were the ones most regularly attended by the students. On the other hand, the circle of scholars around Mutianus had made Erfurt one of the two or three leading centres of German humanism. Again, it so abounded in religious foundations as to be called 'a little Rome'. It had experienced emotional religious revivals and had rebuilt two of its churches upon a grandiose scale. This complexity was paralleled in its political life. Though ranked as the sixth most populous place in Germany, Erfurt had abandoned its claims to be an imperial city. It belonged to an isolated territory under the lordship of the distant Archbishop-Elector of Mainz. Yet this area was surrounded by the lands of the House of Wettin, with the result that the Elector of Saxony also claimed a special authority over Erfurt.

These two connections complicated the 'normal' rivalries between council, burghers, and students. All these groups stood in opposition to the phalanx of Mainz officials and supporters permanently resident in Erfurt, upholding the archbishop's rights, collecting his revenues and deriving support from his considerable patronage. On the other hand Erfurt did not participate in the Saxon Estates, yet could only trade through a screen of Saxon customs duties, payable in addition to those demanded by the archbishop. To these peculiar conditions could be added some severe economic problems. Though the chief European market for woad, then so extensively used for dyeing textiles, Erfurt had failed to develop any important secondary manufactures. At the meeting-place of several major trade-routes, it had long served as gateway to the Slav lands, but since

[13] On Erfurt, my information comes largely from my associate R. W. Scribner. Of the older books, those by P. Kalkoff and F. W. Kampschulte require corrections, but are still useful. See also M. von Hase.

1500 had largely ceded this role to Leipzig, the managerial and financial centre of the rapidly expanding copper and silver mines in the region. To this tale of multiple tensions and a declining economy, the academic population added its special problems. Like that of Cologne, the university of Erfurt was not only old and well-attended, but a civic foundation. It owed little more than titular obedience to the archbishop, but all too readily it became a factor in city politics. In the 'mad year' of 1509 local grievances had boiled over amid great destruction and intermittent bloodshed wrought mainly by the mob and the student malcontents. Yet the recollection of these events—and of the seven long years of faction and intrigue which followed them—may well have had a sobering effect upon participants in the Reformation. There remained a widespread desire to prevent the new struggle developing to the old danger-point. Moreover the city council proved itself astute and unscrupulous: it was to play off the Mainz interest against the Saxon Electors, and the latter against their Catholic cousin Duke George, ruler of the Albertine lands of the Wettins. As we shall see, the council even manipulated in its own interest the rebellious peasantry of 1524-5.

From the summer of 1519 to that of 1521 the Erfurt humanists, led by Luther's friend Crotus Rubeanus and by his future associates Justus Jonas and the Augustinian Johannes Lang, obtained a strong footing within the hitherto theologically-dominated university. As yet, however, these men stood for reforms of the type advocated by Erasmus, and during these early years they seem not to have realized the more disturbing implications of Luther's theology. Chosen rector of the university in 1520, Crotus wrote advising Luther not to become involved in the ugly political debates, above all not to get his name added to that of Huss in the martyrologies. In fact some of the older masters and city clerics were pressing the university to publish the papal Bull against Luther; but, sensing violent anti-papalism among the students and younger graduates, the authorities refused. An Erfurt pamphlet, circulating late in 1520 and printed in May 1521, denounced this 'heretical' Bull on behalf of the masters and bachelors: it claimed that if the Prophets, the Gospels and St. Paul had spoken the truth, then Martin Luther was also teaching true Christianity. About this time Lang suggested to Spalatin that the strongly-defended city could serve as a place of refuge for Luther. When in April 1521 Luther stayed at Erfurt on his way to the Diet of Worms, he was formally received by Crotus and other university officials, being greeted with warmth not only by these former colleagues but by the other citizens, a large body of whom followed him for some distance when he departed on the next stage of his journey.

These actions inspired the deans of the collegiate chapters to prosecute the canons who had greeted Luther, but they were soon intimidated by student hostility and dropped the plan. In May Crotus marked the end of his period of office with an official report: it ended with an artistic device displaying his own arms surrounded by those of a bevy of humanists and reformers, including Erasmus, Reuchlin, Mutianus and Luther. He also spoke of the last-named as one who had 'dared as the first after many centuries to chastise Roman pride with the sword of Holy Scripture'. Eobanus Hessus likewise celebrated Luther's recent visit by a poem hailing him as the man who had completed the work of Erasmus by restoring the pure Word of God. Perhaps the first of the Erfurt group to draw theologically abreast of Luther was Jonas, but the evidence coincides with his move in June–July 1521 to Wittenberg, whence he wrote letters contrasting Wittenberg's amazing progress in godly learning with the cold conservatism of Erfurt. Meanwhile a deadlock ensued at the latter, where the deans denounced the supporters of the now outlawed Luther as heretics. So challenged, Lang for the first time wrote a self-defence which amounted to a full-fledged championship of Luther the Reformer. By this time the 'Martinist' students had decided that mere verbal protests made no impact upon the entrenched forces of the Church, and they decided upon a violent demonstration. Helped by journeymen, apprentices, and even by peasants coming in to market, they spent two nights (11–12 June) demolishing forty-four houses belonging to the canons, as well as the consistory court. This *Pfaffensturm* was meticulously planned, and the city council, which doubtless rejoiced at the lesson administered to the over-mighty clerics, did nothing to restrain it until, having served this purpose, it threatened to get out of hand and had to be terminated. The anticlericalism of the students, who resented the attack on Lang, must have differed in quality from that of the working-class burghers who, like those we observed in the Baltic cities, are known to have resented the tax immunities of the cathedral and the collegiate churches. And whatever its role in these events, the city council used them to force the chapters into paying protection money. Some of Luther's admirers openly greeted the riot as a triumph for the Reformation, and before long the pope was complaining to Erfurt's overlord, Albrecht of Mainz, that the rector of the university had organized the affair. As for the Erfurt humanists, they could hardly do other than join with the theologians in the official apology issued by the university.

In the period which followed, progress toward a Lutheran Church settlement occurred by gradual stages. During the last months of 1521 monks and nuns began to leave their houses. In March 1522, having obtained permission from the Thuringian authorities of their Order, Lang and fourteen other Augustinians abandoned their convent. Shortly afterwards the council gave permission to four priests of known Lutheran sympathies to preach at specified churches: they included Lang, who now decisively took the lead in the Erfurt Reformation, even to the extent of defending clerical marriage. The movement was also guided from Wittenberg by Luther, who in former years had witnessed the capacity of the Erfurt population for violence and now counselled caution and forbearance. Accompanied by Melanchthon, he briefly visited Erfurt in October 1522 and preached in the church of the merchants, which was already managed by a group of his ardent admirers. In July 1523 communion was first administered to the laity in both kinds, while in the same month local priests began to contract marriages without opposition from the council. During this year the utterances of a number of ex-monks and semi-educated popular preachers encouraged Luther's former tutor von Usingen to depict the movement as essentially illiberal and anti-intellectual, a notion which soon occurred even to those who did not share von Usingen's conservative zeal. Eobanus, though committed to the Reformation, protested to Luther and other correspondents that in place of the old superstitions various new menaces were arising: libertinism, contempt for secular authority, attacks upon learning as an impious luxury. Such strictures, thought by some to be aimed at Lang, prompted the latter to preach and publish a university sermon reconciling Lutheran Scriptural doctrine with classical studies. From this position he proceeded to denounce the radical enthusiasts who wanted to abandon that very learning which had contributed so greatly to revive the Gospel and to liberate it from servitude to scholasticism. Lang also took this opportunity to assert that the recent fall in student enrolment at Erfurt did not spring from barbarism but from lack of funds, a situation aggravated by a recent cut in grants to the university made by the impoverished council.

From this stage, it is true, the financial needs of a city in economic decline began to influence both political and religious developments. Reduced to borrowing money from Duke George of Saxony and seeking financial guarantees from Frankfurt-am-Main, the council imposed taxes unpopular with the lower orders. Consequently it had strong motives to deflect this resentment toward the ecclesiastical corporations, which as usual had declined to contribute. By April 1524 peasant revolts in the vicinity began to suggest new pressures which might be applied to the churchmen. Eberlin von Günzburg, a newcomer to Erfurt but already a popular preacher, was ordered to soothe a large gathering of irate citizens, who threatened to join the peasants. On the other hand, agents of the council, some of them Lutherans, went forth to treat with the insurgents and then deliberately admitted them within the walls on condition they swore not to injure the interests of the citizens. There soon proved to be method in this madness. The peasants, having been allowed to despoil the houses of the clergy, destroyed the archbishop's prison together with the *Mainzerhof*, the headquarters of his officials, stores and records. Though the Erfurt council as a whole probably did not take the decision to admit the rebels, it must incur responsibilty for allowing—and perhaps organizing—this calculated violence. It was primarily concerned not to establish Lutheranism but to weaken and intimidate the archbishop and the ecclesiastical chapters. Yet soon afterwards, having induced the peasants to withdraw peacefully, the council completed the organization of the city parishes along Lutheran lines, and on the death of the Elector Frederick it offered professorships to Luther and Melanchthon. As soon as the revolt collapsed, the city recovered control over the peasantry in its own countryside, executed four ringleaders and then opened negotiations with Archbishop Albrecht. Here the councillors obtained the backing not merely of Frederick's successor, the Protestant Elector John, but that of his Catholic cousin Duke George. Seeing them moving into the orbit of Saxony, the hitherto lethargic Albrecht demanded full compensation for himself and the Erfurt clergy, together with a restoration of orthodox services. In 1526 the council again recognized his overlordship but protested that total restitution was far beyond its means. On the religious issue it temporized, allowing Catholic services, though without sermons, in four parish churches and in the two collegiate foundations. As sometimes happened with the frequently-changing membership of German city councils, the Catholic families recovered some degree of influence two years later, but even they tended to place municipal independence and finance before the archbishop's continuing claims.

In March 1530, rather than see Erfurt pass totally under Saxon influence, Albrecht concluded an agreement at Hammelburg. In return for a general amnesty, the city paid him a moderate amount in compensation, and a lesser sum by easy instalments to the collegiate chapters. Yet the most interesting clauses of the Hammelburg document are those arranging a religious compromise. In the cathedral, the important church of St. Severus and two monastic churches, Catholic services were to be permitted. On the other side, the Evangelicals received guaranteed possession of ten parish churches, while the archbishop promised to play a completely neutral role in religious matters within Erfurt. The settlement at Hammelburg should be regarded as something more significant than a mere reflection of the Recess of Speyer (1526), which had temporarily and in vague terms offered freedom of conscience. Rather did it anticipate the situation recommended for the imperial cities by the Peace of Augsburg a quarter of a century later. Implicitly it recognized a separation of Church and state, rejection of Rome being distinguished from secular disobedience. In the years which followed it provided a precedent for a number of German cities which arranged similar compromises. Erfurt's unscrupulous handling of the Peasants' Revolt thus became the prelude to a far more impressive achievement.

If they had simply bowed to the popular cry for Lutheran Reform, the German cities would have contributed less than in fact they did to the centuries ahead, to the delicate balance of European religion and culture. When the old yearning for peace within the walls was seriously threatened, many cities had the good sense to thrust aside those ideals of fanaticism and uniformity which would have ruined them. As exponents of practical toleration their needs and traditions put them far in advance of most princely and ecclesiastical states. To the Erfurt model, it must be freely acknowledged, there contributed a 'machiavellian' group of burghers and a lax archbishop, himself deeply responsible for the scandals leading up to the revolt of Martin Luther. Somehow—or so it may seem to our more tolerant eyes—providence used the children of this world to confound the godly.

9

The Imperial Cities and the Decline of Urban Reformation

Having independently examined a few of the many available test-cases, we stand better prepared to consider the patterns of urban Reformation attained by modern synthesis, especially by that of Bernd Moeller in his *Reichsstadt und Reformation*.[1] Yet before approaching this brief but seminal account, some cautionary thoughts would seem appropriate, the more so since the imperial cities, about sixty-five in number at this period, fail to illustrate all the significant features of the Reformation in urban society. We are here concerned less with the political influence of cities than with their social accessibility to the Reformation. And in this regard it must be remarked that apart from these sixty-five *Reichsstädte*—subject only to the emperor and summoned to the Diet—there were over 2,000 territorial cities or towns (*Landstädte*) subject to princes. What happened in princely places like Wittenberg, Marburg and Heidelberg owed little to popular or municipal initiatives, yet it still remains an integral element of Reformation history. Again, by no means all the *Landstädte* were small. A few were larger than many of the imperial cities and a considerable number proudly and justly called themselves *Freistädte*, since under their oligarchic councils they could boast internal independence. And this apart,

[1] Though I have used several of the city histories upon which his work is largely based, this chapter has heavy debts to Moeller's *Reichsstadt und Reformation*. For details on its editions in French and English, see the Bibliography below. See also note 1 to ch. 8 above, and the broad general article on German and Swiss cities by Basil Hall. On the late medieval social and constitutional structures see H. Planitz.

their citizens might well enjoy more personal freedom than, say, the people of a meticulously-governed *Reichsstadt* like Nuremberg. Conversely, a number of the imperial cities, whatever their legal status, contained a couple of thousand citizens or less; while some were so hemmed in by powerful princes that they could scarcely be regarded as independent states within the imperial framework.

Of the largest non-imperial cities we have already studied one in Erfurt, a place of well over 20,000 inhabitants when in 1501 the young Luther first attended its prestigious university. A striking contrast appeared at Wittenberg, the miniature capital of the Electors of Saxony. When in 1502 Frederick the Wise followed up his rebuilding programme at the castle and the Rathaus by founding a university, the town's population numbered only one-tenth that of Erfurt. Later on Duke George, whose own capital at Dresden was no great metropolis, declared of Luther that 'for a single monk coming from such a hole to undertake a Reformation was quite intolerable'. Others, including Luther himself, spoke just as slightingly of Wittenberg. Even so, thanks to two great university teachers supported by an enthusiastic faculty and by faithful princes, Wittenberg attained a fame throughout the empire and Europe which might have been envied by the greatest towns and which came to overshadow that of Erfurt itself. Admittedly the reputation of Wittenberg depended upon academic not civic achievement. Ranging in economic importance between Erfurt and Wittenberg were such places as the three other non-imperial cities which we have examined in some detail: Rostock, Wismar and Stralsund. All in all, it seems clear that any future exhaustive study of the urban contribution to the Reformation will not be limited to the imperial cities, so many of which had attained their status through somewhat fortuitous processes and were not earning it by their size, or by their political, economic and cultural influences.

With this safeguard in mind, we shall proceed to some general quantification in the light of recent research, and then pass on to Moeller's Reformation statistics. We have seen how difficult it was to eradicate the new religious beliefs once they had established themselves in a self-governing walled town. On the other hand the majority of both imperial and princely cities were small communities which could react readily to the stimuli provided by a few Lutheran missionaries. That they were compact, numerous and self-centred enabled them to play their unique role in the history of the Reformation. In point of size only Cologne could begin to compare with the major capitals of western Europe such as Paris, Antwerp, London, Milan, Venice and Naples.

Regarding the total population of many individual towns we have information of a sort. Where they exist, censuses of food-consumers made in time of emergency provide our firmest figures. Otherwise we can try to extrapolate from other data: lists of taxpayers or muster-rolls of able-bodied males, numbers of hearths or houses. Different sources can often be collated to attain reasonably solid results. After the large overestimates current in the last century and the probable underestimates of more recent years, the latest trend is to enlarge the latter, though marginally. The latest survey by Hektor Ammann gives Cologne a total of over 40,000 and certain others figures exceeding 20,000. These latter are far from numerous: in Upper Germany Strassburg, Metz, Nuremberg, Augsburg—plus of course Vienna and Prague, also within the empire. Further north, besides Cologne and Erfurt the over-20,000 list consists of Lübeck, Magdeburg and, by the year 1500, Danzig. In terms of imperial taxation and therefore of reputed wealth, Cologne, Nuremberg and Ulm came first, closely followed by Strassburg and Lübeck, then by Augsburg, Frankfurt and Metz. Below these very large places there were perhaps ten German cities with figures between 10,000 and 20,000; below them possibly as many as 200 medium-sized or smallish ones having 2,000 to 10,000 inhabitants. The rest ranged for the most part between 500 and 2,000, though there existed some dwarfs with less than 500, yet having urban constitutions.[2]

Hence if we must use crude phrases such as 'a typical German city', we should prudently envisage a little walled town with far less than 10,000 people: Dinkelsbühl rather than Rothenburg, let alone Nuremberg. We should think of a concentrated society, where power and wealth belonged to the few, but a place where

[2] For these estimates see H. Ammann; further information in H. Mauersberg.

almost everybody knew everybody else and where the population could assemble in the main market-place. But what proportion of the nation lived in urban communities? Here the regional variations are great: in some regions, especially in the north, towns were far more thinly scattered than in others. So far as the imperial cities are concerned, a glance at the appropriate map in Putzger's historical atlas (or any of its derivatives) will show that the vast majority lay in the south between Nuremberg and Alsace. In a German or a Swiss region of average urban distribution, perhaps a quarter of the population lived in towns, though naturally a sizeable proportion of any urban community worked in or for agriculture. This is especially true of the very small towns, yet again not uniformly, since some even of the smallest contained considerable groups of textile or mining workers. This rough estimate of a quarter may be compared with those made for the Netherlands, the most highly urbanized region of northern Europe, where the proportion of town-dwellers in the sixteenth century has been estimated as nearly one-half.

Depending chiefly upon Moeller, we may now give some of the more striking facts and figures concerning the imperial cities and their reception of the Reformation. The *matricula* of the empire drawn up at the Diet of Worms in 1521 enumerated under the heading 'Free and Imperial City' a total of eighty-five places, but Moeller ranks only sixty-five as unquestionably imperial cities. According to his count, more than fifty of these sixty-five officially accepted the Reformation in the course of the sixteenth century, more than half becoming fully and finally Protestant, others proceeding to tolerate a Protestant alongside a Catholic community or *vice versa*. In the cases of a mere handful, the Reformation scored a temporary success but was later on suppressed. Of the sixty-five cities only fourteen never tolerated Protestantism for any period, and most even among these had to fight hard to avoid tolerating it. Moeller could find only five very small places in Swabia and Alsace which seem never to have been seriously touched by the Reformation, though even this impression may be due to defective evidence.[3] If then we ask whether the attitude of the more independent urban communities

[3] B. Moeller, *Imperial Cities and the Reformation*, trans. and ed. H. C. E. Midelfort and M. U. Edwards, p. 41.

was favourable to the Reformation, the answer must be a very decided affirmative. So far as concerns the crisis of the Reformation, relatively too much has been said about the godly prince and the formula *cujus regio ejus religio*.

Equally decisive is Moeller's analysis of the prevalent social causation. In the imperial cities the Reformation was not a patrician movement; he fully confirms the earlier judgment of another distinguished authority Franz Lau, who wrote, 'The Reformation was never the work of a city council.' The initiative and the vitality of the movement depended on the populace, though the latter often appear to have been motivated not simply by gospel preaching but also by those old and negative emotions: anticlericalism and in particular rage against the abuse of Indulgences. At this stage one might again recall the group of letters from eminent Catholics stating that Protestantism was a popular movement and of course thinking none the better of it simply because it had attracted the rabble. Indeed, it was not always disinterested or spiritually impressive. At Speyer in 1525 the citizens suddenly refused to pay their church dues, saying that pious foundations were fraudulent and useless to the dead and the living. In 1524–5, alongside the Peasants' Revolt, the populace of Frankfurt-am-Main forced through a Reformation, together with various secular demands, amid street-fighting and the looting of monasteries. Two years later the artisans of Hamburg demanded the punishment of their Catholic priests, who, they argued, 'have led us poor people into error with their Indulgences and holy purgatory'. Such were aggravated cases of an already old-established anticlericalism, sometimes, as at Wendelstein in 1525–6, qualified by documentary evidence of a genuine Scriptural congregationalism. In any town the balance could tip over with apparent suddenness. In one year processions, pilgrimages, miracles, entries into religious houses appear to be proceeding normally. Yet, a couple of years later the Protestant preachers and printers are at work and vociferous groups demanding that Catholic institutions be dismantled. Of all such cases that of Regensburg is perhaps the most striking: in 1520–21 a record number of pilgrimage plaques were sold at the fashionable shrine of the Virgin, where 200 miracles were reported. By 1522 a sizeable Lutheran group had come into being and the city printer was publishing the works of Luther. The Regensburg Lutherans sallied forth into Bavaria and soon became a thorn in the side of the Bavarian government when it decided upon persecution.[4]

City councillors commonly responded to popular pressure on the medieval assumption that the life of the city embraced both the temporal and the spiritual welfare of its citizens. Laymen had long managed their own educational and charitable services. Meanwhile their concept of salvation as a municipal service had arisen in part as the concomitant of a jealousy directed against episcopally-sponsored salvation. We have already noticed how deliberately the fourteenth-century citizens of Lübeck outbuilt their bishop. Likewise, even the superb west façade and tower of Strassburg cathedral, built by the citizens from 1277, seems a conscious celebration of their newly-won independence from the bishop. On the firm foundation of such old rivalries, exacerbated by Indulgences, citations to Rome, clerical tax privileges and other grievances, Protestantism was able to build. The city represented the greater loyalty, while the hierarchy, the papacy, the Church Universal itself, could claim not only a lesser but a dwindling loyalty. In Basil Hall's words, 'You belonged to your town not only visibly by residence, but invisibly in the mystical sense of identity with it.'[5]

Again, after all we have written in previous chapters, we need but briefly to recall that the German Reformation was an urban event at once literary, technological and oratorical. Long ago the city had displaced the monastery as the chief home of the literate element, both clerical and lay, in medieval society. Cities kept chronicles, recorded important happenings and diplomatic transactions. If they wanted to preserve their integrity and privileges, they had to be conscious of history and precedent. Since the fourteenth century they had introduced

[4] L. Theobald, *Die Reformationsgeschichte der Reichsstadt Regensburg*, i (Munich, 1936), pp. 33ff; cf. B. Moeller, *Imperial Cities and the Reformation*, p. 59; F. Lau and E. Bizer, p. 22, n. 13; G. Strauss, 'The Religious Policies of Dukes Wilhelm and Ludwig', p. 361.

[5] B. Hall, p. 112. R. W. Henderson ('Sixteenth Century Community Benevolence', in *Church History*, xxxviii (1996)) has argued that the secularization of charity in the later Middle Ages was followed in cities like Strassburg, Nuremberg and Geneva by the attempt of the Reformers to 'resacralize' charity as an ecclesiastical institution.

jurists into their affairs and combined elements of Roman law with ther local and customary legislation. Latterly they had employed humanists as their leading officials, and could therefore negotiate on equal intellectual terms with sovereign states. In the cities dwelt not merely the authors, editors and printers, but also a very high proportion of the literate public. We have again already insisted upon the interlocking within urban society of the spoken with the printed word, for then, as now, ideas were most surely mediated by personalities.

From one important angle, the Reformation forms a natural climax to the laicization of the medieval urban community. Yet it was a process carried out with the powerful aid of friars and other unprivileged clerics, who in the end made such notable and numerous contributions to Lutheran missionary effort. We often see the German municipalities as islands in a sea of princely and feudal power. Should we not likewise regard them as islands in a sea of prelatical power? Having in former times expelled their bishops, influenced appointments to canonries and in effect chosen their own parish clergy, was it not logical that town governments should proceed in this self-sufficiency to complete the controls they had already in large measure established over their own ecclesiastical life? At this point one might profitably recall the earlier history of Cologne, often accepted in our period as a prime 'ecclesiastical city' with its conservative theologians and canonists, its numerous convents and churches.[6] Yet the image of this 'German Rome' can be deceptive. After two centuries of struggle, Cologne had in 1288 defeated its archbishop at the battle of Worringen and had thenceforth developed as a free imperial city, acknowledging only the emperor as its overlord. As for the subsequent archbishops, they gave up their Cologne palace and lived in their outlying castles at Godesberg, Lechenich, Zons and Poppelsdorf. From 1500 they normally resided at Bonn, while on his initial entry into Cologne an archbishop had first to make a solemn declaration that he would keep inviolate the rights and liberties of the city. In its essentials this pattern applied to many other German cities, several of outstanding importance, such as Mainz, Worms, Speyer, Strassburg, Regensburg and Magdeburg. Highly conscious of

[6] See p. 154, n. 17 above.

their medieval history, such communities knew that its most meaningful episode had been the shaking-off of episcopal over-lordship in order to become *Freistädte*, enjoying internal self-government.

Some modern scholars have claimed that the coming of the Reformation revitalized—for a time at least—the communal sense of responsibility, the interest of the common people in city government. Even groups of unprivileged citizens played active parts in expediting Reformation measures. Moreover the belief seems to have been widespread that such action commended a city to God, proving it worthy of his spiritual and material favours. This competition for divine prizes seems an obvious outcome of the civic salvation service which remained a prominent feature of sixteenth-century religion throughout Europe. To exemplify it one could cite both municipal councils and municipal theologians, and these not only in Germany. The list would doubtless be headed by Zwingli at Zürich and Calvin at Geneva, yet it could as easily reach back to urban revivalists of earlier generations, especially to Savonarola, who loudly proclaimed his Florence as the favoured city of God.[7] Elsewhere the phenomenon could almost as readily assume national proportions. Such aspirations combined the practical and the Scriptural in much the same manner as the nationalist religiosity of the English Elizabethans, or as Milton's conviction that God entrusted his crucial tasks to his Englishmen. Thus a German townsman could thank Providence for his thick walls as fervently as Shakespeare, through the mouth of John of Gaunt, thanks it for the silver moat which encircled his island, guarding it against infection and the hand of war. Of course, in stressing these old anticlerical prejudices and group-insurance attitudes, we modern historians may easily underestimate the more genuinely revivalist currents within late medieval Catholicism and within the response to early Protestant missionaries. Our secularism can easily expose us to the dangers of anachronism, blunt our minds to mixed motives, even make us undervalue the pervasive character both of the *devotio moderna* and of the more or less informed Gospel Christianity of these early Reformation years.

[7] I have in mind the *Trattato circa il reggimento e governo della città di Firenze* (1498).

The case of Swabia's leading city is so singular as to demand special attention. Augsburg was a place of such wealth and influence that it might well have seemed destined to play a part in Reformation history comparable with those of Nuremberg and Strassburg.[8] True, its wealth was of recent growth and largely based upon profits from the new overseas and oriental commerce initiated not by Germans but by the Iberian states. And unlike the two greater cities, Augsburg could boast very few old patrician families; amongst these the most distinguished and wealthy was that of the Welsers, who in the next generation were to marry a daughter to a Habsburg archduke. These few patricians depended, however, upon alliance with the rising groups of financier-merchants, whose headquarters were concentrated within this one place. The Fugger, Baumgartner and Imhoff families, which together with the Welsers headed this group, were not officially taken into the patrician circle until 1538. Their wealth and their problems depended not merely upon colonial imports but upon the fact that they financed the house of Habsburg. This became especially true of the Fuggers, who in return for large and ever-growing loans were granted enormous concessions, including the Habsburg mines in the Tyrol and Hungary. And since no one could sue or foreclose upon the emperor, the Augsburg bankers—and with them innumerable smaller people in that city—depended upon the retention of imperial goodwill. Hence Augsburg's attachment to the emperor was less traditional, less sentimental and more mercenary than that of Nuremberg. On the other hand the Fuggers also strove to justify their profits in the eyes of God and man by founding in 1519 Europe's first large-scale social settlement, to this day a prominent feature of Augsburg and a functioning charity for the Catholic poor.

This situation might have remained tolerable but for the disturbing influence of the Reformation upon both the middle

---

[8] On the earlier Reformation and class conflict in Augsburg see the full narrative to 1537 in the first two volumes of F. Roth, *Augsburgs Reformationsgeschichte* (Munich, 1901, 1904). Roth's third and fourth volumes (1907, 1911) carry the complicated story to 1555. H. Baron's comparisons with Nuremberg and Strassburg are valuable. On the social and financial background in Augsburg see also R. Ehrenberg; G. von Poelnitz, *Die Fugger* (2nd edn., Frankfurt, 1960).

groups and the populace. Despite the spectacular magnates, the actual constitution of Augsburg had developed along more democratic lines than that of most cities: the guilds shared some executive functions with the patricians, while on the council representing the citizenry they outnumbered their social superiors. Moreover, during the 1520s the populace and the guildsmen became ever more strongly attracted not merely by Lutheran but by Zwinglian and even sectarian beliefs. Had popular opinion been given its head, Augsburg would have turned Protestant as soon as Strassburg and Nuremberg. As things stood, the dependence of the poor upon the rich, and that of the rich upon the Habsburgs, produced an appalling dichotomy which Augsburg failed to resolve. Until 1530 the Fuggers, supported by that minority of the leading families who were Catholic or at least pro-Habsburg, strove with success to prevent an open *rapprochement* with the Protestant princes and cities. Subsequently, however, the shift was forced on by the larger council which represented the citizen body, with the result that by 1536 Augsburg had joined the Schmalkaldic League. When in 1546–7 war came at last, the financiers actually withdrew from the city to avoid incrimination in the emperor's eyes, and with it the forfeiture of their immense concessions. On the defeat of the League, Charles ignored the pleas of Anton Fugger on behalf of his fellow-citizens, and he frightened Augsburg into accepting changes more sweeping than any he imposed elsewhere during that brief period of his triumph. In effect the guilds were stripped of effective power and subjected to a council of Catholic patricians, under whom Lutheranism survived only amid difficulties and upon a reduced scale. Distrusted by contemporaries, and later censured by historians, the city of Augsburg may deserve more sympathy than it has been accorded. Its fate seems to have been unwittingly decided by the amazing enterprise of its bankers years before the revolt of Martin Luther. Its whole social-economic structure, together with its exposed geographical position, prevented it from riding the storm unscathed. As Hans Baron so clearly demonstrated, Augsburg exemplifies the severity of the problems besetting a city in which the material interests of the establishment, and even those of the people, clashed with the spontaneous adherence of the latter to Protestant beliefs.

Some day no doubt more detailed biographical studies will examine the work of urban Protestant preachers and ministers between 1520 and the Peace of Augsburg. Their letters rather than their theological works tell us how the Reformation took root and consolidated itself. In Thuringia were Wenceslaus Link at Altenburg, Friedrich Myconius at Weimar and Gotha, Jakob Strauss at Eisenach. Further south Osiander worked at Nuremberg, Brenz at Schwäbisch Hall, Zell, Bucer and Capito at Strassburg, Theobald Billican at Nördingen, Heinrich von Kettenbach and Konrad Sam at Ulm, Ambrosius Blaurer and Johann Zwick at Constance, Oecolampadius, Johannes Frosch and Urbanus Rhegius at Augsburg.[9] Few of those working in the south had come down from Wittenberg, or dwelt devoutly on the pronouncements of the Wittenberg oracles. Many, though in a broad sense disciples of Luther, drew inspiration also from other sources. Some, like Balthazar Hubmaier at Waldshut and Christoph Schappeler at Memmingen, were Zwingli's disciples operating deep in Germany. From early days Zwinglianism became strong at Ulm; while at Augsburg the Reformers preferred its eucharistic theology to that of Luther. At Strassburg Bucer was one of the chief creators of the Reformed as distinct from the Lutheran tradition, while Capito came in from the angle of reformist humanism. Elsewhere in later years a few of the missionary clerics ceased to support the Protestant cause altogether. Thus from the beginning the Word was not preached in identical terms throughout Germany; this can be proved merely from the sermons which have survived from these years.

By the same token the city councils reacted to popular pressure with greatly varying speed and decision. The swift and masterful line taken at Nuremberg was equalled at few other places. To cite an extreme of hesitancy, Reformers were operating in Regensburg as early as 1522 while the Reformation did not achieve final acceptance there until 1542. The religious future of a city was not necessarily decided above the heads of its people. If it thought fit, a council might determine the matter by organizing a vote of the guilds or of a general assembly of citizens. This happened at Constance in 1528, at Biberach in 1529, at

[9] I take this list largely from F. Lau and E. Bizer, pp. 22–3, who supply references.

Memmingen, Ulm, Weissenburg, Heilbronn and Esslingen in 1529–31. A variant occurred at Kempten in 1533, where the citizens were allowed a free vote on images in church; 800 voted against images and 174 in favour.[10] We need scarcely add that authority did not trouble to count the modest 'don't knows'; such were in fact rare birds in the sixteenth century. At Goslar in 1528 the council deliberately made the citizens accomplices by causing each one to swear on oath:

> If the council and the said city should find themselves in distress and adversity as a result of the abolition of the Mass and other ceremonies, or on account of the Holy Gospel (which is now preached as it should be in all its purity and clarity), I promise to show myself obedient, putting my life and goods at the service of your noble council and of the town of Goslar, as long as I shall be a citizen and inhabitant. May God help me: He and his Holy Gospel.[11]

We have traced in several northern cities the close links between the early Reformation and the widespread campaigning to resist taxation and democratize city constitutions. A similar situation developed also at Göttingen and several other places, yet in view of the known exceptions and dubious cases this pattern cannot be made a universal principle of Reformation politics in the German urban setting. Moreover the democratic movement proved brief. Quite apart from the rising powers of the princes, it cannot be argued that in general the internal power structures of the cities were more democratic in 1555 than they had been in 1520.

At present there remain a number of unfinished assignments in regard to Reformation history at the municipal level. We need comparative studies concerning police and order-keeping during periods of internal crisis: for example, a study of the guilds as forces of order and change within major cities like Cologne, where guilds are known to have continued to be influential in this regard. A different set of problems arises from the control exercised by cities over their extramural territories. Several city councils ruled over extensive lordships, governing their bailiffs

---

[10] B. Moeller, *Imperial Cities and the Reformation*, p. 95, citing O. Erhard, *Die Reformation der Kirche in Kempten* (Kempten, 1917), p. 37.

[11] H. Hölscher, *Die Geschichte der Reformation in Goslar* (Hanover, 1902) is based upon texts from the city archives: this oath is printed on p. 32.

and peasantry with an authority as absolute as that exercised by any prince. One of the best-documented examples is that of Ulm, which ruled a province of some 300 square miles, said to contain about 60,000 inhabitants. Ulm did not finalize its ecclesiastical revolution until the years 1531–2, yet it then did so with a deliberation and thoroughness applied to every part of its domain. In the May of 1531 the council summoned both the city parish priests and those of the countryside to the Rathaus, examined them upon eighteen articles of religion, ejected a few diehards from their benefices, promoted a few priests to preaching functions, and spared those of the slow-moving or ignorant who showed reasonable promise of conversion to the Evangelical viewpoint. The attitude of each cleric to the articles was summarized, showing that only a small minority took a firm line in either direction. Their standard response was to the effect that they were unlearned men, ready to be guided by scholars and by the city council in matters that were too high and difficult for them. A few stalled more purposefully by replying that they thought as the Church had always prescribed, or that they would accept the Recess of Augsburg, or submit to the commands of the emperor. Later on visitors despatched to the parishes assessed the situation by collecting reports from the lay officials upon the clergy, and *vice versa*. Hardly any of these humble and slow-moving parsons can be depicted as early representatives of a reformed Catholicism; did they not rather exemplify, like so many of their kind throughout Europe, the blessedness of the poor in spirit ? At all events, they look to me genuine simpletons rather than smart prevaricators. Doubtless reassured by the weakness of the apparent opposition, the council moved forward purposefully during the rest of 1531 and throughout the subsequent year. Under the influence of Sam and Blaurer it arranged a conclusive series of visitations, sermons, synods and Church orders. A city Reformation was being imposed also upon a largely passive agrarian society: the atmosphere and the problems resembled those of a little princely state rather than those of a walled town.[12]

[12] F. Keidel, 'Ulmische Reformationsakten von 1531 und 1532', in *Württembergische Vierteljahrshefte für Landesgeschichte, Neue Folge, Jahrgang iv* (1895), pp. 255–342.

Our remaining theme in this chapter must concern the division of the Protestant cities between those which followed Luther and those which adhered for a while to the Reformed tradition initiated by Zwingli and then developed, still in broad consonance with the Swiss, by Bucer and his Strassburg associates.[13] If we examine the situation in the late 1530s we find a fairly clear geographical distribution. The north and east were Lutheran, led by the great imperial Hanseatic ports with the princely cities of their hinterland like Brunswick, Lüneburg, Magdeburg, Göttingen. Also Lutheran were the central provinces of Thuringia and Franconia, with Nuremberg, Windheim and Weissenburg; so again were the Hessian towns along with Frankfurt and Worms. On the other hand, the cities of the southwest and the extreme south became Reformed: this group includes not only Strassburg and the lesser Alsatian towns but also those of Swabia, from Esslingen in the north to Constance in the south, from Augsburg in the east to the Rhine in the west. On the map the Lutheran area is much bigger, but many of the places involved were not imperial cities and came increasingly under the influence of their princely overlords, who by the late 1530s had for the most part turned Lutheran. On the other hand, the imperial cities had more scope for spontaneous partisanship, and a high proportion of them, heavily grouped in the southwest, kept in close touch with the great Reformed block of the Swiss Confederation. The only considerable town in this area to remain Lutheran throughout the earlier phases of the Reformation was Reutlingen, and even here some of the citizens had maintained close contact with Zwingli and Bucer.

What was the nature of this division between Lutheran and Reformed? Why did it occur along these geographical lines? Then as later, theologians pointed to the Marburg Conference of 1529 and saw the ecclesiastical division as based on a sharp divergence of eucharistic doctrine, a divergence which obstinately persisted, despite the fact that Bucer and Calvin modified and refined the rationalizing eucharistic beliefs of Zwingli. Of course, within their limits the theologians were right: how right we realize when we look in detail at the Marburg Conference of

[13] On this theme I largely follow B. Moeller, *Imperial Cities and the Reformation*, pp. 95ff.

1529 and witness the high degree of agreement reached between Lutherans and Zwinglians on all other doctrines save that of the eucharist. And it would be plainly wrong to imagine that eucharistic doctrine mattered only to theologians. How difficult it must have been for any thoughtful man, nurtured in Catholicism as all this generation had been, to pronounce the nature of the divine presence in the Mass a matter of uncertainty, let alone one of indifference. Inevitably the Protestants pontificated in their turn upon the meagre evidence contained in Holy Writ, and they proceeded to differ from one another. Even more inevitably, the Catholics, conditioned by centuries of policing against eucharistic heresies, kept this emotive theme well to the forefront of the doctrinal battle. So it remained for half a century, in the end contributing almost as much to the Reformed *versus* Lutheran dichotomy as to the greater gulf between Catholic and Protestant.

Even so, the theological division by no means exhausts this complex historical division between Lutheran and Reformed. Other factors, intellectual, social, political, played their parts in an effective if unquantifiable manner. On the level of political thought, for example, another rift between Luther and the Reformed thinkers soon came to the fore, and it was not simply and solely a rift between Luther, the loyal subject of a prince, and the republican city leaders, a rift between the subject-mind and the citizen-mind. At first sight Luther may well seem one who exalted the secular state. In *Christian Nobility* he swept away what he called 'the first wall' erected around itself by the Roman Church: the claim that the temporal power had no right to intervene in ecclesiastical affairs. Luther also made the clergy fully responsible within the secular community, and he announced the sanctification of secular tasks done in faith. In practice he even encouraged princes to nominate commissions of clerics and laymen who should draw up Church Orders and supervise the management of churches. On the other hand Luther would not accord to the state, whether city or princedom, any direct role in salvation; each man and woman must remain perilously, individually, face to face with God in his saving or damning omnipotence. The true Church, its members known only to God, remained a little flock of believers amid the crowd of the luke-warm and the unbelievers. Obviously there could be no question of a merger between secular state and true Church. It thus happened that the principle one might caricature as Group Salvation Incorporated—that apotheosis of the medieval city—passed over to the Reformed, not to the Lutheran churches. It was to find its triumph in Geneva and in the many little Genevas from Scotland to Transylvania.

Luther's secular state had been assigned by God to a basic yet unglamorous task: the curbing of evil men in this dark sublunary world. That his reasoning was theological and Scripturally based, one cannot doubt. Yet it remains also a fair observation that Luther was a friar brought up in humble little towns, maturing in the exceptionally confused atmosphere of Erfurt and prospering in the small princely capital of Wittenberg. At all events, Reformers who had known more august urban settings read some very different messages into the same Bible. From the early days both Zwingli and Bucer showed a more pronounced urban emphasis, a more sweeping concept of civic responsibility. They were citizens of free cities and stood firm by the expansive traditions we have observed in so many places. An activist instrument of the Word, Zwingli saw Church and state as charged to harness themselves together and to set about preparing the first stage of salvation: the erection of God's city on earth. The civil magistrates, indispensable to the prosperity of the Church, should administer discipline when appealed to by the parish, if necessary by imposing secular punishments. Conversely the Reformed churches must help the state, for they alone could educate the citizen to govern with equity and intelligence. Again, the state must obey the law of God, which is not only drawn from the Scriptures but expounded by preachers and prophets. Assuming the lead at Zwingli's death, Bucer significantly enlarged and modified Zwingli's simple theocracy into a communal ethic based on the principle of love, a concept he was still elaborating throughout his last years in England. Constructing there his major work *De Regno Christi*, he went on to plan a community wherein the civil and the ecclesiastical life are closely interfused. In social content at least, he stood very near to the English mid-Tudor 'Commonwealth men', idealistic advocates of a just society based on strict morality and the blunting of the profit motive.[14] Meanwhile in Geneva, Calvin was actually exploring the practicalities of a civic theocracy, one highly conscious of its own theological and philosophical bases. Hence there appears an unbroken line of development from the late medieval urban community to the Presbyterian tradition, but Luther does not stand in that line. At the same time one must hasten to add that this broad dichotomy need not be held to dictate all the local results. Dare we insist, for example, that the unusually authoritarian tone of city government in Nuremberg inevitably made that city embrace Lutheran rather than Reformed beliefs?

In addition one might well stress other aspects of this ideological difference between the Lutheran and the Reformed. Into the minds of both Zwingli and Bucer humanist social concepts penetrated much more deeply than into the mind of Luther. They respected those ideals of civic humanism which had originated well over a century earlier in Florence. They have much to say about the *publica utilitas* and the *tranquillitas* of the *respublica*. And while Zwingli grew up breathing the good Swiss mountain air, Bucer as a young Dominican friar had imbibed something almost as bracing: the anti-tyrannical passages in the prescribed text by St. Thomas Aquinas. Both these men lacked the pig-headed grandeur of Luther; they were less prophets than ecclesiastical statesmen, Zwingli seeking to extend the Reformation both through Switzerland and into Germany, Bucer tirelessly striving alongside the politician Philip of Hesse[15] to knit together the Reformed with the Lutheran powers. Yet their ecumenism, even that of Bucer, had distinct limitations. The Reformed could sincerely long for agreement with the Lutherans and yet naïvely expect the Lutherans to go nine-tenths of the way to meet them.

[14] On the English writers see W. R. D. Jones, *The Tudor Commonwealth 1529–1559* (1970). On Bucer see H. Eells; J. Courvoisier, *La notion d'église chez Bucer* (Paris, 1933); W. Pauck, ch. 3; and the same author's earlier work in *De regno Christi: Das Reich Gottes auf Erden* (Berlin and Leipzig, 1928). The Bucer literature is voluminous: see E. G. Léonard, pp. 402–5. On Bucer and Zwingli as 'free' citizens, B. Moeller, pp. 75–90, and compare H. Baron, 'Calvinist Republicanism' in *Church History*, viii (1939).

[15] On Philip see A. O. Hancock; H. J. Hillerbrand, *Landgrave Philipp of Hesse*. For a select German bibliography on Philip and the Hessian Reformation see S. Skalweit, pp. 435–6; F. Lau and E. Bizer, p. 51.

Again, in so many cases the original choice did not prove to be the final choice. Why did the Swabian and Alsatian towns so readily accept the Bucerian Reformed tradition for three or four decades, and then to so great an extent relinquish this tradition in favour of Lutheranism? During the 1530s and 1540s there is no doubt that these places were Reformed, not Evangelical: their austere liturgies resembled those of the Swiss; their hatred of images was marked, their antipathy toward Luther's eucharistic doctrine loudly expressed. Moeller argues that mere proximity to the Swiss should not be pressed too heavily, if only because the slide in the Reformed direction continued for some time after Zwingli fell at Kappel in 1531; in other words, that the Reformed cause continued to expand even during the years when the Swiss had drawn in their horns and were trying to adjust their own confused affairs rather than manage those of the Germans. Whatever the weight of this contention, there can be no doubt about the infectious character of Reformed beliefs within southern Germany itself. Amid the growing perils of princely intervention, the cities tended to stand and move together. The smaller Alsatian towns were naturally disposed to imitate Strassburg. In fact the towns which first turned Protestant speedily sought to pull in others by sending them missionaries, of whom Bucer and Ambrosius Blaurer were among the most prominent. In fact a parallel inter-city movement occurred in the Lutheran north, headed by Luther's friends Bugenhagen and Amsdorf; while at least one famous Lutheran missionary Johann Brenz tried for a time to operate in the south at Reutlingen (1527) and Heilbronn (1531).

This 'natural' southern predilection for the Reformed faith seems to have sprung in no small part from the fact that humanist values and their civic corollaries were not limited to a few choice spirits but had penetrated society to a marked degree. We have, it is true, acknowledged that the absence of humanist schools did not greatly retard the acceptance of Lutheran beliefs in the northern cities. Yet in the south the Reformation did acquire a distinctive quality from the intellectuals and publishers who represented old humanist and semi-popular traditions. Not merely Strassburg but its small neighbour Schlettstadt had boasted leading humanist teachers when Lübeck and Bremen lay almost untouched by the new learning. Even Erfurt, where humanism was long treated as a reinforcement for the old university arts course, the *trivium*, could scarcely be held to rival these Alsatian cities. Nationalism and anti-papalism had issued more readily from Alsatian mouths and printing presses: Sebastian Brant had denounced the pope as Antichrist even more readily than Luther.

Whereas in the north religious unrest tended to reopen old social and economic fissures, the more intellectual tone of southern town society provided a perfect foundation for teachers like Zwingli and Bucer, who by contrast could gain only power-less handfuls of northern supporters. In addition, the southern guildsmen and lower orders had long played a creative role in city government, especially in Alsace. Again in contrast, as we observed along the Baltic, the attempts of north German citizens to hoist themselves into power alongside the rise of Lutheranism found little support from local traditions, either civic or intellectual. In other words, the area of most active communal and humanist traditions coincides with the area of Bucerian Reform. Certainly some contemporaries identified democratic politics with both Reformed and sectarian religion. For example, when the wavering city of Augsburg was striving to regain the good opinion of the emperor, its agents argued that it had no religious Radicals, because the good old patrician families still ran Augsburg's affairs!

What we have said regarding this great division applies to the later 1520s and the 1530s. Yet events were to prove that the religious frontiers between Catholic, Lutheran and Reformed Germany had been anything but permanently settled during these years. Orthodox Lutheranism began to gain mass support among the secular rulers. Until 1525 only one prince had played a significant hand in the origins of the Lutheran Reformation, and even so in a devious and covert fashion. Frederick the Wise, though the greatest relic-collector in Germany, had nevertheless protected Luther ever since the Indulgence quarrel. His actions are conventionally but not quite adequately explained by pride in his new university and by the influence of pro-Lutheran councillors like Spalatin. A recent historian[16] has laid stress

[16] Cf. T. Borth, *passim*, together with the broader view by W. D. J. Cargill Thompson in *Journal of Theological Studies*, xxiv (1973).

upon the deep-seated rivalry between the houses of Wettin and Hohenzollern, to which latter belonged Albrecht of Mainz, the beneficiary of the Indulgence campaign. The Hohenzollerns had assiduously collected great ecclesiastical offices held in the past by cadets of the house of Wettin: the Grand Mastership of the Teutonic Order, the sees of Halberstadt, Magdeburg and now Mainz. By striking at Indulgences aimed to benefit the Hohenzollerns, Luther would have acquired claims to the protection of any Saxon Elector. Whatever his precise objectives, Frederick's actions from 1517 have done much to make historians overestimate the share of the princes in the origins of the Lutheran Reformation. For eight years his favours were not only concealed but unique. Even for a decade after 1525 the adherence of the princes was a slow, piecemeal process.

Electoral Saxony and the new Duchy of Prussia went Protestant in 1525, then Hesse in 1526, and Brunswick-Luneburg soon afterwards. Yet the major extension of princely Lutheranism belonged to the middle and later 1530s. Württemberg, Pomerania and Nassau accepted the Reform in 1534, Electoral Brandenburg in 1538, Albertine Saxony on the death of Duke George in 1539, Mecklenburg-Schwerin and Brunswick-Calenburg the following year. From this stage the princes gradually assumed political leadership of the Reformation while the role of the free cities declined. Thus a second Reformation, stabilizing yet sterilizing, followed upon the popular and enthusiastic Reformation of the cities. Across most of northern Germany ecclesiastical laws were applied and reforms enforced by the legal authority of the princes. One major ruler, Joachim II of Brandenburg, even sought a personal solution through a prolonged experiment in fence-sitting and mediation between the Catholic and Protestant causes. Meanwhile on the other side, the Habsburgs and the Wittelsbachs by threats and rewards caused several city governments to waver or even to rejoin the Catholic cause, this despite the continuing popularity of the new beliefs within their walls. The pressures brought to bear upon these cities were still secular, for the Jesuits were not yet reconverting the masses. The case of Biberach, where a small Catholic council managed to hold in check a large Protestant majority of citizens, provides an extreme example of Habsburg influence aided by some local virtuosity. In 1546–7 came the Schmalkaldic War and the triumph of the emperor at Mühlberg; then from 1548 to 1552 a process whereby about thirty cities—uncaptured, yet yielding to the threat of Habsburg force—had their constitutions abrogated and Catholic oligarchies and bureaucracies installed. Bucer himself and many other Reformed leaders sorrowfully shook the German dust from their feet and made their way to the England of Edward VI or to some other place of refuge. At last in 1552 there followed the Treaty of Passau and the definitive Peace of Augsburg three years later. These settlements ignored all the divisions of the Protestants; they mentioned only 'those of the old religion' and 'those of the Augsburg Confession', that is, Catholics and Lutherans. The seventeenth section of the Peace of Augsburg specifically provided that 'all others not belonging to the aforesaid two religions are not to be included in this Peace, but wholly excluded'. For the remaining Bucerian Reformed cities there was no offer involving *cujus regio ejus religio*.[17]

The services of Charles V to Catholicism had been great, but at this moment they were transcended by the splendour of his services to Lutheranism. As a result of the Augsburg settlement, a number of cities, even Strassburg, sought to extricate themselves from war and misery by turning orthodox Lutheran. Not long after Bucer's death his Reformed colleagues who had stayed to maintain the struggle found themselves treated with intolerance by Lutheran authorities: with much the same intolerance as the latter manifested toward both Catholics and sectarians. And as Lutheranism surrendered so much of its remaining liberalism, the populace in the southern cities counted for less and less in Church affairs. The pastors appointed by the magistrates were apt to become obedient and efficient city functionaries. Even as it extended its hold upon those portions of the south which remained Protestant, Lutheranism became more institutionalized, more unproductive of popular

---

[17] For a general assessment of the Peace of Augsburg, see H. Tüchler's article translated in H. J. Cohn, *Government in Reformation Europe*. On the political history of the German Reformation from the death of Luther to the Peace of Augsburg, see especially S. Skalweit, chs. 7, 8; and the still more detailed H. Lutz, *Christianitas Afflicta* (Göttingen, 1956).

enthusiasm, more academic and even scholastic in its religious thinking. It entered upon the so-called Age of Orthodoxy and, though enlivened by fine music and hymnology, it remained stodgily unproductive of religious and social ideas until the rise of Pietism in the later decades of the seventeenth century. To these epithets one is tempted to add the word monolithic, but only in regard to the period following 1580, when after a fierce internal struggle Orthodox Lutheranism overcame the Philipist party.

This breakdown of the old Bucerian Reformed south was followed not only by some marginal Jesuit reconquests to Catholicism but also by the incursion into Germany of a new and harder-hitting version of the Reformed faith: Calvinism. In 1563 the Elector Frederick III led the Palatinate into the Calvinist cause, made Heidelberg its German intellectual centre, and started that long train of events which led his descendant to the catastrophe of the White Mountain. The small principalities of Anhalt and Nassau also turned Calvinist; yet they were followed by only one imperial city, that of Bremen, isolated in its north-western corner. Even in these places Calvinism failed to establish its distinctive ecclesiastical patterns, for there emerged churches organized along Lutheran lines even while professing Calvinist beliefs. What the Bucerian Reformed cause had lost was not to any marked extent regained by its successor, the Calvinist Reformed cause. This collapse has been all too little acknowledged as a turning-point in German affairs. That the Reformed religion lost its hold on the imperial cities of Swabia and Alsace we should doubtless regret, because that religious outlook might have furnished a firm basis for ideas of civic freedom and political independence. The survival would have expanded what might be dubbed the Swiss-thinking element among the Germanic peoples, and possibly in later days it might have tipped the balance toward liberty and diversity. What if southern Germany had stayed Bucerian, while the Hanseatic north-west and Lower Saxony had drawn closer to their Dutch, Scandinavian and English associates? At all events the spectacle of the liberal and charitable Martin Bucer exiled in Cambridge can arouse some far-reaching speculations, some of history's more attractive might-have-beens. Does it not symbolize one of the 'hard luck stories' so thickly scattered across German history?

Thus in the German cities the long decline of the civic and communal sense had been arrested for a time by the lively influence of humanism, and still more by the popular enthusiasms of the Reformation. But, as with the revolt of the Netherlanders against Philip of Spain, once the major storm had spent itself the old rulers were found still sitting in the seats of power. In Germany from the 1550s onward the powers and pretensions of city magistrates and councillors grew; caught in a web of nepotism and self-seeking, the burgher failed to become more of a citizen and less of a subject. And in the background lay a process of economic decline, springing essentially from the patterns of that new Atlantic and Baltic world economy which left High Germany not only high but dry. The Hanseatic ports remained on the new *mappa mundi*, but Augsburg's population fell by half, while even that of Nuremberg remained stationary until the nineteenth century. In Frankfurt we recall the magic early pages of Goethe's *Dichtung und Wahrheit*: a delightful background for the boyhood and youth of genius, yet something of a world in trance until the coming of the industrial revolution. Yet whatever the extent and nature of their decline, whatever formalism tended to beset their religion once sectarianism had been repressed and democratic enthusiasm had faded, the old German cities continued to provide settings for civilized and humane living. Even in our day the decentralization of German public life has done much not only to foster genius but to prevent the triumph of barbarism. When the present writer returned to Germany during the last months of war and the first of peace in 1945, he found himself reflecting on this theme, and not without emotion. From beneath the physical and spiritual rubble, the Germany of Renaissance, Reformation and Enlightenment quickened and sprouted in a thousand places: it soon began to grow again into warmth and fragrance, and it grew first of all in the musical and religious life of the city churches.

10

The German Reformation:
A Changing Historiography

Having sought to depict some of the developments in modern Reformation studies, the writer must above all avoid leaving the impression that a scholarly Valhalla has now been attained. This implication of a mellow finality perhaps remains the most serious criticism to be brought against the otherwise deservedly famous synthesists of the last generation. Before summarizing my conclusions and stressing their highly provisional character, I may promote a greater realism by first glancing at a few landmarks along the route which has brought historians to their present positions. With regard to the Reformation, a subject of such magnitude and continuing interest, historiography remains in its own right a meaningful aspect of history. Over the intervening periods few branches of culture have been subjected to greater changes of emphasis; and if anything may be confidently predicted, it is that recent approaches and generalizations will undergo extension and correction during the decades to come. Apart from changing attitudes and interests, there still await discovery rich mines of factual information, especially concerning the social and mental history of the period. And there remain a good many German cities and districts, any one of which would abundantly justify the expenditure of twenty years' work or more by some experienced scholar.

During the middle and later sixteenth century the Lutherans made surprisingly few notable contributions to the historiography of their own Reformation.[1] In some cases this failure to write

[1] The most useful handbook on historiography for our present purpose

recent history sprang from their preoccupation with earlier ages, wherein they sought precedents and justifications for themselves, sins and shortcomings in papalist Christianity. For example, among the first Lutheran historians was the Englishman Robert Barnes, whose *Lives of the Roman Pontiffs* only reached the twelfth-century pontificate of Alexander III. These were written under the eye of Luther, who added a preface before the book appeared at Wittenberg in 1536. Equally partisan was that unattractive but monumental compilation by Flacius Illyricus and his colleagues, *The Magdeburg Centuries* (Basle, 1559–74), which failed to pass beyond the end of the thirteenth. It nevertheless helped to establish the type and the context of 'universal' Church history, foreshadowing to no small extent the lines of research since favoured by that odd abstraction from the fabric of human experience. To this group of writings belongs also John Foxe's Latin *Commentaries* (Strassburg, 1554) which, even when brought up to date in 1559, formed merely the kernel of the enormous *Acts and Monuments of the Christian Martyrs* (London, 1563). By then Foxe had been influenced by Crespin's *Le Livre des Martyrs...depuis Jean Hus* (Geneva, 1554), another large collection also involving pertinacious labour upon the source-materials, yet conceived in a less partisan spirit. These two deserve mention here, since one striking fact concerning German historiography of the Reformation is its lack of a Foxe or a Crespin,[2] a lack perhaps attributable to the relative paucity of Lutheran as opposed to Anabaptist martyrs, or again to the

is E. Fueter. P. Joachimsen, *Geschichtsauffassung und Geschichtsschreibung* is essential on the historical writing of the German humanists. Equally indispensable, especially in regard to Church history, is E. C. Scherer. G. Wolf has a good, though now dated, 48-page chapter on the historiography of the Reformation. F. Schnabel, and B. Gebhardt, *Handbuch der deutschen Geschichte*, ii are both useful tools for historiographical study. For recent publications see especially the *Archiv für Reformationsgeschichte*, *Luther Jahrbuch* and *Church History*. In English, brief accounts appear in J. P. Dolan, ch. 1 and in H. E. Barnes, *A History of Historical Writing* (2nd edn., New York, 1962), ch. 6. Bibliographical guidance on early Lutheran historians is given by H. Scheible, *Die Anfänge der reformatorischen Geschichtsschreibung* (Gütersloh, 1966).

[2] The most serviceable edition of Crespin's *Histoire des Martyrs* is edited by D. Benoit (3 vols., Toulouse, 1885–9). A third comparable martyrology is that of the Netherlander Haemstede: cf. J.-F. Gilmont, 'La genèse du martyrologe d'Adriaen van Haemstede' in *Revue d'histoire ecclésiastique*, lxiii (1968).

non-militant spirit which beset Lutheranism after the Peace of Augsburg. Had a systematic record of suffering and devotion ever been compiled, it could at least have depicted the German Reformation for what it was: a movement owing much to the common people. But this did not constitute an attractive spectacle in Melanchthon's world which, as we shall shortly observe, produced a very different historian in Johannes Sleidan. There were other writers, it is true, who saw the Lutheran Reformation from more religious and popular viewpoints, but for one reason or another they did not fill the German gap. That industrious and able writer Heinrich Bullinger did not even intend to do so, since he concerned himself with the early Reformation in German-speaking Switzerland: indeed, he sought both by exclusion and inclusion to depict the Swiss Reformation as a process independent of Luther. Again, that German Lutheran writers should have overcome the cult of personality was hardly possible, since they stood so near to the immense corpus of Luther's writings, pervaded so richly by his spirit. Yet Luther himself did not find a great contemporary or near-contemporary biographer. Johann Mathesius published in 1566 his *Histories of Martin Luther's ... Life and Death.* Such value as may be found in this pleasant but undistinguished work lies in anecdotal detail compiled by a non-intellectual memoirist incapable of writing a critical or historical biography of his hero. Nevertheless hagiography had begun its course, and at no stage has it lacked nourishment at the hands of pious moralists, soulful theologians and even innocent psychiatrists, all consciously or unconsciously tending to turn the German Reformation into a one-man story.

There remains the massive work of Sleidan, which deserves far more attention than the rest, since it set the tone and methodology of German and European Reformation history at least until the nineteenth century.[3] Johannes Philippson was born in 1506

---

[3] On Sleidan see the biography by W. Friedensburg and his correspondence, well edited by H. Baumgarten. Among other contributions are those by P. Joachimsen, *Geschichtsauffassung und Geschichtsschreibung*; E. C. Scherer; and the article by F. W. Kampschulte. Personally I have made most use of E. Menke-Glückert (ch. 4), who is also valuable (ch. 3) on the Melanchthon school and outlook. Bibliographical notes are in E. Fueter (Paris, 1914), p. 247. A useful bibliography and selection of texts

or 1508 at Schleiden in the Eifel, received a thorough humanist training at Liège, Cologne and Louvain, then from 1533 pursued legal studies in Paris and Orléans. Recommended to Cardinal Jean du Bellay, archbishop of Paris, he became an agent of the group headed by this distinguished family, the group which sought to ally France with the Schmalkaldic League. When he joined the du Bellays, Sleidan was already a student of the French historians: in 1537 he published Latin translations from Froissart, and in 1545–8 two volumes containing a free Latin version of Commines. Returning to Germany and settling in Strassburg, he finally committed himself to the Protestant Reformation, which for the rest of his life he regarded as a miraculous work of God. In 1545 Sleidan urged the leaders of the Schmalkaldic League to ensure that, just as Commines had created a true picture of his age, so now a worthy memorial of their own still greater age should be erected. 'For you it is to provide that all men should experience what has been transacted through you, and that they should learn to honour therein the unspeakable wisdom and power of God.' At this stage the League appointed him its official historian and gave him special access to its archives, demanding nevertheless that the resultant work should be examined by its representatives.

Sleidan had in fact been collecting his materials for several years, but progress was interrupted by his exacting employers, who realized that they now had another diplomat in their pay and in 1545 sent him to England on a mission to secure support from Henry VIII. Though two years later he had completed his first four books, covering the period 1517–25, the emperor's victories over the League now demanded a period of caution. During a part of the years 1551–2 he represented Strassburg at the Council of Trent, but thenceforth he surmounted the remaining obstacles with amazing industry. In 1555 the first edition of his *Commentaries*, a folio volume of some 940 pages in twenty-five books, was being distributed from Strassburg: its full title might be translated: *Commentaries on the State of*

covering the historical objectives of Melanchthon, Sleidan, Flacius and the Centuriators is in H. Scheible, *Die Anfänge der reformatorischen Geschichtsschreibung*.

Religion and Public Affairs under Emperor Charles V.[4] To Sleidan's credit, the zealous Catholics blamed him for his partisanship, the zealous Protestants for his moderation and his disclosures. In later years his French equivalent La Popelinière was to receive similar treatment. Characteristically, Melanchthon thought that Sleidan had revealed many things best left in eternal silence. But the poor historian had little time to taste of fame or contumely, since in the October of 1556 he succumbed to the pestilence then raging throughout Europe. Nevertheless he had just published another book destined to fame. This was the little outline of ancient history called *On the Four Chief Empires*, subsequently used by the Jesuits and also much expanded by tormentors of the young.

Until displaced by nineteenth-century research, the *Commentaries* remained the most scholarly and best-documented survey of the German Reformation. In his Preface and again in an *Apology* written for the second edition shortly before his death, Sleidan expresses his ideals in the words *candor* and *veritas*. These he claims to have attained by discounting the common reports and basing his story upon public records, by adding nothing of his own but leaving the documents to the judgment of the reader. Virtually using Ranke's famous phrase, he says he will write 'just as everything happened'. He reproaches Cardinal Pole and Cochlaeus as slanderers of the Protestant religion; and it must be acknowledged that in comparison with these rivals, or with the Protestant Centuriators, he provides a model of impartiality. On the other hand Sleidan shows the defects of his virtues, for he entertained an austere and self-abnegating concept of the historian's task. A high proportion of his text consists of quoted or summarized state papers: all too literally does he 'stick to the documents'. One must grant him his point that civil and religious history 'are interwoven one with another, so that it was impossible to separate them'. Yet in fact Sleidan provided a highly externalized and political version of the movement, dominated as he was by his legal training, by the official source-materials and by his

---

[4] Sleidan was widely read abroad in the original Latin. There are also, for example, two English translations: those by John Daus (1560) and G. Bohun (1689).

models Caesar, Livy, Commines—historians who never had to describe a phenomenon remotely resembling the Reformation. If his account of Luther as a man of religion seems to us quite perfunctory, how much more so his references to religion on the lower social levels. Armed with the general fear of social chaos and the ancient notion that history should blaze forth the lives and deaths of princes, he says all too little about religious motivation and wholly underestimates the constructive role of the people.

Thus did humanist ideals, even in the service of an industrious and noble mind, reject some significant aspects of Reformation history. And it can scarcely be pleaded on Sleidan's behalf that such limitations remained universal in his day. Foxe and Crespin were writing the history of the common people, while books on spirituality abounded, and were soon to produce biography with a psycho-religious dimension, as in Ribadeneira's *Life of Ignatius Loyola* (Naples, 1572). Yet for good or ill, Sleidan's dignified, documented, largely political narrative passed into tradition as the 'standard' form of Reformation history. In the cases of not a few authors this form has remained 'standard' even into our own century, and most evidently among the English, ever bemused by the personalities of the Tudor monarchs, the acts of parliament, the state reformation in general. But we have not yet exhausted the influences bearing upon Johannes Sleidan. A number of clues indicate that he was writing under the strong influence of Melanchthon, who had taught not only Sleidan's scheme of the four world monarchies, but also the wider notion that history forms a succession of divinely predestined events and patterns. 'God transfers and stabilizes the Kingdoms.'[5] Moreover, Melanchthon was a primary source for the idea that history is philosophy teaching by example. 'All the world is God's theatre in which he displays examples of all our duties.' Hence history involved a pedagogic search for heroes and a turning away from the unpleasant spectacle of fallen man-in-the-mass. The political aristocracy of Guicciardini was no more exclusive than the theological aristocracy of Melanchthon. The disciple Sleidan created a textbook for the *Praeceptor Germaniae*, the all-German pedagogue Philip Melanchthon. Still later, but

[5] E. Menke-Glückert, p. 49.

in a similar context, Samuel Pufendorf was to speak of 'the useful science of history', directed toward 'the youth of high rank' who would some day hold 'offices of state'.

This moralistic, high-class history envisaged no human progress, but rather (along with the *Book of Daniel* and Melanchthon's pessimistic anthropology) the cyclical struggle of a corrupt mankind. All too gradually, historians of the German Reformation liberated themselves from such patterns. Yet the best of them also strove to maintain and develop Sleidan's ideal of objectivity. In 1692, the year of his death, Veit Ludwig von Seckendorf finished his *History of Lutheranism*, a work seeking to unite a strict and theologically-minded piety with an impartial adherence to the sources. He found the most meaningful episode of the Reformation in Luther's German Bible and in the initial conversion of so large a part of the German people. Thereafter he saw anticlimax: the depressing assumption of authority by politicians, and those scandalous internal divisions which Protestants should have been trying to heal. Meanwhile, under the leadership of P. J. Spener, the Pietist movement had pervaded the Lutheran churches, softening their scholastic dogmatism and calling for a revival of the Evangelical outlook and a resumption of the spiritual Reformation. In this tradition Gottfried Arnold published between 1700 and 1712 his *Non-Partisan History of Churches and Heretics*, exalting the young Luther an as apostle of renewal, but devaluing Luther the middle-aged creator of institutions and orthodoxies. In due course this liberal Pietism allied with the rationalizing tenor of the age to produce in the heavily-documented and wide-ranging works of J. L. von Mosheim new standards of exhaustiveness and accuracy. While Mosheim did not reject the supernatural, his main emphasis when he reached the Reformation lay upon its character as a logical reorganization of Christianity, a triumph of reason which had paved the way toward the advances of his own day. Mosheim's *Institutes of Ecclesiastical History* (1737–41) preserved an antiquated form in according a chapter to each century of the Christian era. On the other hand its ponderous annotation and scrupulous examination of sources make it a forerunner of the age of Ranke. By virtue of his massive learning Mosheim long dominated the international field; for example the English translation was to be edited as late as 1863 by William Stubbs, one of the fathers of 'scientific' history in Britain. Meanwhile in western Europe Mosheim's contemporaries Hume, Voltaire, Gibbon and Robertson were all carrying forward more or less analogous interpretations, deploring the intolerance of the early Reformers but welcoming their movement as a precursor of the Enlightenment.

In some respects the attitudes of Leopold von Ranke toward the Reformation did not mark a notable advance on those of his recent predecessors. Believing human history a providential patterning of both secular and religious forces, Ranke achieved little original insight into the theological issues and touched all too rarely upon the rugged forces underlying the Reformation. Based largely upon a heroic study of the rediscovered acts of the imperial Diets, his *German History in the Era of the Reformation* (1839–47) seems nowadays disproportionately political, even though more than once he does turn aside to sketch the social progress of the new beliefs. Ranke's Luther is essentially the 'good German' who rallies a confused nation and its princes not merely in order to reform the Church but also to preserve the structure of its empire. Alongside this rather stolid but still valuable narrative may be placed another of his early books, the *History of the Popes* (1834–6), a beautifully ordered account, with some important chapters on the Reformation and Counter Reformation as they affected Germany. It was Ranke who originated our modern usage of the term and the concept 'Counter Reformation'.

Despite their conscientious striving for objectivity, the works of Ranke understandably failed to satisfy the German Catholic historians of his day, and *The Reformation* (1846–8) of J. J. Ignaz von Döllinger directly challenged their dark picture of the late medieval Church and papacy. Stressing the element of reform during the century preceding Luther, Döllinger went on to express his conviction that the Reformation brought about a decline in German morality and religion. It need hardly be added that the puritanical diatribes of Lutheran moralists themselves could be used after a fashion to buttress this contention. Similarly, in his eight-volume *History of the German People at the Close of the Middle Ages* (1874–91) the patriotic Johannes

Janssen not only blamed treacherous alien forces—monopoly-capitalism and the Jews—for the ills of Germany, but laid stress on the devotional life of the pre-Reformation period, its expansion of school and university education, the number of Bibles available in German before Luther. However tendentiously he selected these factors, Janssen's work nevertheless contributed toward a more balanced view of German religion and thought during the century preceding the Reformation. Moreover, it encouraged others to explore spirituality on the social level. A similarly creative role could not be attributed to another partisan work, *Luther and Lutheranism* (1904) by the Dominican Heinrich Denifle, who, though so erudite in this and other fields, could make of Luther little more than a monster of spiritual pride and moral depravity. These years did indeed see a certain decline of objectivity amongst many historical writers, both Protestant and Catholic. At the same time, the Jesuit Hartmann Grisar (*Luther*, 1911) relieved Luther from the grosser aspersions of Denifle, while nevertheless sternly condemning the Evangelical theology. And so far as the charges of turpitude were concerned, H. Boehmer's *Luther in the Light of Modern Research*, widely translated and greatly developed since the original edition of 1906, effectively silenced the stories current from Cochlaeus to Denifle.

Behind the spectacular controversies and the eye-catching *magna opera* of the century 1830–1930, there were occurring developments far more vital to recent scholarship. In the great Weimar Edition of Luther's works we observe but one of the many editorial and bibliographical enterprises upon which modern historiography has been built. Many *Flugschriften* were collected and republished, a close study of the work and correspondence of the German humanists and early Reformers inaugurated. The 'Luther Renaissance' among the theologians was headed by Karl Holl and by an ever-growing group of Swedish, German, American and British scholars.[6] Though it often incorporated imaginative superstructures, this movement has had profound implications even for historians, who would be rash to enter the Reformation field without some grasp of its

[6] A good notion of the movement may be gained, for example, from the text and bibliography of E. G. Rupp, *The Righteousness of God*.

achievements. By contrast the advancing disciplines of psychology and sociology seem as yet to have brought few fresh insights into our field. Thus far the psychological evidence on Luther has not been convincingly handled; in any event, moreover, what interests historians in the personality of Luther—his creative and destructive intellect, his charismatic qualities—cannot be 'explained' by reference to youthful maladjustments which he must have shared with millions of undistinguished contemporaries. Again, Marxism encouraged historians to explore those social-economic factors which undoubtedly underlay the progress of the Reformation. Yet Marxist dogma did not convince even Marxist historians that the Reformation should be dismissed as an epiphenomenon of social-economic forces, or as a new opiate administered to the people by the ruling and exploiting classes. Max Weber's inversion, whereby Calvinist puritanism became the parent of modern capitalism, is demonstrably weaker still; but in any case its author and his followers did not even seek to apply it to the Lutheran Reformation. Of greater interest was *The Social Teaching of the Christian Churches* (1912) by Ernst Troeltsch:[7] it has a special relevance to Reformation studies in its division of Christianity into three 'types': the Church-type, territorialist and accommodating toward the world; the sect-type, withdrawing, exclusivist, well exemplified by Anabaptism; and the 'Spiritualist' type, seeing the essence of religion not in Luther's Scriptural fidelity but in the spiritual enlightenment described by a whole group of early Protestant mystics like Denck, Franck and Schwenckfeld. Such concepts have obvious dangers, yet Troeltsch himself presents them as a series of helpful models, not as precise categorization; he acknowledges that his three 'types' were variously intertwined, and that many individuals moved freely from one affiliation to another. In the years which followed, rapid progress occurred in the study of Anabaptist and Spiritualist religion: here the Mennonite Society has taken the lead in publishing or re-publishing a large body of hitherto unknown or unfamiliar source-materials. Regarding the Radicals, the complexities have grown with every decade, and it has become increasingly clear

---

[7] *Soziallehren der christlichen Kirchen und Gruppen* (Tübingen, 1912; English translation by O. Wyon, 1931).

that a collective term like 'the Radical Reformation' has not so close a link with historical reality as terms like 'Lutheran Reformation' or 'Church of England'.

Today historians of the Reformation are thus heirs to some varied and expanding traditions. In mere quantitative terms no individual historian can hope to attain a mastery even of the secondary sources, let alone the primary materials, across the whole field. Yet we now stand prepared to describe the causes and character of the Reformation on a far greater number of levels than those envisaged by our predecessors; most notably on the grass-roots level, where life has been for several decades enlivened by the increasingly purposeful and not merely antiquarian study of regional and local history. The common people of that day are now allowed to have minds and spirits; they too are seen not as mere economic functionaries but as subject to complex and conflicting motives and aspirations. We have liberated ourselves from the Sleidanian tradition. Today Reformation historians should presumably seek to derive all they can from a multitude of disciplines: theology, literary criticism, the histories of art and of philosophy, economic, legal, administrative, social and political studies. And surely more will choose not merely to pursue specialist researches but to synthesize the work of others, overleaping in that process the old subject-boundaries, creating sober yet imaginative modes of communication between areas once separated by academic custom. This work of synthesis must involve failures, misunderstandings, omissions and lapses. Though seldom successfully pursued by writers without research experience, it remains no practicable task for purists, pedants, individualists who will trust no other man's deductions from the original sources. It can afford to disdain the timidity or the spiritual pride which has made some scholars consecrate a lifetime to a couple of articles. In short, synthesis must involve writing books which form challenges to write better ones, books which will inevitably be replaced, attacked and patronized by others which climb upon their shoulders.

Of this sort, the present essay forms a very modest, a rough-and-ready, example. A great deal of its information comes at second hand; and if a reader unfamiliar with the literature of the

German Reformation would know why this must be so, he should peruse the seven ponderous volumes of Schottenloher's bibliography of German history during the period 1517–85, which contain more than 65,000 printed items![8] My own scope has been restricted in the sense that it comprehends not the whole enormous panorama of the Reformation, but merely the most crucial and formative stage of the Lutheran Reformation in Germany. We have sought to explore the causal phenomena, rational and sub-rational, social and intellectual, religious and secular. Despite the apparent suddenness of the popular response to Luther, this response had attained weight from a lengthy accretion of theory and grievance. It had developed layer upon layer: the age-old antagonism between Roman Church and German empire, the prophecies of millennial revolution, the nationalist manifestos of the humanists, the cloud of anticlerical complaints. All these nevertheless coexisted with a fund of popular pietism, sometimes externalized and superstitious, sometimes in the tradition of German mysticism and its offshoot, the *devotio moderna*. It was most naïve to suppose that in 1517–20 religious people, even the more conservative members of the ruling class, saw Luther's movement in terms of a head-on collision between Catholic piety and heretical innovation. As late as 1524 Lazarus Spengler was asserting that the nation did not face a schism but a series of theological differences, which could be tolerated—given goodwill and moderation—just as the clashes between Thomists, Scotists and Occamists had been tolerated in earlier days. And many years later there were mediating theologians like Georg Witzel,[9] and fence-sitting rulers like Joachim II of Brandenburg.

Amongst the stimulants to popular and middle-class revolt, humanist criticism, whether Erasmian or German nationalist, remains hard to evaluate with any precision. Yet we cannot doubt that the attacks made by the generation of Brant and Erasmus upon clerical abuses and superstitions, still more the humour and bitterness of Ulrich von Hutten and his associates,

---

[8] Approximately ten times the number of entries in Conyers Read's *Bibliography of British History, Tudor Period* (2nd edn., 1959).

[9] For a review of Witzel's position, see J. P. Dolan, pp. 371–82. Further bibliographies on both Joachim II and Witzel are in S. Skalweit, p. 440.

managed to percolate into mass opinion. Also at work were milder yet equally pervasive forms of nationalism. An intense fascination with German history, topography and local tradition preceded and accompanied the Reformation. Such notions did not remain exclusively those of the educated classes. From Brant and Hutten onwards, but increasingly from 1520, humanists themselves wrote a part of the early vernacular propaganda directed toward the common people, while Luther's own works enshrined no small part of humanist social and historical teachings. On the other hand, it has been shown that during the 1520s a neighbouring school of humanism was far from being a necessary condition for the adherence of a given city to Lutheranism. We are dealing with a longstanding, diffuse but complex atmosphere of satire, moralizing and grievance. The malaise of the people, at bottom social and economic, might in any given place be directed against canons, city oligarchs, or both. Then it was suddenly intensified by an upsurge of pamphleteering and preaching, inspired in the main by the theological orientations deriving from Luther. The secular pressures also arising from Luther's own work need treating with great caution, since with all his failings he cannot be regarded as anything other than an authentic man of religion. Even so, his debt to humanist Biblical scholarship, especially to Reuchlin and Erasmus, seems straightforward and manifest. Likewise, the humanists and their allies the publisher-printers formed a most powerful agency in amplifying Luther's message, or rather those parts of it which could readily be made intelligible to the masses; in particular the blunt appeal to Biblical Christianity against the papacy. We drew attention also to factors sometimes neglected by ecclesiastical historians, especially to Luther's impact upon town populations already acquiring verbal and literary education, people responsive to his plea for education, social service and mutual aid. Nevertheless the genuine religious enthusiasm amongst those people is too well attested—and their secular motivations too varied—to sanction the simplistic Marxist phrase 'early bourgeois revolution' as a satisfactory label for Luther's movement.[10] His promotion of laymen to the priesthood

[10] See, for example, M. Steinmetz, 'Reformation und Bauernkrieg...als frühbürgerliche Revolution' in *Zeitschrift für Geschichtswissenschaft*, xiii

was taken crudely by some anticlerical minds; yet if we may judge from the tracts, the people can hardly have been left ignorant of its deeper implications. As for Luther's specifically social teaching, this arose directly from his religious concepts, which made him inevitably a social thinker but not in any modern sense a 'political thinker'. Though he had somehow to work in the context of the existing German state system, he exercised little influence upon either the philosophical apotheosis or the bureaucratic centralization of the state.

Concerning the theological influences brought to bear upon the developing Luther, we cannot claim to have gleaned novelties where so many minds more erudite have already harvested. At the same time, to shirk some examination of Luther's own intellectual context would have been an obvious dereliction of duty in a survey of this present type. It seemed difficult to attribute Luther's more fruitful concepts, still less his public appeal, to his long sojourn in the sphere of Occamism. On the other hand, his characteristic 'theology of the Cross' had distinct debts to the German mystics, to his counsellor Staupitz, and also to that continuing best-seller, the *Imitatio Christi*. Conventionally but inevitably, we had to stress the force of his attraction toward Augustine, while yet observing that Augustine formed a gateway to the Pauline Epistles, and so to Luther's original interpretation of a central Pauline theme, the interpretation known as Justification by Faith Alone. Psychologically as well as theologically this went beyond Augustine, especially in its emphasis upon the 'extrinsic' doctrine of imputation. Needless to add, a historian would like to know how far this doctrine did in fact promote Luther's mission in society, but the question is probably unanswerable through the surviving evidence. The very term 'Augustine' embraces a whole complex of intervening traditions, not merely a study of Augustine's own works. Within this complex, at once 'ancient', 'medieval' and 'modern', I have ventured to re-assign a limited yet still significant role to the so-called 'forerunners' of the mid-fifteenth century: John of Wesel, Wessel Gansfort

(1965), *Sonderheft*, pp. 35–50. Such Marxist interpretations are reviewed by K. Dienst in *Blätter für Pfälzische Kirchengeschichte*, xxvii (1969) and by L. W. Spitz in *Lutherische Rundschau*, xix (1969).

and Johann Pupper of Goch. That such writers formed confirmatory rather than causal influences might no doubt be argued: a similar but less intimate role could indeed be attributed to John Huss, whom Luther began in 1519 to appreciate as a predecessor.

All in all, every historian armed with some modest theological knowledge must surely feel obliged to stress Luther's originality of thought and expression, together with his strong sense of continuity with the past, his sense of a mission to revitalize rather than to divide Catholic Christianity. His mis-prediction of history and his underestimation of the controlling interest of Rome does not make acceptable the image of the neurotic individualist, the divisive rebel. It must of course be conceded not only that the unwilled results of Luther's career were divisive, but that the divisions arose in some measure from those aspects of his theology which, given the current intellectual constraints of papacy and hierarchy, were bound sooner or later to suffer juridical condemnation as heresy. Never did Rome show itself more clearly as a preserver of its own past. Still more perhaps was schism fostered by Luther's stentorian literary expression, in particular by his stark announcement that the papacy was condemned and lost beyond hope of recovery. Division also arose in marked degree from the cynicism, the self-deception, the despair of laymen high and low: from both Habsburg and anti-Habsburg politics, above all from a nationalist and anticlerical public opinion, which left the papal champion Eck with so small a following in the early years of the struggle. Even had the lightning actually struck Luther at Stotternheim in 1505, some schism larger in scale than that of the Hussites would almost certainly have arisen in Germany, in Switzerland, in the Netherlands. A historian like Janssen showed naïvety in supposing that 'German piety' would necessarily occasion a sense of dutiful obedience to the Rome of Alexander VI and Julius II. Again, it is one thing to assert that a Catholic reforming spirit was already in motion in 1517, quite another to suppose that a general Catholic Reformation would—even without a menacing Luther to spur it on—have arisen on a scale sufficient to avoid the cataclysm then imminent. By that date immense floods of resentment had built up behind the frail dam of traditional ecclesiasticism. The German Catholic Reformation grew but slowly as a strange blend of devotion and fear, and few historians have realized that, in its earlier stages, it was more of a one-man movement than Luther's. For where would it have been without St. Peter Canisius?[11]

The later chapters of this present survey seek to examine the forces of change even as they erupted from their confinement, and especially during the years just after 1520, the years when their nature became clearer, when Luther spoke for a nation still largely united, when he won over not merely the young, the critical, the restive, but also many of those traditional minds which in the longer run would reject his theology. But by the time these disturbed but fundamentally conservative people had rejoined the traditionalist theologians, Luther and his allies had established a firm grip upon the bulk of the nation, especially upon the middle and lower orders in the numerous and politically vital towns of Germany. From this point our essay has concerned not merely the lateral diffusion of ideas between educated men but still more their vertical dissemination into society as a whole. This downward movement is clearly indicated by the gigantic sales of tracts, by the documented adhesion of urban populations, by the recorded views even of magnates and scholars opposed to democratization and religious change alike. The striking agency has seemed to us not merely 'the press' but the ability of both writers and printers to collaborate in producing the cheap pamphlet, written in terms of mass-appeal. The industry geared itself to such a function all the more rapidly since for several decades already it had been issuing popular literature on more or less serious subjects, albeit on a far smaller scale. The evidence shows clearly that the press did not displace the pulpit. Indeed it confirmed and extended the spoken word: to regard the two as 'rival' forces is to divide the indivisible. Some printers ran both with the hare and with the hounds: their inconsistencies suggest that the enormous numerical preponderance of Protestant tracts in 1520–25 owed much to commercial enterprise as well as to religious conviction. But printers can have made money out of Lutheran propaganda only in proportion to its acceptability among a large reading public. To study the

[11] The outstanding biography is J. Brodrick, *Saint Peter Canisius* (1935).

book-making and book-purchasing behaviour of any European nation of the sixteenth century is to become convinced that it bought what it wanted to support its prejudices. For the first time in history, religious and social publicity became big business throughout central Europe, and during the crucial years this apparently decisive medium was ranged behind Luther.

An examination of his fellow-publicists revealed that they sprang from all classes of the community, with the exception of working peasants. Some of them vulgarized Luther's message, while their writings also reflect a wide variety of responses to the crisis. Alongside the work of devout and scrupulous disciples, there extends a spectrum of attitudes ranging from 'enlightened' humanism to 'literary' satire and near-secular protest. Older attitudes are often preserved or revived by the propagandists. The 'obscure men', the ecclesiastical reactionaries, were not allowed to disappear quietly after the work of Crotus and Hutten, while on the sidelines there stands the sturdy peasant critic, the *Karsthans*, even though the role assigned him by Vadianus and other educated writers must not be presumed to reproduce widely prevalent attitudes among real-life peasantry. Likewise, though Luther's Catholic adversaries did not correspond with the unjust image created by the satirists, they did not happen to include a rival figure with charismatic appeal. While able men like Eck and Emser lacked such appeal—and somehow managed to appear even more ultra-clerical than we now suppose them— the one Catholic writer of near-genius was also something of a literary maverick. Thomas Murner did not lack a basic sincerity, but his affinities lay with Erasmus' *Praise of Folly*, even a little with Rabelais: in the last resort he was incapable of creating those monuments of earnest and massive simplicity demanded by the popular mood. Thus Luther was fortunate in the limitations of his opponents: he survived even the embarrassment caused by the Protestant sectarians, and avoided with some little effort the brush of social anarchy with which they soon tarred themselves. Karlstadt and Müntzer both lacked intellectual discretion and worldly wisdom: whatever their initial appeal, they soon embraced the forces most clearly destined for defeat. Surveying these forces, it is hard not to sympathize most warmly with the peasants, who after all did not seek to rule

Germany or to shake off the social bond.[12] On the other hand, even a peasant victory at Frankenhausen would probably have solved no problems: by way of more prolonged anarchy and bloodshed it might have led to a fundamental crisis of civilization and thence to an even greater exploitation of the peasantry. And though we have studied pamphlets according an active role to peasant wisdom, besides pamphlets adapted to peasant understanding, it remains hard to accord to this group, perhaps involving well over half the nation, a creative role in the Lutheran Reformation. The evidence strongly suggests that such peasant aspirations as could be organized were concerned with agrarian rights and legal status. As individuals, peasants were not religious sceptics, but to their group thinking, the Catholic *versus* Lutheran struggle must all too readily have seemed peripheral. How far this happened after the disaster of 1525 remains hard to estimate from the available evidence, but after this experience the peasants did not again appeal to arms. During the generation which followed, a host of pastors both Catholic and Protestant taught them a soporific Christianity and helped to keep them at work on the land. At all events east of the Elbe, their legal and economic privileges continued to decline in favour of their landlords. Meantime their more ardent and prophetic spirits, unsatisfied by routine Lutheranism, turned toward other religions; especially toward Anabaptism, the appeal of which was by no means limited to urban artisans.

While there remain major uncertainties regarding the trends of peasant opinion after the Revolt, the German townsman has become a far better-documented character. To him the last three chapters have been devoted, and without hesitation we have emphasized the crucial nature of his contribution to the Lutheran movement. Here again it must be confessed that many local tasks await historians. So many of the older town histories took parochial views of the Reformation, failing to realize they were dealing with mobile populations, inter-city movements, cases inviting comparisons. Again, all too often they failed to utilize

[12] On the Peasants' Revolt and its Reformation connections, see G. Franz; P. Althaus; F. Lau in *Luther Jahrbuch*. Important passages from the last are translated in K. C. Sessions, *Reformation and Authority. The Meaning of the Peasants' Revolt* (Lexington, Mass., 1968), pp. 94–101. Sessions gives a select bibliography; so does E. G. Léonard, pp. 393–5.

the masses of evidence lying undiscovered in manuscript sources. Even today, the numerous uncompleted assignments in urban history reflect no special discredit on German scholarship: they are still paralleled, for example, in English and Scottish urban history of the sixteenth century. So far as concerns the German municipalities, these unknown factors have not prevented the steady emergence of certain common though by no means universal patterns. At first sight, it is true, the diversities of urban experience during the Reformation seem formidable. The cities, and even the imperial cities, varied enormously in size, influence and independence. Even among the largest and most prestigious, so many seem to display some powerful differential: the financiers at Augsburg, the array of authors, publishers and sectarian immigrants at Strassburg, the strange fragmentation of loyalties at Erfurt, the tenacious influence of ecclesiastical corporations and theologians at Cologne, the exceptional force of Catholic princely houses at Vienna, Munich and Dresden, the very limitations upon municipal independence at Wittenberg, whence the most solid body of religious dogma came forth. Had Switzerland lain within our purview, its urban variety would have proved hardly less impressive.

Drawing gratefully upon the researches of others, we studied Nuremberg, Strassburg, various Baltic cities, and Erfurt; then examined the broad picture of events in the imperial cities as revealed by Bernd Moeller and other synthesists. These processes convinced the writer—and he hopes the reader—that the Reformation arose in its greatest strength within the cities, that it arose largely because of their social structures and dynamics, their class struggles, their longstanding anticlericalism, their literacy and mental liveliness, their strong self-protective urge toward internal unity, their ability to evade wholesale coercion by the emperor. Their resilience appeared most clearly after the disasters suffered by the Lutheran princes in 1546–7. Faced by France and the Turks, rent by mutual jealousies and the devout dynasticism of the Habsburgs, the Catholic princes lacked the power to capture many cities, let alone to police them and so eradicate Protestant heresy. The role of cities in the struggle, though most crucial during the formative decade 1520–30, was thus far from being limited to that decade.

Whatever may be said of the rising ecclesiastical powers of princes, or of the ultimate relapse even of the Reformed southern cities into that complacent Lutheran orthodoxy favoured by the Peace of Augsburg, urban Protestantism still remained the solid substructure of the Reformation.

Despite the variations of local interests and policies, something like a common design became detectable in a large group, perhaps in the majority of the German cities. Very broadly speaking, this design corresponds with the archetype already apparent in the Prague of John Huss. A decisive shift to the new beliefs could happen most easily in such compact and 'patriotic' communities, subject indeed to social tensions and yet in the last resort aware that chronic internal disunity might gravely menace their treasured way of life. The German Reformation arose from the assault of preachers and pamphleteers upon the middle and lower orders of the towns, not in the first place from the ruling patriciates, whose first instinct was to identify the demand for religious change with the longstanding secular unrest of their subjects. On the other hand, all classes of laymen and unprivileged clergy could see a common enemy and a common victim in the wealthy chapters and other clerical corporations. Their proud spires dominated the skyline of every major city, yet they had steadily rejected a co-operative civic role; they had preferred to remain 'foreign' elements within the legal and financial structure of the medieval city.

It has been noted that in Baltic cities and elsewhere the 'democratic' groups seeking a share of political control also promoted the religious Reformation, which thus remained the beneficiary when the secular campaigns subsided. The Lutheran Reformation was most fortunate to find a propaganda base within the patronage of Electoral Saxony, but it was also fortunate to arise when throughout most of the cities the old class struggle was still being waged—yet waged spasmodically and often without that degree of bitterness which would have excluded flexible adjustment. The atmosphere usually allowed of compromise and common action, even if a shared ambition to curtail ecclesiastical privilege and wealth were needed to bring the urban classes together. The city councils, seldom distinguished by any sacrificial adherence to Catholicism, often perceived that civic cohesion—and their own retention of power—might be purchased by agreeing to accept an Evangelical Reformation. Like the ruling classes everywhere, they contrived with much success to divert discontent into ecclesiastical channels. Effective imperial displeasure remained a menace, yet a somewhat nebulous one, because the emperor himself was demanding Church reform, and still more because he depended upon urban men and money in order to resist the triumphant Turk.[13] Yet in any event, faced by the choice between his displeasure and the graver evils of internal disruption, a city council would only hesitate on account of the most exceptionally powerful anti-Lutheran conviction or Habsburg affinities. At all events, during the amorphous early 1520s the cities probably ran less political risks in embracing the Reformation than did the princes a few years later.

Along these broad lines arose the commonest pattern of development, a pattern to be seriously broken by external pressures from Catholic princes rather than by any Catholic forces arising from within the cities. Even so, we have observed not merely local variants such as the flocking of radical sectarians to Strassburg but more general complications, especially the serious inroads made for a time by the Reformed, 'Bucerian' wing of Protestantism into the great cluster of cities in the south-west. It has been seen that in their failure at the Peace of Augsburg to grant equal recognition to the Reformed faith the Habsburgs conferred great favours on orthodox Lutheranism, toward which it now paid even these southern Protestants to gravitate. Thus at first sight the Habsburgs might seem to have united rather than divided their religious opponents, but in the longer run the Peace represented a wiser policy for the Catholic powers than they themselves are likely to have realized.

With our eye on civic and civil liberties, we may regret this decline of the Reformed Bucerian tradition, yet it must be conceded that a hard mosaic of Reformed outposts in the south-west, in league with the Swiss and able to negotiate support from the neighbouring power of France, would have brought further dangers not only to the Habsburgs and other Catholic princes but to the whole tottering structure of the Empire. As events in

[13] The relation of the Turkish threat to the Reformation is well surveyed by S. A. Fischer-Galati.

France, in the Netherlands, in Scotland were soon to show, the Reformed religion, remodelled by Calvin, excelled as a sharpener of cutting-edges for political revolution, especially for movements with an anti-monarchical, anti-legitimist tendency. After Augsburg the Lutheran religion could still make local advances, yet it was now restrained from within by a group of Lutheran princes and magistrates satisfied by the treaty privileges assigned them, rulers with more to fear from disruptive movements—either popular or princely—than from their Catholic colleagues in the Diet. When in the earlier phases of the Thirty Years War, Habsburgs, Calvinists, Danes, Swedes and Frenchmen imported dynamic change into the Empire, the successors of these German Lutheran princes remained the most immobile, the last to re-enlist in the defence of their faith against a now aggressive Habsburg Counter Reformation.

In the last resort the present writer must find himself reviewing the story he has outlined in the light of the history of political and mental liberties. These 'free' cities, humanists, printers, preachers, merchants, artisans, embarked upon the Reformation inspired by a variety of motives, only in part related to what we now regard as the 'history of freedom.' Moreover, to no small extent they soon found the Lutheran leadership taken over by rulers, often paternalist but always potentially oppressive; rulers whose virtues, when the main crisis came in 1620, proved the supine virtues of legalism rather than those of religious and political liberty. In the longer run our western liberties must acknowledge profound debts to the Reformed, Puritan and sectarian traditions, left by the Lutherans to fight for what they could grasp. And while the young Luther, with his appeal both to a national and a spiritual freedom, played an honourable part in the origins of all three movements, the mature Luther, his emphasis on spiritual fulfilment at the price of political quiescence, must bear no little responsibility for the changes which beset his movement and with it the fate of the German nation. Yet even before 1530 the alternative of prolonged religious and social confusion had come to present Lutheranism with its greatest menace. Again, though the central European cities contained precious elements of liberalism, Luther and his associates could not prevent their economic and political decline. Likewise they could not have foreseen and prepared for those conflicts which culminated in the Thirty Years War. Less still could Luther, Melanchthon or Sleidan have foreseen the harsh and calculating leadership within the Lutheran world attained in later centuries by the enterprising, insecure and hence militarist state of Prussia. However diverse modern judgments must remain on the doctrinal issues and solutions, to the sixteenth-century Germans of all social classes must be attributed some victories for a commonsense by no means strikingly common elsewhere in Europe. They finally demonstrated that within the structure of the empire, sometimes even within that of a single city, two or more religions could coexist, however precariously, for a long period. On the social and political plane, Luther's contemporaries and their sons should be judged by that substantial peace which reigned for more than half a century after Augsburg and was finally broken by human error rather than by inexorable forces: by the reckless irresponsibility of Frederick Elector Palatine and by the equally reckless reaction of the Emperor Ferdinand II.

The present writer has worked for most of his career in the field of English local and regional history, which for forty years he has seen as the key to a more significant social and mental history of England. In Germany similar tasks have long been in progress, yet as in Britain they might be done on a larger scale and with a closer regard to the great problems of national and supranational history. Ever increasingly we need to study German local history, and especially in its urban settings, in order to understand German national history. So stimulated, we shall see more clearly than ever that neither an examination of Luther's own thinking, nor a description of the clash of imperial and princely powers, nor even an analysis of the interaction between the social classes and the politicians, can significantly explain the series of movements and changes which set the stage for a new era. Likewise it would avail little to enunciate any one causal theory, still less to coin a meaningless formula like 'the general crisis of the sixteenth century'. The important principle is to recognize our hosts at this historical reception. At least for the present writer, they are not Luther, Melanchthon and the princes; they are the millions who then formed the German

nation. The nation is both hero and anti-hero of this story, and
it is even more complicated than the conventional hero, Martin
Luther. One can hardly wonder that the majority of historians
have assumed the easier task and turned biographers. The
dramatic developments of the age arose partly from a mixture
of more or less discernible intellectual trends, partly from an
obscurer turmoil of prejudices, emotions, aspirations, com-
pounded of spiritual and material elements, the sort of turmoil
always apparent when genuine ideas as well as mere grudges
penetrate downward to the popular level. Great changes are
inevitably complex changes, and hard to analyse with precision
and certitude from the voluminous yet still fragmentary evidence
which has come down from the sixteenth century. And mixed
with the ideological trends are material and technological
factors demanding due acknowledgement—in this case formidable city walls enclosing innumerable printing presses. Even
contemporaries saw that printing had vitally affected the outcome, though they ascribed its timely appearance to the machinations of divine providence.

Had all these currents not been running with vigour by the
early years of the sixteenth century, and in particular had
turbulent forces not been at work within the cities, how could an
intellectual have emerged from obscurity to interpret the age in
the light of the Bible and to impose at least a degree of order
upon the confused scene? We have tried to show that Luther,
for all his obstinacy, was a respondent to forces, as well as a
promoter and a creator of forces. Mutually, the person and the
nation interacted upon the broad scale and in the rapid tempo
made possible by printing. It needed this spiral growth of
ideological and popular tensions to bring forth Luther's genius
as pamphleteer and preacher, to create that prophetic sense of
mission which carried him into the unforeseen, and over one
crisis into the next. Welling up from beneath his feet, the social
forces gave birth not to the man's peculiar inward tensions but
to capacities which should interest historians still more: to his
wonderful outgoing and organizing qualities. At least for a few
years, the sheer power to communicate, based upon a sensitive
knowledge of the popular idiom, enabled him to give a clearer
shape to the social and spiritual pressures which had already

developed his own gifts. Yet threatened from the first by Radicalism as well as by conservatism, his personal grip upon the situation steadily weakened, even though in the last resort the convictions or ambitions of many rulers and city councils impelled them to freeze their subjects in Lutheran postures. From this second crisis, with Luther's personal spirit in decline, there emerged an Evangelical Church which in view of the untoward circumstances developed a rather surprising degree of spiritual vitality. And without doubt, this residue of vitality owed a great deal to the urban and academic culture which—spearheaded by the university of Wittenberg—had produced the first crisis and had provided a younger apostolate working in or near Luther's tradition.

I have stressed the historical effects of Luther's social teachings, and their part—alongside some very different ideologies—in the slow emancipation of European society from its long phase of clerical domination. It cannot be seriously questioned that this perilous libertarianism of 1520 arose quite as much from theological considerations as from Luther's warm personal concern for human souls and family values. On the other hand, we may still ask whether this precise theological basis, even this original and fruitful theology of Justification, had any historically indispensable character. It seems indeed demonstrable that a large sector of the German populace soon developed strong inclinations toward both Zwinglian and sectarian beliefs in part rejected by Luther. It cannot credibly be maintained that everything in Luther's system of ideas was uniquely and categorically required in order to marshal the confused trends of the day, and to establish something like a national Church. Despite the man's enormous impact upon German society, the evidence leaves us free to doubt whether the mass of his lay followers during the early years had grasped more than a bunch of religious slogans. Even among his better-educated supporters, a large number speedily dissented from him upon such critical issues as Justification and the eucharist. Again, there seems no reason to suppose that many people could have distinguished between his original solutions and those passages wherein he was merely popularizing Augustine or restating the views of lesser forerunners. On the contrary, one can fairly ask how far, and among what social groups, Luther's appeal would have survived a dramatic reputation for originality. Here was a dubious distinction which in that age needed to be played down. The strength of his case lay in its power to achieve or seem to achieve a close fidelity, a plain man's fidelity, to something more venerable than the papacy: the Gospel. Of course there remained many thousands of Germans, heirs to the medieval visionaries, who did value originality in the sense that they sought a radically new deal in spiritual, ecclesiastical and social life. But these enthusiasts did not stay with Luther, and from the early 1520s they were turning to Anabaptism and to the other sects. Later on, amid the revulsion from extremism after the horrors of Münster, activist minds must in all likelihood have been attracted toward the Reformed faith rather than back into Lutheranism. Reformed Protestantism was at least seeking to alter society by direct action: it wanted to create authentic 'cities of God', even though upon the basis of Zwingli's, Bucer's and Calvin's Biblical humanism. Upon exegeses more sophisticated than those current among the radical sects, Reformed cities thus attempted to recover control of the popular and progressive elements within the Reformation.

We have seen that in Bucerian Germany this experiment enjoyed only a limited and often short-lived success. Its solid triumphs came in Switzerland and the Netherlands. But since its failures in Germany sprang largely from politics, especially from the anti-Reformed discrimination exercised by the Peace of Augsburg, they cannot be used to bolster that alleged indispensability of Luther's own teaching which we have ventured to reject. In short, by 1517 the German masses had their faces averted from Rome and were ready to march. That their willingness to march did not depend upon the theological niceties of leaders may be demonstrated from the actual behaviour of other Germanic groups: those of Switzerland and the Netherlands. Even at the height of his influence, Luther the theologian never looked like becoming a one-man Council of Trent for the Protestant half of Europe. His influence over the tumultuous hopes and hatreds of German society was less masterful than either the hagiographers or the believers in a 'magisterial Reformation' would have us suppose. At no stage was the

German nation to be neatly manipulated by its major prophet. A hero of history is after all a creation of the people. By contrast, there have been many great souls, many superb communicators who have nevertheless failed to qualify for a monument in the echoing statuary-hall of the past. The heroic scale cannot be attained by mere genius: it must be thrust upon a man—and ultimately withdrawn from him—by some marvellous concatenation of circumstances. While Luther's own spirit lacked neither charisma nor intellect, it was the surge of forces within the nation, the forces which in this essay we have sought to describe, which elevated him to one of the rare titanic roles of western history. So chosen and so raised up, he became one of those who in posterity's wondering eyes have seemed to preside over the breaking of nations. Even so, historical realism clearly obliges us to explore a host of causal dimensions, amongst which the biographical remains but one. The greater the hero, the more pressing the obligation.

General Bibliography

Only a few city histories are listed here, though others occur in the notes above. A bibliography of such will be found in the German and French editions of B. Moeller, *Reichsstadt und Reformation*, detailed below. Again, readers requiring select bibliographies on the Reformation throughout Europe should consult, for example, H. J. Grimm, *The Reformation Era* (New York and London, 1965); that by L. W. Spitz in *Luther, Erasmus and the Reformation*, ed. J. C. Olin and others; S. Skalweit, pp. 419–45; E. G. Léonard, i. 356–432: only the English edition of Léonard, in which the bibliographies were corrected and extended by H. H. Rowley, is worth using. For a list of bibliographical surveys see S. E. Ozment, *The Reformation in Medieval Perspective*, pp. 253–6.

Where no place of publication is given, the book was published in London.

Adam, P., *L'Humanisme à Sélestat* (Sélestat, 1962).

Allen, P. S., *The Age of Erasmus* (Oxford, 1914).

Althaus, P., *Luthers Haltung im Bauernkrieg* (Basle, 1953).

Ammann, H., 'Wie gross war die mittelalterliche Stadt?', in *Die Stadt des Mittelalters*, ed. C. Haase (Darmstadt, 1969).

Andreas, W., *Deutschland vor der Reformation* (6th edn., Stuttgart, 1959).

Atkinson, J., *Martin Luther* (1968).

Bainton, R. H., *Women of the Reformation in Germany and Italy* (Minneapolis, 1971).

Studies on the Reformation (Boston, 1963).

Here I Stand: A Life of Martin Luther (New York, 1950).

'Psychiatry and History. An Examination of Erikson's *Young Man Luther*', in *Religion and Life* (winter no., 1971).

Baron, H., 'Religion and Politics in the German Imperial Cities during the Reformation' in *English Historical Review*, lii (1937).

Baumgarten, H. (ed.), *Sleidans Briefwechsel* (Strassburg and London, 1881).

Ben-Sasson, H. H., *The Reformation in Contemporary Jewish Eyes* (*Israel Acad. of Sciences and Humanities Proc.*, iv, no. 12; Jerusalem, 1970).

Benzing, J., *Die Buchdrucker des 16 und 17 Jahrhunderts im deutschen Sprachgebiet* (Wiesbaden, 1963).
See also Works of Reference.

Berger, A. E. (ed.), *Die Sturmtruppen der Reformation. Ausgewählte Flugschriften der Jahre 1520–25* (Leipzig, 1931).
Lied-Spruch-und Fabeldichtung im Dienste der Reformation (Leipzig, 1938).
Die Schaubühne im Dienste der Reformation (2 vols., Leipzig, 1935–6).
Satirische Feldzüge wider die Reformation. Thomas Murner. Daniel von Soest (Leipzig, 1933).

Betten, F., 'The Cartoon in Luther's Warfare against the Church', in *Catholic Historical Review*, v (1925).

Bieder, T., *Geschichte der Germanenforschung* (Leipzig and Berlin, 1921–5).

Blochwitz, G., 'Die antirömischen deutschen Flugschriften der frühen Reformationszeit (bis 1522) in ihrer religiös-sittlichen Eigenart', in *Archiv für Reformationsgeschichte*, xxvii (1930).

Böckmann, P., 'Der gemeine Mann in den Flugschriften der Reformationszeit', in *Deutsche Vierteljahrschrift für Literaturwissenschaft und Geistesgeschichte*, xxii (1944).

Boehmer, H. (trans. J. W. Doberstein and T. G. Tappert), *Road to Reformation* (Philadelphia, 1946).

Boesch, B. (ed.) (trans. R. Taylor), *German Literature. A Critical Survey* (1971).

Bohnenstädt, E., *Kirche und Reich im Schrifttum des Nikolaus von Cues* (*Sitzungsberichte der Heidelberger Akademie der Wissenschaften, Jahrgang 1938–9*, no. 1, Heidelberg, 1939).

Bonorand, C., *Vadians Weg vom Humanismus zur Reformation und seine Vorträge über die Apostelgeschichte* (St. Gallen, 1961).

Borchardt, F. L., *German Antiquity in Renaissance Myth* (Baltimore and London, 1971).

Bornkamm, H., *Luther im Spiegel der deutschen Geistesgeschichte* (Heidelberg, 1955).

(trans. M. H. Bertram), *Luther's World of Thought* (St. Louis, 1958).

Borth, W., *Die Luthersache (Causa Lutheri) 1517–1524: Die Anfänge der Reformation als Frage von Politik und Recht* (Lübeck and Hamburg, 1970).

Bouyer, L. (trans. A. V. Littledale), *The Spirit and Forms of Protestantism* (Westminster, Md., 1956).

Burger, H. O., *Renaissance, Humanismus, Reformation. Deutsche Literatur im europäischen Kontext* (Bad Homburg, Berlin, Zürich, 1969).

Cargill Thompson, W. D. J., 'The "Two Kingdoms" and the "Two Regiments": some Problems of Luther's *Zwei-Reich-Lehre*', in *Journal of Theological Studies*, xx (1969).

Carlson, E. M., *The Reinterpretation of Luther* (Philadelphia, 1948).

Carsten, F. L., *The Origins of Prussia* (1954).
Princes and Parliaments in Germany (Oxford, 1959).

Chrisman, M. U., *Strasbourg and the Reform* (New Haven and London, 1967).

Christensen, C. C., 'Municipal Patronage and the Crisis of the Arts in Reformation Nuernberg', in *Church History*, xxxvi (1967).
'Iconoclasm and the Preservation of Ecclesiastical Art in Reformation Nuremberg', in *Archiv für Reformationsgeschichte*, lxi (1970).

Clasen, C.-P., 'The Sociology of Swabian Anabaptism', in *Church History*, xxxii (1963), pp. 150–86.
'Medieval Heresies in the Reformation', in *ibid.*, pp. 391–414.

Anabaptism: a Social History, 1525–1618 (Ithaca and London, 1972).

Clemen, O. C., *Johann Pupper von Goch* (Leipzig, 1896).

Flugschriften aus den ersten Jahren der Reformation (4 vols., Leipzig and New York, 1907–11).

Die lutherische Reformation und der Buchdruck (Leipzig, 1939).

Cohn, H. J., *The Government of the Rhine Palatinate in the Fifteenth Century* (1965).

'The Early Renaissance Court in Heidelberg', in *European Studies Review*, i (1971).

(ed.), *Government in Reformation Europe 1520–1560* (New York, 1972).

Cohn, N., *The Pursuit of the Millennium* (rev. edn., 1970).

Cranz, F. E., *The Development of Luther's Thought on Justice, Law and Society* (Cambridge, Mass., 1959).

Dannenbauer, H., *Luther als religiöser Schriftsteller, 1517–1520* (Tübingen, 1930).

'Germanisches Altertum und deutsche Geschichtswissenschaft' in *Philosophie und Geschichte*, xxxv (1935).

Dickens, A. G., *Martin Luther and the Reformation* (1967).

Diederichs, P., *Kaiser Maximilian I als politischer Publizist* (Jena, s.a., ?1932).

Dillenberger, J., *Martin Luther. Selections from his Writings* (New York, 1961).

Dohna, L. Graf zu, *Reformatio Sigismundi, Beiträge zum Verständnis einer Reformschrift des 15. Jahrhunderts* (Göttingen, 1960).

Dolan, J. P., *History of the Reformation* (New York, 1965).

Dollinger, P. (trans. D. S. Ault and S. H. Steinberg), *The German Hansa* (1970).

Douglass, E. J. D., *Justification in Late Medieval Preaching. A Study of John Geiler of Kaisersberg* (Leiden, 1966).

Ebeling, G. (trans. R. A. Wilson), *Luther: an Introduction to his Thought* (Philadelphia, 1964).

Eckertz, G., 'Die Revolution in der Stadt Köln im Jahre 1513', in *Annalen des historischen Vereins für den Niederrhein*, xxvi–vii (1874).

Eells, H., *Martin Bucer* (New Haven, 1931).

Ehrenberg, R. (trans. H. M. Lucas), *Capital and Finance in the Age of the Renaissance* (1928).

Eisenstein, E. L., 'The Advent of Printing and the Problem of the Renaissance', in *Past & Present*, xlv (1969).

'L'avènement de l'imprimerie et la Réforme', in *Annales, Économies, Sociétés, Civilisations*, no. 6 (Paris, 1971).

Elton, G. R., *Reformation Europe 1517–1559* (1963).

Febvre, L., and Martin, H.-J., *L'apparition du livre* (Paris, 1958).

Fife, R. H., *The Revolt of Martin Luther* (New York, 1957).

Fischer-Galati, S. A., *Ottoman Imperialism and German Protestantism 1521–1555* (Cambridge, Mass., 1959).

Forster, L. W. (ed.), *Selections from Conrad Celtis* (Cambridge, 1948).

Franz, G., *Der deutsche Bauernkrieg* (4th edn., Darmstadt, 1952). See also *Works of Reference: Bibliographie de la Réforme*.

Friedensburg, W., *Johannes Sleidanus* (Leipzig, 1935).

Friedenthal, R. (trans. J. Nowell), *Luther* (1970).

Fueter, E., *Geschichte der neueren Historiographie* (Munich and Berlin, 1911; French translation by E. Jeanmaire as *Histoire de l'historiographie moderne*, (Paris, 1914).

Gebhardt, B., *Die Gravamina der deutschen Nation gegen den römischen Hof* (2nd edn., Breslau, 1895). See also *Works of Reference*.

Gerrish, B., *Grace and Reason* (Oxford, 1962).

Götze, A., *Die Hochdeutschen Drucker der Reformationszeit* (Strassburg, 1905).

Gotthelf, F., *Das deutsche Altertum in den Anschauungen des sechszehnten und siebzehnten Jahrhunderts* (Berlin, 1900).

Gravier, H., *Luther et l'opinion publique* (Paris, 1943).

Green, V. H. H., *Luther and the Reformation* (1964).

Grimm, H. J., 'Luther's Conception of Territorial and National Sovereignty' in *Church History*, xvii (1948).

'The Human Element in Luther's Sermons', in *Archiv für Reformationsgeschichte*, xlix (1958).

'The Relations of Luther and Melanchthon with the Townsmen', in *Luther and Melanchthon*, ed. V. Vajta (Göttingen, 1961).

'Social Forces in the German Reformation', in *Church History* xxxi (1962).

'Lazarus Spengler, the Nürnberg Council, and the Reformation', in *Luther for an Ecumenical Age*, ed. C. S. Meyer (St. Louis, 1967).

'The Reformation and the Urban Social Classes in Germany', in J. C. Olin (ed.), *Luther, Erasmus and the Reformation*.

Grossmann, M., 'Wittenberg Printing, Early Sixteenth Century' in *Sixteenth Century Essays and Studies* (Foundation for Reformation Research, St. Louis, 1970).

Hall, B., 'The Reformation City', in *Bulletin of the John Rylands Library*, liv (1971).

Hancock, A. O., 'Philipp of Hesse's View of the Relationship of Prince and Church', in *Church History*, xxxv (1966).

Harbison, E. H., *The Christian Scholar in the Age of the Reformation* (New York, 1956).

Hase, M. von, *Bibliographie der Erfurter Drucke von 1501–1550* (*Archiv für die Geschichte des Buchwesens*, 1966).

Haupt, H., *Ein oberrheinischer Revolutionär aus dem Zeitalter Kaiser Maximilians I* (*Westdeutsche Zeitschrift für Geschichte und Kunst, Ergänzungsheft*, viii, Trier, 1893).

Headley, J. M., *Luther's View of Church History* (New Haven and London, 1963).

Heinsius, M., *Das unüberwindliche Wort. Frauen der Reformationszeit* (Munich, 1951).

Hermelink, H., *Die religiösen Reformbestrebungen des deutschen Humanismus* (Tübingen, 1907).

Hertz, F., *The Development of the German Public Mind* (1957).

Heymann, F. G., 'The Hussite Revolution and the German Peasants' War', in *Medievalia et Humanistica*, new series, no. 1 (1970).

Hildebrandt, F., *Melanchthon: Alien or Ally?* (1946).

Hillerbrand, H. J., *The Reformation in its Own Words* (1964).

Landgrave Philipp of Hesse 1504–1567 (Foundation for Reformation Research, St. Louis, 1967).

'The Spread of the Protestant Reformation of the Sixteenth Century: a Historical Case-Study in the Transfer of Ideas', in *South Atlantic Quarterly*, lxvii (1968).

Hitchcock, W. R., *The Background of the Knights' Revolt* (Berkeley and Los Angeles, 1958).

Holborn, H., *A History of Modern Germany. The Reformation* (1965).

— (trans. R. H. Bainton), *Ulrich von Hutten and the German Reformation* (New Haven and London, 1937; New York, 1966).

Holborn, L., 'Printing and the Growth of a Protestant Movement in Germany from 1517 to 1524', in *Church History*, xi (1942).

Hubatsch, W., *Albrecht von Brandenburg-Ansbach. Deutschordens-Hochminister und Herzog in Preussen, 1490–1568* (Cologne and Berlin, 1960). Excerpts are translated in H. J. Cohn (ed.), *Government in Reformation Europe*.

Hurstfield, J. (ed.), *The Reformation Crisis* (London, 1965; New York, 1966).

Hyma, A., *The Christian Renaissance* (rev. edn., Hamden, Conn., 1965).

— *The Brethren of the Common Life* (Grand Rapids, Mich., 1950).

Ibach, H., *Leben und Schriften des Konrad von Megenberg* (Berlin, 1938).

Iserloh, E., *Reform der Kirche bei Nikolaus von Kues* (Wiesbaden, 1965).

Jannasch, W., *Reformationsgeschichte Lübecks vom Petersablass bis zum Augsburger Reichstag 1515–1530 (Veröffentlichungen zur Geschichte der Hansestadt Lübeck*, Band 16, Lübeck, 1958).

Janssen, J. (trans. M. A. Mitchell and A. M. Christie), *History of the German People at the Close of the Middle Ages* (17 vols., 1896–1925).

Jedin, H. (trans. E. Graf), *A History of the Council of Trent* (2 vols., 1957–61).

Joachimsen, P., *Geschichtsauffassung und Geschichtsschreibung in Deutschland unter dem Einfluss des Humanismus* (Leipzig, 1910).

— 'Der Humanismus und die Entwicklung des deutschen Geistes' and 'Tacitus im deutschen Humanismus', in his *Gesammelte Aufsätze*, ed. N. Hammerstein (1970). An English translation of the former article is in G. Strauss (ed.), *Pre-Reformation Germany*.

Die Reformation als Epoche der deutschen Geschichte (Munich, 1951).

Joachimsohn, P., *Gregor Heimburg* (Bamberg and Munich, 1891).

Kalkoff, P., *Humanismus und Reformation in Erfurt, 1500–1530* (Halle, 1926).

Kampschulte, F. W., *Die Universität Erfurt in ihrem Verhältnisse zu dem Humanismus und zu der Reformation* (2 vols., Trier, 1858–60).

'Uber Johannes Sleidanus als Geschichtsschreiber der Reformation' in *Forschungen zur deutschen Geschichte*, iii (1863).

Kekow, R., *Luther und die Devotio Moderna* (Düsseldorf, 1937).

Kiessling, E. C., *The Early Sermons of Luther and their Relation to the Pre-Reformation Sermon* (Grand Rapids, Mich., 1935).

Koenigsberger, H. G., 'The Reformation and Social Revolution', in J. Hurstfield (ed.), *The Reformation Crisis* (London, 1965; New York, 1966).

(ed.) *Luther. A Profile* (New York, 1973).

(with Mosse, G. L.), *Europe in the Sixteenth Century* (1968).

Kreider, R., 'Anabaptism and Humanism', in *Mennonite Quarterly Review*, xxvi (1952).

Kück, E. (ed.), *Die Schriften Hartmuts von Cronberg* (Halle, 1899).

Landeen, W. A., 'The Beginnings of the *Devotio Moderna* in Germany', in *Research Studies of the University of Washington*, xix (1951).

'The *Devotio Moderna* in Germany', in *ibid.*, xxi–xxii (1953–4).

'Martin Luther and the *Devotio Moderna* in Herford', in K. A. Strand (ed.), *The Dawn of Modern Civilization* (Ann Arbor, Mich., 1962).

Lau, F., 'Der Bauernkrieg und das angebliche Ende der lutherischen Reformation als spontaner Volksbewegung', in F. Lau (ed.), *Luther Jahrbuch*, xxvi (1959).

(trans. R. H. Fischer), *Luther* (1963).

Lau, F. and Bizer, E. (trans. B. A. Hardy), *A History of the Reformation in Germany to 1555* (1969).

Leff, G., *Heresy in the Later Middle Ages* (2 vols., Manchester, 1967).

Legge, T., *Flug-und Streitschriften der Reformationszeit in Westfalen 1523–1583* (Münster, 1933).

Léonard, E. G. (ed. H. H. Rowley), *A History of Protestantism*, i, *The Reformation* (1965).

Liebing, H., and Scholder, K. (eds.), *Geist und Geschichte der Reformation* (*Festgabe Hanns Rückert*, Berlin, 1966).

Lortz, J. (trans. R. Walls), *The Reformation in Germany* (2 vols., London and New York, 1968).

McDonough, T. M., *The Law and the Gospel in Luther: A study of Martin Luther's Confessional Writings* (Oxford, 1963).

Mackinnon, J., *Luther and the Reformation* (4 vols., 1925–30). *The Origins of the Reformation* (1939).

Mauersberg, H., *Wirtschafts- und Sozialgeschichte zentraleuropäischer Städte in neuerer Zeit* (Göttingen, 1960).

Menke-Glückert, E., *Die Geschichtsschreibung der Reformation und Gegenreformation* (Leipzig, 1912).

Meyer, C. S., 'A Dialog or Conversation between a Father and his Son about Martin Luther's Doctrine', in C. S. Meyer (ed.), *Luther for an Ecumenical Age* (St. Louis, 1967).

'Erasmus and Johann Reuchlin', in *Moreana*, xxiv (1969).

'Christian Humanism and the Reformation: Erasmus and Melanchthon', in *Concordia Theological Monthly*, xli (1970).

Meyer, H., *Lupold von Bebenburg: Studien zu seinen Schriften* (H. Grauert (ed.), *Studien und Darstellungen aus dem Gebiete der Geschichte*, vii, Freiburg, 1909).

Moeller, B., 'Die deutschen Humanisten und die Anfänge der Reformation', in *Zeitschrift für Kirchengeschichte*, viii (1959). For an English translation see the next item.

Reichsstadt und Reformation (Gütersloh, 1962; French translation as *Villes d'Empire et Réformation*, Geneva, 1966; English translation by H. C. E. Midelfort and M. U. Edwards as *Imperial Cities and the Reformation*, Philadelphia, 1972. This last also includes the foregoing item and another esssay by Moeller, but not the bibliographies of the German and French editions.).

'Frömmigkeit in Deutschland um 1500', in *Archiv für Reformationsgeschichte*, lvi (1965); English translation in G. Strauss (ed.) *Pre-Reformation Germany*, and in S. E. Ozment (ed.), *The Reformation in Medieval Perspective*.

Mommsen, K., 'Die *Reformatio Sigismundi*, Basel und die Schweiz', in *Schweizerische Zeitschrift für Geschichte*, xx (1970).

Mosse, G. L., see Koenigsberger, H. G.

Most, R., 'Der Reichsgedanke des Lupold von Bebenburg', in *Deutsches Archiv für Geschichte des Mittelalters*, iv (1941).

Newald, R., *Probleme und Gestalten des deutschen Humanismus* (Berlin, 1963).

Newman, L. I., *Jewish Influence on Christian Reform Movements* (New York, 1925).

Oberman, H. A., 'Facientibus Quod in se est Deus non Denegat Gratiam: Robert Holcot O. P. and the Beginnings of Luther's Theology', in *Harvard Theological Review*, lv (1962), reprinted in S. E. Ozment (ed.), *The Reformation in Medieval Perspective*.

The Harvest of Medieval Theology (Cambridge, Mass., 1963).

Forerunners of the Reformation (1967).

Olin, J. C., Smart, D. S. and McNally, R. E. (eds.), *Luther, Erasmus and the Reformation. A Catholic-Protestant Reappraisal* (New York, 1969).

Olin, J. C. (ed.), *Desiderius Erasmus: Christian Humanism and the Reformation* (New York, 1965).

Overfield, J. H., 'A New Look at the Reuchlin Affair', in *Studies in Medieval and Renaissance History*, viii (1971).

Ozment, S. E., *Homo Spiritualis: A Comparative Study of the Anthropology of Johannes Tauler, Jean Gerson and Martin Luther in the Context of their Theological Thought* (Leiden, 1969).

(ed.), *The Reformation in Medieval Perspective* (Chicago, 1971) [includes the Editor's own essay, 'Homo Viator: Luther and Late Medieval Theology'].

Panofsky, E., *Albrecht Dürer* (3rd edn., 2 vols., London and Princeton, 1948).

Pascal, R., *The Social Basis of the German Reformation* (1933).

Pauck, W., *The Heritage of the Reformation* (rev. edn., Glencoe, Ill., 1961).

Paul, U., *Studien zur Geschichte des deutschen Nationalbewusstseins im Zeitalter des Humanismus und der Reformation* (Berlin, 1936).

Pelikan, J., 'Luther's Attitude to John Huss', in *Concordia Theological Monthly*, xix (1948).

Luther the Expositor (companion vol. to the American Edition of Luther's Works, St. Louis, 1959).

From Luther to Kierkegaard (St. Louis, 1950).

Obedient Rebels: Catholic Substance and Protestant Principle in Luther's Reformation (New York, 1964).

Peuckert, W.-E., *Deutsche Volksglaube des Spätmittelalters* (Stuttgart, 1942).

Pfeiffer, G. (ed.), *Nürnberg-Geschichte einer europäischen Stadt* (Munich and Nördlingen, 1971).

Planitz, H., *Die deutsche Stadt im Mittelalter* (Cologne, 1954).

Post, R. R., *The Modern Devotion* (Leiden, 1968).

Ranke, L. von (trans. S. Austin), *History of the Reformation in Germany* (3 vols., 1845–7; one vol., ed. R. A. Johnson, 1905). The translation is incomplete; full German edn., 6 vols., Munich, 1925–6).

Reeves, M., *The Influence of Prophecy in the Later Middle Ages* (Oxford, 1969).

Riess, H., *Motive des patriotischen Stolzes bei den deutschen Humanisten* (Berlin, 1934).

Ritter, G., 'Die geschichtliche Bedeutung des deutschen Humanismus', in *Historische Zeitschrift*, cxxvii (1923).

'Romantische und revolutionäre Elemente in der deutschen Theologie am Vorabend der Reformation', in *Deutsche Vierteljahrsschrift für Literaturwissenschaft und Geistesgeschichte*, v (1927), translated in S. E. Ozment (ed.), *The Reformation in Medieval Perspective*.

'Lutheranism, Catholicism and the Humanistic View of Life', in *Archiv für Reformationsgeschichte*, xliv (1953).

Luther his Life and Work (1963).

Rupp, E. G., *The Righteousness of God: Luther Studies* (1953).

Luther's Progress to the Diet of Worms (1951).

'Word and Spirit in the First Years of the Reformation', in *Archiv für Reformationsgeschichte*, xlix (1958).

'Luther's Ninety-Five Theses and the Theology of the Cross', in C. S. Meyer (ed.), *Luther for an Ecumenical Age* (St. Louis, 1967).

Patterns of Reformation (1969).

Rupp, E. G. and Drewery, B., *Martin Luther* (*Documents of Modern History*, 1970).

Saarnivaara, U., *Luther Discovers the Gospel* (St. Louis, 1951).

Schade, O., *Satiren und Pasquille aus der Reformationszeit* (3 vols., Hanover, 1856–8).

Schäfer, E., *Luther als Kirchenhistoriker* (Gütersloh, 1897).

Scharfe, S., *Religiöse Bildpropaganda der Reformationszeit* (Göttingen, 1951).

Scheel, O., *Dokumente zu Luthers Entwicklung* (*bis 1519*) (2nd ed., Tübingen, 1929).

Scherer, E. C., *Geschichte und Kirchengeschichte an den deutschen Universitäten* (Freiburg, 1927).

Schildhauer, J., *Soziale, politische und religiöse Auseinandersetzungen in den Hansestädten Stralsund, Rostock und Wismar im ersten Drittel des XVI. Jahrhunderts* (Wismar, 1959).

Schmidt, C., *Histoire littéraire de l'Alsace à la fin du XVe et au commencement du XVIe siècle* (2 vols., Paris, 1879).

Schmidt, M., 'Luthers Schau der Geschichte', in F. Lau (ed.), *Luther Jahrbuch*, 1963.

Schottenloher, K., *Flugblatt und Zeitung. Ein Wegweiser durch das gedruckte Tagesschrifttum* (Berlin, 1922).

(ed.), *Flugschriften zur Ritterschaftsbewegung des Jahres 1523* (Münster, 1929).

See also Works of Reference.

Schubert, H. von, *Lazarus Spengler und die Einführung der Reformation in Nürnberg* (ed. H. Holborn, *Quellen und Forschungen zur Reformationsgeschichte*, xvii, Leipzig, 1934).

Schultze, A., *Stadtgemeinde und Reformation* (Tübingen, 1918).

Schwiebert, E. G., 'The Reformation from a new Perspective', in *Church History*, xvii (1947).

Luther and his Times (St. Louis, 1950).

'New Groups and Ideas at the University of Wittenberg', in *Archiv für Reformationsgeschichte*, xlix (1958).

Scribner, R. W., *Reformation, Society and Humanism in Erfurt, c. 1450–1530* (unpublished Ph.D. thesis, London University, 1972).

Senger, A., *Lupold von Bebenburg* (Bamberg, 1905).

Sessions, K. C., *Reformation and Authority. The Meaning of the Peasants' Revolt* (Lexington, Mass., 1968).

Siggins, I. D. K., *Luther* (Edinburgh, 1972).

Skalweit, S., *Reich und Reformation* (Berlin, 1967).

Spinka, M., *Advocates of Reform: From Wyclif to Erasmus* (*Library of Christian Classics*, xiv, Philadelphia, 1953).

Spitz, L. W., 'The Conflict of Ideals in Mutianus Rufus', in *Journal of the Warburg and Courtauld Institutes*, xvi (1953).

'Reuchlin's Philosophy: Pythagoras and Cabala for Christ', in *Archiv für Reformationsgeschichte*, xlvii (1956).

Conrad Celtis, the German Arch-Humanist (Cambridge, Mass., 1957).

'Ideas of Liberty in German Humanism', in *Church History*, xxxi (1962).

The Religious Renaissance of the German Humanists (Cambridge, Mass., 1953).

'The Third Generation of German Renaissance Humanists', in A. R. Lewis (ed.), *Aspects of the Renaissance* (Austin, Texas, 1967).

'Scholarship in the Renaissance: German Humanism', in *Renaissance Quarterly*, xxi (1968).

Sponagel, L., *Konrad Celtis und das deutsche Nationalbewusstsein* (Bühl-Baden, 1939).

Srbik, H. von, *Geist und Geschichte vom deutschen Humanismus bis zur Gegenwart* (2 vols., Munich, Salzburg and Vienna 1950–51).

Steinberg, S. H., *Five Hundred Years of Printing* (rev. edn., 1961).

Steinmetz, D. C., *Misericordia Dei. The Theology of Johannes von Staupitz in its Late Medieval Setting* (Leiden, 1965).

Stemmermann, P. H., *Die Anfänge der deutschen Vorgeschichtsforschung* (Quakenbrück, 1934).

Stokes, F. G. (ed.), *Epistolae Obscurorum Virorum: The Latin Text with an English Rendering* (1909).

Strauss, G., 'The Religious Policies of Dukes Wilhelm and Ludwig of Bavaria in the first Decade of the Protestant Era', in *Church History*, xxviii (1959).

'Topographical-Historical Method in Sixteenth-century German Scholarship', in *Studies in the Renaissance*, v (1958).

Sixteenth Century Germany: its Topography and Topographers (Madison, Wisc., 1959).

Historian in an Age of Crisis. The Life and Work of Johannes Aventinus, 1477–1534 (Cambridge, Mass., 1963).

Nuremberg in the Sixteenth Century (New York, 1966).

'Protestant Dogma and City Government: the Case of Nuremberg', in *Past & Present*, xxxvi (1967).

(ed.), *Manifestations of Discontent in Germany on the Eve of the Reformation* (Bloomington, Ind., 1972).

(ed.), *Pre-Reformation Germany* (1972) [translates ten valuable German articles].

Stupperich, R., 'Der Humanismus und die Wiedervereinigung der Konfessionen', in *Schriften des Vereins für Reformationsgeschichte*, clx (1936).

'Die Frau in der Publizistik der Reformation', in *Archiv für Kulturgeschichte*, xxxvii (1955).

Thompson, L. S., 'German Translations of the Classics between 1450 and 1550', in *Journal of English and Germanic Philology*, xlii (1943).

Thomson, S. H., 'Luther and Bohemia', in *Archiv für Reformationsgeschichte*, xliv (1953).

Tillmanns, W. G., *The World and Men around Luther* (Minneapolis, 1959).

Todd, J. M., *Martin Luther, A Biographical Study* (1964).

Tracy, J. D., 'Erasmus becomes a German', in *Renaissance Quarterly*, xxi (1968).

Trinkaus, C. E., 'The Religious Foundations of Luther's Social Views', in J. Mundy, R. Emery and B. Nelson (eds.), *Essays in Medieval Life and Thought* (New York, 1955).

Uhrig, K., 'Der Bauer in der Publizistik der Reformation', in *Archiv für Reformationsgeschichte*, xxxiii (1936).

Ullmann, K. H., *Reformatoren vor der Reformation* (2 vols., Hamburg, 1841–2); English translation, *Reformers before the Reformation*, 1885).

Volz, H., 'Flugschriften der Reformationszeit', in K. Galling (ed.), *Die Religion in Geschichte und Gegenwart* (3rd edn., vol. ii, Tübingen, 1958).

Bibel und Bibeldruck in Deutschland im 15. und 16. Jahrhundert (Mainz, 1960).

Watson, P. S., *Let God be God: an Interpretation of the Theology of Martin Luther* (1947).

Williams, G. H., *The Radical Reformation* (1962).

Wolf, E., *Staupitz und Luther. Ein Beitrag zur Theologie des Johannes von Staupitz und deren Bedeutung für Luthers theologischen Werdegang* (Leipzig, 1927).

Wunderlich, P., *Die Beurteilung der Vorreformation in der deutschen Geschichtsschreibung seit Ranke* (Erlangen, 1930).

Zeeden, E. W., *The Legacy of Luther* (1954).

Zinnhobler, R., 'Johannes Fabers Leichenrede auf Maximilian I', in *15 Jahrbuch des Musealvereins Wels* (Wels, 1968–9).

Zins, H., 'The Political and Social Background of the Early Reformation in Ermeland', in *English Historical Review*, lxxv (1960).

Zweynert, E., *Luthers Stellung zur humanistischen Schule und Wissenschaft* (Chemnitz, 1895).

Works of Reference

[Abbreviations appear in square brackets.]

Aland, K., *Hilfsbuch zum Lutherstudium* (Berlin, 1957).
    Repetitorium der Kirchengeschichte, iii, *Reformation und Gegen-reformation* (Berlin, 1967).
Allgemeine deutsche Biographie (56 vols., Leipzig, 1875–1912). [*ADB*]
Archiv für Geschichte des Buchwesens, ed. B. Heck and B. Wendt (12 vols., Frankfurt, 1958–72).
Benzing, J., *Lutherbibliographie. Verzeichnis der gedruckten Schriften Martin Luthers zu dessen Tod* (3 vols., Baden-Baden, 1965–6).
Bibliographie de la Réforme, fasc. i, *Allemagne*, ed. G. Franz (3rd edn., Leiden, 1964).
Dictionnaire d'histoire et de géographie ecclésiastiques, ed. A. Baudrillart and others (Paris, 1912–).
Dictionnaire de Théologie Catholique, ed. A. Vacant and others (21 vols., Paris, 1899–1967). [*DTC*]
Encyclopedia of the Lutheran Church, ed. J. Bodensieck (3 vols., Minneapolis, 1965).
Erman, W., and Horn, E., *Bibliographie der deutschen Univer-sitäten* (3 vols., Leipzig and Berlin, 1904–5; photo-reprint, Hildesheim, 1965).
Gebhardt, B., *Handbuch der deutschen Geschichte* (8th edn., Stuttgart, 1954).

Hauck, A. (ed.), *Realencyclopädie für protestantische Theologie und Kirche* (24 vols., Leipzig, 1896–1913).

Keyser, E., *Bibliographie zur Städtegeschichte Deutschlands* (Cologne and Vienna, 1969).

Lexikon für Theologie und Kirche, ed. J. Höfer and K. Rahner (10 vols., Freiburg, 1957–65).

Luther, M., *D. Martin Luthers Werke*. (*Weimarer Ausgabe*, 1883–). [*WA*] [*Briefwechsel* vols.: *WA Br*]

Neue deutsche Biographie (1952–). [*NDB*]

New Catholic Encyclopedia (15 vols., New York, 1967). [*NCE*]

New Schaff-Herzog Encyclopedia of Religious Knowledge (13 vols., Grand Rapids, Mich., 1949–50).

Oxford Dictionary of the Christian Church, ed. F. L. Cross (1957). [*ODCC*]

Pegg, M. A., *A Catalogue of German Reformation Pamphlets (1516–1546) in Libraries of Great Britain and Ireland* (*Bibliotheca Bibliographica Aureliana*, xlv, Baden-Baden, 1973).

Die Religion in Geschichte und Gegenwart (3rd edn., ed. K. Galling, 6 vols., Tübingen, 1956–62).

Schnabel, F., *Deutschlands geschichtliche Quellen und Darstellungen in der Neuzeit* (Leipzig and Berlin, 1931).

Schottenloher, K., *Bibliographie zur deutschen Geschichte im Zeitalter der Glaubensspaltung 1517–1585* (6 vols., Leipzig, 1933–9; vol. vii [Stuttgart, 1962] covers the years 1938–60]. [Schottenloher]

Short Title Catalogue of Books printed in the German-speaking Countries and German Books printed in other Countries, from 1455 to 1600 now in the British Museum (1962).

Stokes, L. D., *Medieval and Reformation Germany…A Select Bibliography* (Historical Association, 1972).

Wörterbuch zu Dr. Martin Luthers deutschen Schriften, ed. P. Dietz (Hildesheim, 1961–).

Wolf, G., *Quellenkunde der deutschen Reformationsgeschichte* (3 vols., Gotha, 1915–23).

Index

Bold numerals represent chapter numbers

The Fontana Economic History of Europe

To be completed in six volumes, each book is made up of individual sections written by a leading European or American specialist. For the convenience of students each section is published separately in pamphlet form as soon as possible, the volumes appearing when all the contributions have been received.

The general editor of the series is Carlo M. Cipolla, Professor of Economic History at the Universities of Pavia and California, Berkeley.

'There can be no doubt that these volumes make an extremely significant addition to the literature of European economic history, where the need for new large comparative works has long been felt . . . It is overall a project of vision and enormous value.'

Times Literary Supplement

Already published

1. The Middle Ages

Contributors: Cipolla: J. C. Russell: Jacques Le Goff: Richard Roehl: Lynn White Jr.: Georges Duby: Sylvia Thrupp: Jacques Bernard: Edward Miller.

2. The Sixteenth and Seventeenth Centuries

Contributors: Cipolla: Roger Mols: Walter Minchinton: Hermann Kellenbenz: Aldo de Maddalena: Domenico Sella: Kristof Glamann: Geoffrey Parker.

3. The Industrial Revolution

Contributors: André Armengaud: Walter Minchinton: Samuel Lilley: Gertrand Gille: Barry Supple: R. M. Hartwell: J. F. Bergier: Paul Bairoch: Donald Winch: M. J. T. Lewis.

4. The Emergence of Industrial Societies

Part 1: Contributors: Claude Fohlen: Knut Borchardt: Phyllis Deane: N. T. Gross: Luciano Cafagna: Jan Dhondt & Marinette Bruwier.
Part 2: Contributors: Lennart Jörberg: Gregory Crossman: Jordi Nadal: B. M. Biucchi: William Woodruff: B. R. Mitchell.

In preparation

5. The Twentieth Century

6. Contemporary Economics

Fontana History

Fontana History includes the well-known History of Europe, edited by J. H. Plumb and the Fontana Economic History of Europe, edited by Carlo Cipolla. Other books available include:

Lectures on Modern History Lord Acton

The Conservative Party from Peel to Churchill
Robert Blake

A Short History of the Second World War
Basil Collier

American Presidents and the Presidency
Marcus Cunliffe

The English Reformation A. G. Dickens

The Norman Achievement David C. Douglas

The Practice of History G. R. Elton

Politics and the Nation, 1450-1660 D. M. Loades

Ireland Since the Famine F. S. L. Lyons

Britain and the Second World War Henry Pelling

Foundations of American Independence J. R. Pole

A History of the Scottish People T. C. Smout

The Ancien Regime and the French Revolution
Tocqueville

The King's Peace 1637-1641 C. V. Wedgwood

The King's War 1641-1647 C. V. Wedgwood

Fontana Politics

The English Constitution Walter Bagehot
edited by R. H. S. Crossman

The Backroom Boys Noam Chomsky

For Reasons of State Noam Chomsky

Peace in the Middle East Noam Chomsky

Problems of Knowledge and Freedom Noam Chomsky

Marx and Engels: Basic Writings
edited by Lewis S. Feuer

Edmund Burke on Government, Politics and Society
edited by Brian Hill

Governing Britain A. H. Hanson and Malcolm Walles

Machiavelli: Selections
edited by John Plamenatz

Sakharov Speaks Andrei D. Sakharov

To the Finland Station Edmund Wilson

Fontana History of Europe

Praised by academics, teachers and general readers alike, this series aims to provide an account, based on the latest research, that combines narrative and explanation. Each volume has been specifically commissioned from a leading English, American or European scholar, and is complete in itself.

The general editor of the series in J. H. Plumb, lately Professor of Modern History at Cambridge University, and Fellow of Christ's College, Cambridge.

In Preparation